OFFICIAL BLUE BOOK OF UNITED STATES COINS™

The Official BLUE BOOK®

HANDBOOK OF

UNITED STATES COINS™

With Premium List

R.S. YEOMAN

EDITED BY

KENNETH BRESSETT

62nd Edition

Containing mint records and wholesale prices for U.S. coins from 1616 to the present time, including Colonials, Regular Issues, Commemoratives, Territorials, Gold, Proof Sets, and Mint Sets. Information on collecting coins—how coins are produced—mints and mint marks—grading of coins—location of mint marks—preserving coins—starting a collection—history of mints and interesting descriptions of all U.S. copper, nickel, silver and gold coins. Fully illustrated.

Printed in Canada

Important Notice

THIS BOOK IS *NOT A RETAIL PRICE LIST*

Premium prices are the average amount dealers will pay for coins (according to condition) if required for their stock.

IF YOU HAVE COINS TO SELL

The publisher of this book is not in the rare coin business; however, the chances are that the dealer from whom you purchased this book is engaged in the buying and selling of rare coins—contact him first. In the event that you purchased this book from a source other than a numismatic establishment, consult your local telephone directory for the names of coin dealers (they will be found sometimes under the heading of "Stamp and Coin Dealers"). If you live in a city or town that does not have any coin dealers, it is suggested that you obtain a copy of one of the trade publications or check the internet in order to obtain the names and addresses of many of the country's leading dealers. Information or sample copies may be obtained by writing to the individual publisher.

Current average *retail* valuations of all U.S. coins are listed in Whitman's *A Guide Book of United States Coins*™ by R. S. Yeoman, Whitman Publishing, LLC, Atlanta, GA ($15.95 Hardcover; $12.95 Coil Bound).

www.whitman**books**.com

Whitman® Publishing, LLC
PUBLISHING SINCE 1934

www.whitman**books**.com

Sell or Auction
Your Coins For
TOP
DOLLAR
With over 150,000 clients
spending $250 million+
with us annually,
Heritage has to
pay you more.
Why settle for less?
CALL TODAY
1-800-US COINS
Ext. 111
(24-hour voicemail)
BB@HeritageCoins.com
STILL BUYING?
Join the world's most popular
numismatic website:
www.HeritageCoins.com/bb
(special offer).
Our 100,000+ online members
enjoy dozens of benefits,
all totally FREE!
HERITAGE
Galleries & Auctioneers
World's Largest Numismatic Dealer and Auctioneer
3500 Maple Avenue, 17th Floor
Dallas, Texas 75219
1-800-US COINS (1-800-872-6467) Ext. 111

Foreword

Since 1941, annually revised editions of this *Handbook* have aided thousands of people who have coins to sell or are actively engaged in collecting United States coins. The popular coin-folder method of collecting by date has created ever-changing premium values, based on the supply and demand of each date and mint. Through its panel of contributors, the *Handbook* has, over the years, reported these changing values. It also serves as a source of general numismatic information to all levels of interest in the hobby.

The values shown are representative prices paid by dealers for various United States coins. These are averages of prices assembled from many widely separated sources. On some issues slight differences in price among dealers may result from proximity to the various mints or heavily populated centers. Other factors, such as local supply and demand or dealers' stock conditions, may also tend to cause deviations from the prices listed. While many coins bring no premium when circulated, they usually bring premium prices in Uncirculated and Proof.

CONTRIBUTORS TO THE SIXTY-SECOND EDITION

Special Consultants: Philip Bressett,
Tom Hallenbeck, and Mary Sauvain

Gary Adkins
David Akers
John Albanese
Buddy Alleva
Dr. Richard S. Appel
Michael Aron
Richard M. August
Richard A. Bagg, Ph.D.
Mitchell A. Battino
Lee J. Bellisario
Jack Beymer
Mark R. Borckardt
Q. David Bowers
J. H. Cline
Elizabeth W. Coggan
Alan R. Cohen
Gary Cohen
Marc Crane
John West Dannreuther
Tom DeLorey
Silvano Di Genova
Kenneth Duncan
Sheridan Downey
Col. Steven Ellsworth
John Feigenbaum
Jeff Garrett
Dennis M. Gillio
Ronald J. Gillio
Ira M. Goldberg
Lawrence S. Goldberg
Kenneth M. Goldman
J. R. Grellman
Ron Guth
James Halperin
John Hamrick
Gene L. Henry
Karl D. Hirtzinger
Jesse Iskowitz
Steve Ivy
James J. Jelinski
A. M. Kagin
Donald H. Kagin
Bradley S. Karoleff
John J. Kraljevich, Jr.
Richard A. Lecce
Robert B. Lecce
Julian M. Leidman
David Leventhal
Stuart Levine
Kevin Lipton
Denis W. Loring
Andy Lustig
Chris McCawley
Robert T. McIntire
Dwight N. Manley
Harry Miller
Lee S. Minshull
Robert Mish
Scott P. Mitchell
Michael C. Moline
Paul Montgomery
Charles Moore
Thomas Mulvaney
Richard Nachbar
Chris Napolitano
Paul Nugget
John M. Pack
Robert M. Paul
William P. Paul
Joel Rettew, Jr.
Robert J. Rhue
Tom Rinaldo
Greg Rohan
Maurice Rosen
Leonard R. Saunders
Mary Sauvain
Cherie Schoeps
Richard J. Schwary
James A. Simek
Richard E. Snow
William J. Spencer
Lawrence Stack
David M. Sundman
Anthony J. Swiatek
Anthony Terranova
Jerry Treglia
Frank E. Van Valen
Fred Weinberg
Douglas Winter
Mark S. Yaffe

COLLECTING COINS

Numismatics or coin collecting is one of the world's oldest hobbies, dating back several centuries. Coin collecting in America did not develop to any extent until about 1840, as our pioneer forefathers were too busy carving a country out of wilderness to afford the luxury of a hobby. The discontinuance of the large-sized cent in 1857 caused many people to attempt to accumulate a complete set of the pieces while they were still in circulation. One of the first groups of collectors to band together for the study of numismatics was the Numismatic and Antiquarian Society of Philadelphia, organized on January 1, 1858. Lack of an economical method to house a collection held the number of devotees of coin collecting to a few thousand until Whitman Publishing and other manufacturers placed the low-priced coin boards and folders on the market some years ago. Since that time, the number of Americans collecting coins has increased many-fold.

The Production of Coins

To collect coins intelligently it is necessary to have some knowledge of the manner in which our coins are produced. They are made in factories called "mints." The Mint of the United States was established at Philadelphia by a resolution of Congress dated April 2, 1792. The Act also provided for the coinage of gold eagles ($10), half-eagles and quarter-eagles, the silver dollar, half-dollar, quarter-dollar, dime (originally spelled "disme") and the half-disme or half-dime; the copper cent and half cent. According to the Treasury Department, the first coins struck were one-cent and half-cent pieces, in March of 1793 on a hand-operated press. Most numismatic authorities consider the half-disme of 1792 as the first United States coinage, quoting the words of George Washington as their authority. Washington, in his annual address, November 6, 1792, said, "There has been a small beginning in the coining of the Half-Dimes, the want of small coins in circulation calling the first attention to them." In the new Philadelphia Mint are a number of implements, from the original mint, and some coins discovered when the old building was wrecked. These coins included half-dismes, and the placard identifying them states that Washington furnished the silver and gave the coined pieces to his friends as souvenirs.

Prior to the adoption of the Constitution, the Continental Congress arranged for the issuance of copper coins under private contract. These are known as the "Fugio cents" from the design of the piece, which shows a sundial and the Latin word "fugio"—"I Fly" or, in connection with the sundial, "Time Flies." The ever appropriate motto, "Mind Your Business," is also on the coin.

In the manufacture of a given coin the first step is the cutting of the "die." Prior to the latter part of the nineteenth century dies for United States coins were "cut by hand." Briefly this method is as follows: The design having been determined, a drawing the exact size of the coin is made. A tracing is made from this drawing. A piece of steel is smoothed and coated with transfer wax, and the tracing impressed into the wax. The engraver then tools out the steel where the relief or raised effect is required. If the design is such that it can all be produced by cutting away steel, the die is hardened and ready for use. Some dies are not brought to a finished state, as some part of the design can perhaps be done better in relief. In that case, when all that can be accomplished to advantage in the die is completed, it is hardened, a soft-steel impression is taken from it, and the unfinished parts are then completed. This piece of steel is in turn hardened and, by a press, driven into another piece of soft-steel, thus making a die which, when hardened, is ready for the making of coins.

This hand method of cutting dies accounts for the many die varieties of early United States coins. Where the amount of coinage of a given year was large enough to wear out several dies, each new die placed in the coining press created another die variety of that year. The dies being cut by hand, no two were exactly alike in every detail, even though some of the major elements such as head, wreath, were sunk into the die by individual master punches. Of the cents dated 1794, over sixty different die varieties have been discovered.

Hundreds of dies are now used by the mints of the United States each year, but they are all made from one master die, which is produced in the following manner:

After the design is settled upon, the plaster of paris or wax model is prepared several times the actual size of the coin. When this model is finished an electrotype (an exact duplicate in metal) is made and prepared for the reducing lathe. The reducing lathe is a machine, working on the principle of the pantograph, only in this case the one point traces or follows the form of the model while another and much smaller point in the form of a drill cuts away the steel and produces a reduced size die of the model. The die is finished and details are sharpened or worked over by an engraver with chisel and graver. The master die is used to make duplicates in soft-steel which are then hardened and ready for the coining press. To harden dies, they are placed in cast-iron boxes packed with carbon to exclude the air, and when heated to a bright red are cooled suddenly with water.

In the coinage operations the first step is to prepare the metal. Alloys that have been used are: silver coins, 90% silver and 10% copper; five-cent pieces, 75% copper and 25% nickel; one-cent pieces, 95% copper and 5% zinc. (The 1943 cent consists of steel coated with zinc; and the five-cent piece 1942-1945 contains 35% silver, 56% copper and 9% manganese.) Under the Coinage Act of 1965, the composition of dimes, quarters and half dollars was changed to eliminate or reduce the silver content of these coins. The copper-nickel "clad" dimes, quarters, halves and dollars are composed of an outer layer of copper-nickel (75% copper and 25% nickel) bonded to an inner core of pure copper. The silver clad half dollar and dollar have an outer layer of 80% silver bonded to an inner core of 21% silver, with a total content of 40% silver. Current cents are made from a core of 99.2% zinc, 0.8% copper, with a plating of pure copper.

Alloys are melted in crucibles and poured into molds to form ingots. The ingots are in the form of thin bars and vary in size according to the denomination of the coin. The width is sufficient to allow three or more coins to be cut from the strips.

The ingots are next put through rolling mills to reduce the thickness to required limits. The strips are then fed into cutting presses which cut circular blanks (planchets) of the approximate size of the finished coin. The blanks are run through annealing furnaces to soften them; next through tumbling barrels, rotating cyclinders containing cleaning solutions which clean and burnish the metal, and finally into centrifugal drying machines.

The blanks are next fed into a milling machine which produces the raised or upset rim. The blank is now ready for the coining press.

The blank is held firmly by a collar, as it is struck under heavy pressure varying from 40 tons for the one-cent pieces and dimes to 170 tons for silver dollars. Upper and lower dies impress the design on both sides of the coin. The pressure is sufficient to produce a raised surface level with that of the milled rim. The collar holding the blank for silver or clad coins is grooved. The pressure forces the metal into the grooves of the collar, producing the "reeding" on the finished coin.

How a Proof Coin Is Made

Selected dies are inspected for perfection and are highly polished and cleaned. They are again wiped clean or polished after every 15 to 25 impressions and are replaced frequently to avoid imperfections from worn dies. Coinage blanks are polished and cleaned to assure high quality in striking. They are then hand fed into the coinage press one at a time, each blank receiving two blows from the dies to bring up sharp, high relief details. The coinage operation is done at slow speed with extra pressure. Finished proofs are individually inspected and are handled by gloves or tongs. They also receive a final inspection by packers before being sonically sealed in special plastic cases.

Certain coins, including Lincoln cents, Buffalo nickels, Quarter eagles, Half eagles, eagles, and Double eagles, between the years 1908 and 1916, were made with a matte or sandblast surface. Matte proofs have a dull frosted surface which was either applied to the dies, or produced by special treatment after striking.

Mints and Mint Marks

In addition to the Philadelphia Mint, the U.S. government has from time to time established branch mints in various parts of the country. At the present time a branch mint operates in Denver. Starting in 1968, proof sets and some of the regular coins were produced at the San Francisco Assay Office. The Denver Mint has operated since 1906. A mint was operated at New Orleans from 1838 to 1861 and again from 1879 to 1909. Mints were also in service at Carson City, Nevada, from 1870 to 1893; at Charlotte, North Carolina, from 1838 to 1861; at Dahlonega, Georgia, from 1838 to 1861; and at San Francisco since 1854.

Coins struck at Philadelphia before 1979 (except 1942 to 1945 five-cent pieces) do not carry a mint mark. The mint mark is found only on coins struck at the branch mints. It is a small letter, usually found on the reverse side. The Lincoln cent is one exception to the rule. All coins minted after 1967 have the mint mark on the obverse. The letters to signify the various mints are as follows:

"C" for Charlotte, North Carolina (on gold coins only).
"CC" for Carson City, Nevada.
"D" for Dahlonega, Georgia (gold coins only, 1838 to 1861).
"D" For Denver, Colorado (from 1906 to date).
"O" for New Orleans, Louisiana.
"P" for Philadelphia, Pennsylvania.
"S" for San Francisco, California.
"W" for West Point, New York.

The mint mark is of utmost importance to collectors because the coinage at the branch mints has usually been much smaller than at Philadelphia and many of the early branch mint pieces are very scarce.

DISTINGUISHING MARKS

The illustrations and explanations in this section will help the collector identify certain well-known varieties.

HALF CENTS OF 1795–1796 SHOWING LOCATION OF POLE TO CAP

The end of the staff or pole lies parallel with the line of the bust, which is pointed. The die-maker, probably through error, omitted the pole on some of the dies of 1795 and 1796.

Pole to Cap

No Pole to Cap

Stemless Wreath

Stems to Wreath

STEMLESS WREATH VARIETY OF HALF CENTS AND LARGE CENTS

Observe the reverse side for this variety. Illustrations at left show both stemless and stems to wreath types for each comparison—stemless wreath found on 1804, 1805, 1806 Half cents. 1797, 1802, 1803 Large cents.

1804 HALF CENT PROTRUDING TONGUE OR SPIKED CHIN VARIETY

Details showing differences in 1804 plain 4 and crosslet 4. Note serif on horizontal bar of figure 4 as shown at right.

Plain 4

Crosslet 4

THE 1856 FLYING EAGLE CENT

Collectors are advised to inspect any 1856 Flying Eagle cent carefully. A few tests will aid in establishing genuineness of this cent, as follows:

THE DATE

The 6 in the date should be as illustrated. If the lower half is thick, it is probably an altered 1858. A magnifying glass will often reveal poor workmanship.

The figure 5 slants slightly to the right on a genuine 1856. The vertical bar points to the center of the ball just beneath. On the 1858, this bar points *outside* the ball. (Compare the two illustrations.)

THE LEGEND

The center of the O in OF is crude and almost squared on the genuine 1856, but on the large letter 1858 it is rounded.

The letters A and M in America are joined in both the 1856 and large letter 1858, but they join at a slight angle on the 1856, while the bottom of the letters form a smooth curve on the 1858 large letter cent.

Large Letters

1858 FLYING EAGLE CENT

Letters A and M in the word AMERICA are joined on the LARGE LETTER variety. They are separated on the SMALL LETTER variety.

Small Letters

1864 BRONZE INDIAN HEAD CENT WITH "L" ON RIBBON

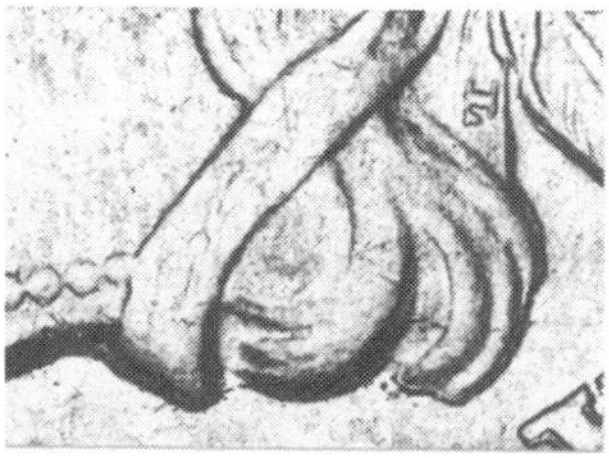

A small "L," the initial of the designer Longacre, was added to the Indian design late in 1864 and was continued through 1909. For coins in less than fine condition, this small letter will often be worn away. The point of the bust is rounded on the 1864 variety without "L"; pointed on the variety with "L." The initial must be visible, however, for the 1864 variety to bring the higher premium. If the coin is turned slightly so that the Indian faces the observer, the highlighted details will usually appear to better advantage.

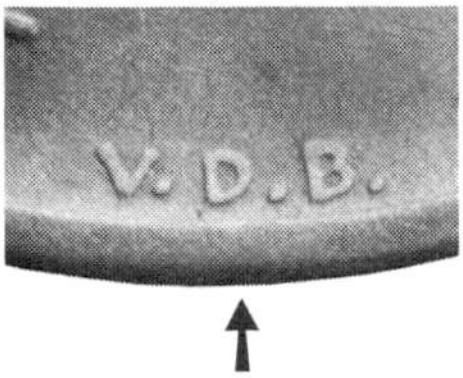

During 1909 initials appeared on the reverse. Starting in 1918 they appear below the shoulder.

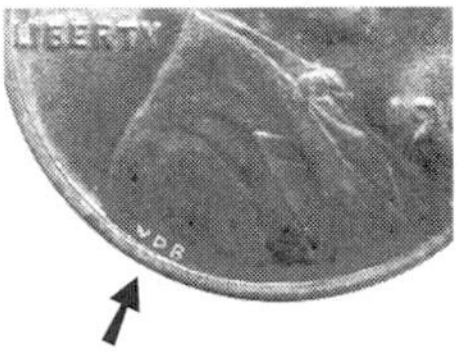

1918-S Quarter
8 Over 7
A variety of this kind is rarely found in coinage of the twentieth century.

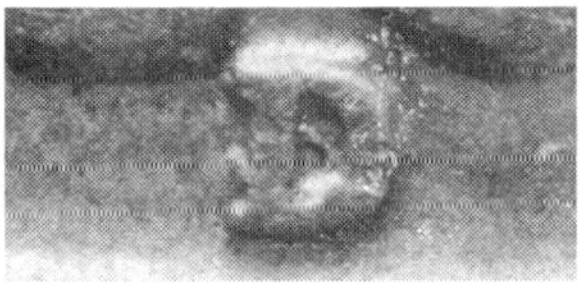

1938 D over S Nickel Variety

1942 Dime with 2 over 1

1955 Cent Error
"Doubled Die" Obverse

Large Date Cent
1960

Small Date Cent
1960

Large Date Cent
1982

Small Date Cent
1982

CONDITION OF COINS

Essential elements of the American Numismatic Association grading system

ABOUT GOOD (AG-3) — Very heavily worn with portions of lettering, date and legends worn smooth. The date may be barely readable.

GOOD (G-4) — Heavily worn with design visible but faint in areas. Many details are flat.

VERY GOOD (VG-8) — Well worn with main features clear and bold although rather flat.

FINE (F-12) — Moderate to considerable even wear. Entire design is bold with overall pleasing appearance.

VERY FINE (VF-20) — Shows moderate wear on high points of design. All major details are clear.

CHOICE VERY FINE (VF-30) — Light even wear on the surface and highest parts of the design. All lettering and major features are sharp.

EXTREMELY FINE (EF-40) — Design is lightly worn throughout, but all features are sharp and well defined. Traces of luster may show.

CHOICE EXTREMELY FINE (EF-45) — Light overall wear shows on highest points. All design details are very sharp. Some of the mint luster is evident.

ABOUT UNCIRCULATED (AU-50) — Has traces of light wear on many of the high points. At least half of the mint luster is still present.

CHOICE ABOUT UNCIRCULATED (AU-55) — Evidence of friction on design high points. Most of mint luster remains.

MINT STATE — The terms Mint State (MS) and Uncirculated (Unc.) are interchangeably used to describe coins showing no trace of wear. Such coins may vary to some degree because of blemishes, toning or slight imperfections as described in the following subdivisions.

UNCIRCULATED (MS-60) — Has no trace of wear but may show a number of contact marks, and surface may be spotted or lack some luster.

UNCIRCULATED (MS-63) — Some distracting contact marks or blemishes in prime focal areas. Luster may be impaired.

CHOICE UNCIRCULATED (MS-65) — An above average Uncirculated coin that may be brilliant or lightly toned and has very few contact marks on the surface or rim. MS-67 through MS-62 indicate a slightly higher or lower grade of preservation.

PERFECT UNCIRCULATED (MS-70) — Perfect new condition, showing no trace of wear. The finest quality possible, with no evidence of scratches, handling or contact with other coins. Very few regular issue coins are ever found in this condition.

PROOF (PF-60) — Surface may have several contact marks, hairlines or light rubs. Luster may be dull and eye appeal lacking.

ATTRACTIVE PROOF (PF-63) — Reflective surfaces with only a few blemishes in secondary focal places. No major flaws.

CHOICE PROOF (PF-65) — Brilliant surfaces with no noticable blemishes or flaws. Few scattered barely noticeable marks or hairlines.

IMPORTANT: Damaged coins, such as those which are bent, corroded, scratched, holed, nicked, stained or mutilated, are worth less than those without defects. *Flawless uncirculated coins are generally worth more than values quoted in this book.* Slightly worn coins ("sliders") which have been cleaned and conditioned ("whizzed") to simulate uncirculated luster are worth considerably less than perfect pieces.

Unlike damage inflicted after striking, manufacturing defects do not always lessen values. Examples are: Colonial coins with planchet flaws and weakly struck designs; early silver and gold with weight adjustment "file marks" (parallel cuts made prior to striking); and pieces with "lint marks" (dust or other foreign matter which may mar the surface during striking).

Brief guides to grading are placed before each major coin type in this book.

Preserving and Cleaning Coins

Most numismatists will tell you to "never clean a coin" and it is good advice! Cleaning coins will almost always reduce their value. Collectors prefer coins in their original condition.

Some effort should be made to protect uncirculated and proof coins so they won't need cleaning. Tarnish on a coin is purely a chemical process caused by oxygen in the air acting on the metal or by chemicals with which the coin comes in contact. One of the commonest chemicals causing tarnish is sulphur; most paper, with the exception of specially manufactured "sulphur-free" kinds, contains sulphur due to the sulphuric acid that is used in paper manufacture, therefore do not wrap coins in ordinary paper; also keep uncirculated and proof coins away from rubber bands (a rubber band placed on a silver coin for a few days will produce a black stripe on the coin where the band touched). The utmost in protection is obtained by storing the coin in an airtight box, away from moisture and humidity, and by using holders made of inert materials.

Many coins become marred by careless handling. Always hold the coin by the edge. The accompanying illustration shows the right and wrong way to handle numismatic specimens. It is a breach of numismatic etiquette to handle another collector's coin except by the edge, even if it is not an uncirculated or proof piece.

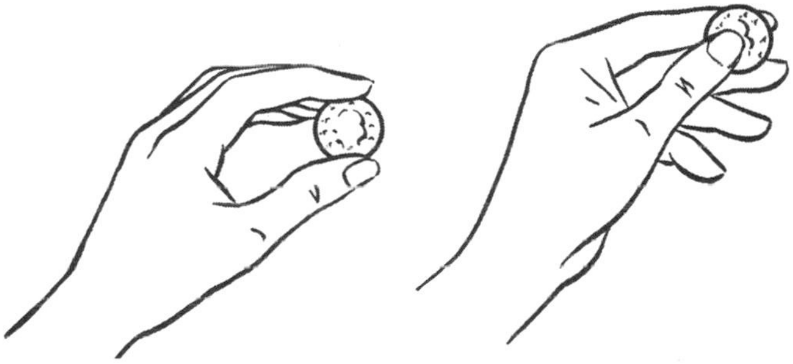

RIGHT WRONG

Starting a Collection

One may start a collection of United States coins with very little expense by systematically assembling the various dates and mint marks of all the types and denominations that are now in general circulation. Whitman's coin folders make this possible.

With the exception of the price paid for the coin folder, collecting coins received in everyday business transactions entails no expense whatever; a Jefferson nickel taken out of circulation, for example, can always be spent for 5 cents if the occasion arises. Filling an album or two out of circulation is probably the best method of determining whether coin collecting appeals to you. Not everyone can be a successful coin collector. It requires patience, intelligence of a high order, and a certain desire to know the meaning behind a lot of things that at first glance appear meaningless. You may not be cut out to be a collector but you'll never know until you look further into the subject, and if by the time an album or two of coins are collected you have no burning desire to acquire many more different coins, you will probably never be a collector. However, the chances are that you will be, because if you have read this far in this book it shows that you are interested in the subject.

Perfection is the goal of every endeavor and coin collecting is no exception. After an album has been filled with circulated specimens, the next step will be to replace them with coins in uncirculated condition, or perhaps to start collecting an obsolete series; in either case, it will be necessary to purchase some coins from dealers or other collectors. The most logical way to keep abreast with the market, or obtain the addresses of the country's leading dealers, is to subscribe to one or more of the trade publications. These magazines carry advertisements of various dealers listing coins for sale. Moreover, through this source the beginner may obtain price lists and catalogs from the dealers.

There are several good reference books available at reasonable prices which will be helpful to the collector who wishes to know more about U. S. coins and paper money. R. S. Yeoman's *A Guide Book Of United States Coins*™ (Red Book) lists retail values of all regular U. S. coins and also lists all coins of the U.S. Colonial period and private and territorial gold coins.

Most coin, book and hobby dealers can supply the following titles:

The Official Red Book®: A Guide Book of United States Coins™ 2005 — R.S. Yeoman

The Official Red Book of Morgan Silver Dollars: A Complete History and Price Guide — Q. David Bowers

The Official Red Book®: A Guide Book of Double Eagle Gold Coins — Q. David Bowers

Coin Collecting: A Beginner's Guide to the World of Coins — Kenneth Bressett

United States Pattern Coins: Experimental, And Trial Pieces — Q. David Bowers

NGC: Grading Guide For Modern U.S. Coins — Richard S. Montgomery & David W. Lange

Coins: Questions & Answers — Clifford Mishler

Join a Coin Club

A beginner should join a "coin club" if he or she is fortunate enough to live in a city which has one. The association with more experienced collectors will be of great benefit. Practically all the larger cities have one or more clubs and they are being rapidly organized in the smaller towns. Trade publications carry information about coin clubs and special events such as coin shows and conventions.

I. THE BRITISH COLONIES IN AMERICA

SOMMER ISLANDS (Bermuda)

This coinage, the first struck for the English colonies in America, was issued about 1616. The coins were known as "Hogge Money" or "Hoggies."

The pieces were made of copper lightly silvered, in four denominations: shilling, sixpence, threepence and twopence, indicated by Roman numerals. The hog is the main device and appears on the obverse side of each. SOMMER ISLANDS is inscribed within beaded circles. The reverse shows a full-rigged galleon with the flag of St. George on each of four masts.

Shilling

	G	VG	F	VF	EF
Twopence	$1,750.	$3,000.	$4,500.	$7,500.	$12,000.
Threepence (*very rare*)					
Sixpence	1,500.	2,600.	4,000.	7,500.	12,500.
Shilling	2,500.	3,500.	4,750.	8,500.	20,000.

MASSACHUSETTS

"NEW ENGLAND" COINAGE (1652)

In 1652 the General Court of Massachusetts ordered the first metallic currency to be struck in the English Americas, the New England silver threepence, sixpence, and shilling. These coins were made from silver bullion procured principally from the West Indies. Joseph Jenks made the punches for the first coins at his Iron Works in Saugus, Massachusetts, close to Boston where the mint was located. John Hull was appointed mintmaster; his assistant was Robert Sanderson.

Note: Early American coins are rare in conditions better than listed and valued much higher.

NE Shilling (1652)

	G	VG	F	VF
NE Threepence (*Unique*)	—	—	—	—
NE Sixpence (*8 known*)	—	—	—	$60,000.
NE Shilling	$6,000.	$15,000.	$30,000.	50,000.

WILLOW TREE COINAGE (1653-1660)

The simplicity of the design on the N.E. coins invited counterfeiting and clipping of the edges. Therefore, they were soon replaced by the Willow, Oak and Pine Tree series. The Willow Tree coins were struck from 1653 to 1660, the Oak Trees 1660 to 1667, and the Pine Trees 1667 to 1682. All of them (with the exception of the Oak Tree twopence) bore the date 1652. Many varieties of all of these coins exist. Values shown are for the most common types.

Sixpence

	F	G	VG	F	VF
Willow Tree Threepence 1652 (*3 known*)	—	—	—	—	—
Willow Tree Sixpence 1652 (*14 known*)	—	$6,000.	$10,000.	$20,000.	$50,000.
Willow Tree Shilling 1652	$ 2,500.	5,800.	9,500.	20,000.	50,000.

OAK TREE COINAGE (1660-1667)

Twopence

Threepence

	G	VG	F	VF	EF	AU
Oak Tree Twopence 1662	$175.	$250.	$400.	$900.	$1,900.	$4,500.
Oak Tree Threepence 1652	180.	275.	550.	1,000.	2,500.	5,000.
Oak Tree Sixpence 1652	175.	275.	550.	1,000.	3,000.	6,000.
Oak Tree Shilling 1652	200.	320.	600.	1,200.	3,100.	6,000.

PINE TREE COINAGE (1667-1682)

The first pine tree coins were minted on the same size planchets as the Oak Tree pieces. Subsequent issues of the shilling were narrower and thicker to conform to the size of English coins.

Shilling,
Large Planchet
(1667-1674)

PINE TREE COINAGE (1667-1682)

Shilling, Small Planchet (1675-1682)

	G	VG	F	VF	EF	AU
Pine Tree Threepence 1652	$225.	$400.	$600.	$1,500.	$2,000.	$3,500.
Pine Tree Sixpence 1652	250.	425.	650.	1,800.	2,100.	3,700.
Pine Tree Shilling, Large Planchet 1652	325.	575.	1,100.	2,250.	3,000.	4,250.
Pine Tree Shilling, Small Planchet 1652	275.	475.	800.	1,950.	2,200.	3,800.

MARYLAND

In 1659 Cecil Calvert, the "Lord Proprietor of Maryland," had coinage struck in England for use in Maryland. There were four denominations: shillings, sixpence, and fourpence (groat) in silver, and a copper penny (denarium). The silver coins have the bust of Lord Baltimore on the obverse, and the Baltimore family arms with the denomination in Roman numerals on the reverse.

Lord Baltimore Shilling

Fourpence (groat)

	G	VG	F	VF	EF	AU
Penny (copper) (*Ex. Rare*)	—	—	—	—	—	—
Fourpence	$600.	$1,200.	$2,750.	$5,750.	$7,500.	$12,000.
Sixpence	525.	975.	2,100.	3,900.	5,750.	7,000.
Shilling	850.	1,500.	2,900.	5,500.	7,400.	11,000.

NEW JERSEY

ST. PATRICK OR MARK NEWBY COINAGE

Mark Newby, who came to America from Dublin, Ireland, in November 1681, brought copper pieces believed by numismatists to have been struck in England c. 1663-1672. These are called St. Patrick coppers. The coin received wide circulation in the New Jersey Province, having been authorized to pass as legal tender by the General Assembly in May 1682. The smaller piece, known as a farthing, was never specifically authorized for circulation in the colonies.

St. Patrick Farthing

	G	VG	F	VF	EF	AU
St. Patrick "Farthing"	$25.	$70.	$200.	$700.	$1,500.	$3,000.
St. Patrick "Halfpenny"	75.	150.	400.	1,000.	2,000.	

II. COINAGE AUTHORIZED BY ROYAL PATENT

AMERICAN PLANTATIONS TOKEN

These tokens struck in nearly pure tin were the first authorized coinage for the British colonies in America. They were made under a franchise granted in 1688 to Richard Holt. Restrikes were made c. 1828 from original dies.

	G	F	EF	AU	UNC
1/24 PART REAL - Tin	$50.	$200.	$500.	$800.	$1,400.
1/24 PART REAL - Restrike	25.	120.	300.	450.	700.

COINAGE OF WILLIAM WOOD

ROSA AMERICANA COINS

William Wood, an Englishman, obtained a patent from George I to make tokens for Ireland and the American colonies. The Rosa Americana pieces were issued in three denominations: halfpenny, penny, and twopence, and were intended for use in America.

Penny

ROSA AMERICANA

	VG	F	VF	EF	AU	UNC
Twopence (no date) motto in ribbon (illustrated)	$60.	$120.	$250.	$500.	$900.	$1,800.
1722, Halfpenny DEI GRATIA REX UTILE DULCI	35.	85.	165.	350.	700.	1,500.
1722, Penny	35.	85.	165.	350.	700.	1,500.
1722, Twopence	55.	120.	210.	450.	850.	1,700.

Halfpenny

Twopence

	VG	F	VF	EF	AU	UNC
1723, Halfpenny	35.	80.	150.	325.	650.	1,300.
1723, Penny	35.	80.	170.	290.	550.	1,200.
1723, Twopence (illustrated)	55.	110.	225.	450.	750.	1,600.

WOOD'S HIBERNIA COINAGE

The type intended for Ireland had a seated figure with a harp on the reverse side and the word HIBERNIA. Denominations struck were halfpenny and farthing with dates 1722, 1723 and 1724. Hibernia coins were unpopular in Ireland, so many of them were sent to the American colonies.

1722 Hibernia Halfpenny | **First Type** | **Second Type**

	VG	F	VF	EF	AU	UNC
1722, Farthing (2nd Type)		$110.	$200.	$435.	$725.	$1,250.
1722, Halfpenny (1st or 2nd Type)	25.	35.	60.	175.	225.	$400.

WOOD'S HIBERNIA COINAGE

1723 Hibernia Farthing

1724 Hibernia Halfpenny

	VG	F	VF	EF	AU	UNC
1723, Farthing	$18.	$29.	$57.	$135.	$175.	$325.
1723, Halfpenny	18.	29.	50.	125.	175.	325.
1724, Farthing	25.	65.	135.	285.	400.	700.
1724, Halfpenny	24.	55.	125.	250.	375.	650.

VIRGINIA HALFPENNY

In 1773 coinage of a copper halfpenny was authorized for Virginia by the English Crown. The style is similar to the regular English coinage. These pieces were never popular, but did circulate by necessity.

	VG	F	VF	EF	AU	UNC
1773, Halfpenny	$30.	$45.	$85.	$175.	$250.	$450.

III. EARLY AMERICAN TOKENS

Struck in America or England for use by American Merchants

LONDON ELEPHANT TOKENS

Struck c. 1672-1684 during the reign of Charles II, the London Token, an early historian states, was produced during the great plague raging in London. The legend on this piece relates directly to that crisis. It has also been stated that the London Token was to have been current in Tangier, Africa, but was never used in that locality. No date appears on this token.

It is unlikely that many ever circulated in America. They are associated with the 1694 pieces through use of a common obverse die.

LONDON ELEPHANT TOKENS

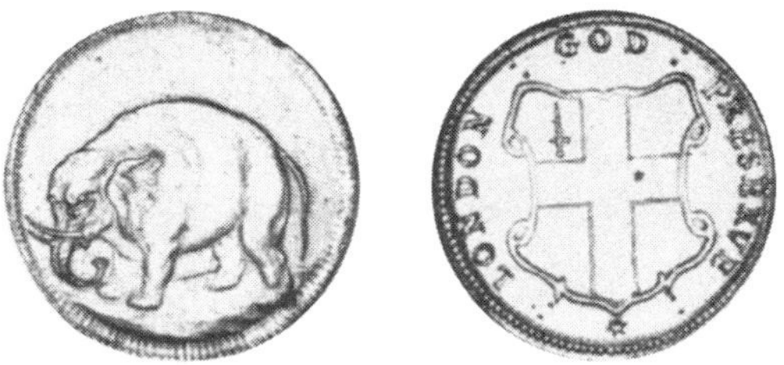

	VG	F	VF	EF	AU	UNC
(1694) Halfpenny, GOD PRESERVE LONDON (Thick or Thin planchet)	$125.	$210.	$360.	$775.	$1,000.	$1,600.

CAROLINA AND NEW ENGLAND ELEPHANT TOKENS

Although no law is known authorizing coinage for Carolina, very interesting pieces known as Elephant Tokens were made with the date 1694. These copper tokens were of halfpenny denomination. The reverse reads GOD PRESERVE CAROLINA AND THE LORDS PROPRIETERS. 1694.

The Carolina pieces were probably struck in England and perhaps intended only as tokens, or possibly as advertising to heighten interest in the Carolina Plantation.

Like the Carolina Tokens, the New England Elephant Tokens were believed to have been struck in England as promotional pieces to increase interest in the American Colonies.

	VG	F	VF	EF
1694, CAROLINA	$1,900.	$3,250.	$5,000.	$8,000.

NEW ENGLAND ELEPHANT TOKEN

	VG	F	VF	EF
1694, NEW ENGLAND	$12,500.	$14,000.	$18,000.	$27,500.

THE NEW YORKE TOKEN

Little is known about the origin of this token. The design of a displayed eagle on a regulated staff with oak leaf finials is identical to the crest found on the arms of William Lovelace, governor of New York 1663-1673. It seems likely that this piece is a token farthing struck by Lovelace for use in New York.

	UNDATED	
	V. Good	**Fine**
Brass	$2,000.	$4,250.

GLOUCESTER TOKEN

This token appears to have been a private coinage by a merchant of Gloucester (county), Virginia. The only specimens known are struck in brass. The exact origin and use of these pieces are unknown.

	Fine
1714, Shilling (brass) (*2 known*)	$17,500.

HIGLEY OR GRANBY COPPERS

The Higley coppers were never officially authorized. All the tokens were made of pure copper. There were seven obverse and four reverse dies. The first issue, in 1737, bore the legend THE VALUE OF THREEPENCE. After a time the quantity exceeded the local demand, and a protest arose against the value of the piece. The inscription was changed to VALUE ME AS YOU PLEASE.

	G	**VG**	**F**	**VF**
1737, THE • VALUE • OF • THREE • PENCE.— 3 Hammers — CONNECTICVT	$3,750.	$5,500.	$10,000.	$20,000.
1737, THE • VALUE • OF • THREE • PENCE.— 3 Hammers — I • AM • GOOD • COPPER	3,950.	6,000.	11,000.	21,000.
1737, VALUE • ME • AS • YOU • PLEASE — 3 Hammers — I • AM • GOOD • COPPER	3,950.	6,000.	11,000.	21,000.
(1737) VALUE • ME • AS • YOU • PLEASE — Broad Axe — J • CUT • MY • WAY • THROUGH	3,950.	6,000.	11,000.	21,000.
1739, VALUE ME AS YOU PLEASE — Broad Axe — J • CUT • MY • WAY • THROUGH	4,500.	7,000.	13,000.	29,000.

HIBERNIA-VOCE POPULI

These coins, struck in the year 1760, were made in Dublin. Like other Irish tokens, some of these pieces found their way to Colonial America.

Farthing 1760 **Halfpenny 1760**

	G	VG	F	VF	EF	AU	UNC
1760, Farthing	$105.	$150.	$225.	$475.	$1,000.	$1,500.	$2,900.
1760, Halfpenny	39.	50.	100.	165.	250.	450.	800.

PITT TOKENS

William Pitt is the subject of these pieces, probably intended as commemorative medalets. The halfpenny served as currency during a shortage of regular coinage.

	VG	F	VF	EF	AU	UNC
1766, Farthing			$5,000.			
1766, Halfpenny (*illustrated*)	$145.	$285.	400.	$950.	$1,300.	$2,100.

RHODE ISLAND SHIP MEDAL

Although this medal has a Dutch inscription, the spelling and design indicate an English or Anglo-American origin. It is believed that this token was struck in England c. 1779-1780 as propaganda to pursuade the Dutch to sign the Treaty of Armed Neutrality. Specimens are known in brass, copper, tin, and pewter. Modern copies exist.

1778-1779
Rhode Island
Ship Medal

	VF	EF	AU	UNC
Rhode Island Ship Medal	$400.	$750.	$1,000.	$1,500.

J. CHALMERS — Annapolis, Maryland

John Chalmers, a silversmith, struck a series of silver tokens at Annapolis in 1783. The shortage of change and the refusal of the people to use underweight coins prompted the issuance of these pieces.

	VG	F	VF	EF	AU
1783, Threepence	$475.	$900.	$1,900.	$3,000.	$4,000.
1783, Sixpence	800.	1,500.	3,000.	5,000.	7,000.
1783, Shilling (*reverse illustrated*)	475.	900.	1,800.	2,750.	4,000.

IV. THE FRENCH COLONIES

None of the coins of the French regime is strictly American. They were all general issues for the French colonies of the New World. The copper of 1717 to 1722 was authorized by edicts of 1716 and 1721 for use in New France, Louisiana, and the French West Indies.

COPPER SOU OR NINE DENIERS

	VG	F	VF
1721-B, (Rouen)	$55.	$110.	$250.
1721-H, (La Rochelle)	40.	65.	100.
1722-H	30.	55.	90.

FRENCH COLONIES IN GENERAL

Coined for use in the French colonies and only unofficially circulated in Louisiana along with other foreign coins and tokens. Most were counterstamped RF (République Française) for use in the West Indies.

	VG	VF	EF	AU
1767, French Colonies, Sou	$28.	$85.	$210.	$350.
1767, French Colonies, Sou. CTSP RF	25.	65.	125.	200.

V. SPECULATIVE ISSUES, TOKENS AND PATTERNS

THE CONTINENTAL CURRENCY

The Continental Currency was probably a pattern issue only and never reached general circulation. It was the first silver dollar size coin ever proposed for the United States. The coins were probably struck in Philadelphia. Many modern copies and replicas exist.

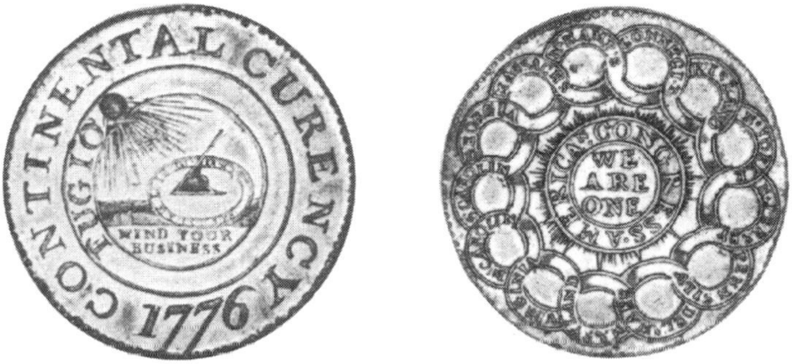

	G	F	VF	EF	AU	UNC
1776, CURENCY, Pewter	$1,100.	$2,500.	$3,000.	$5,500.	$7,000.	$12,500.
1776, CURENCY, Silver		50,000.				
1776, CURRENCY, Pewter	1,200.	2,750.	3,500.	6,000.	8,500.	15,000.
1776, CURRENCY, Pewter, EG FECIT above dt.	1,100.	2,500.	3,000.	5,500.	7,000.	14,000.

NOVA CONSTELLATIO COPPERS

The Nova Constellatio pieces were struck supposedly by order of Gouverneur Morris. Evidence indicates that they were all struck in Birmingham and imported for American circulation as a private business venture.

1783
"CONSTELLATIO"
Pointed Rays

V. Good	$40.
Fine	90.
V. Fine	175.
E. Fine	325.
A. Unc.	600.
Unc.	1,250

1783
"CONSTELLATIO"
Blunt Rays

V. Good	$40.
Fine	100.
V. Fine	200.
E. Fine	375.
A. Unc.	750.
Unc.	1,500.

NOVA CONSTELLATIO COPPERS

1785
"CONSTELATIO"
Blunt Rays

V. Good	$50.
Fine	110.
V. Fine	250.
E. Fine	450.
A. Unc.	800.
Unc.	1,750.

1785
"CONSTELLATIO"
Pointed Rays

V. Good	$40.
Fine	100.
V. Fine	200.
E. Fine	400.
A. Unc.	600.
Unc.	1,250.

IMMUNE COLUMBIA PIECES

These are considered experimental or pattern pieces. No laws describing them are known.

	VF	EF
1785, Copper, Star reverse	5,750	$6,750

1785
George III Obverse

Good	$1,300.
V. Good	1,800.
Fine	2,500.

1785
Vermon Auctori Obverse

Good	$1,400.
V. Good	2,000.
Fine	2,700.
V. Fine	6,000.

1787
IMMUNIS COLUMBIA
Eagle Reverse

Good	$100.
V. Good	210.
Fine	450.
V. Fine	1,200.
E. Fine	2,400.
A. Unc.	3,500.

CONFEDERATIO COPPERS

The Confederatio Coppers are experimental or pattern pieces. This will explain why the die with the CONFEDERATIO legend was combined with other designs such as a bust of George Washington, Libertas et Justitia of 1785, Immunis Columbia of 1786, the New York "Excelsiors," Inimica Tyrannis Americana and others. There were in all thirteen dies struck in fourteen combinations. There are two types of the Confederatio reverse. In one instance the stars are contained in a small circle; in the other larger stars are in a larger circle.

Typical Obverse

Small Circle Reverse

Large Circle Reverse

	VF
1785, Stars in Small circle, various obverses	$7,250.
1785, Stars in Large circle, various obverses	6,750.

SPECULATIVE PATTERNS

1786 IMMUNIS COLUMBIA

Eagle Reverse

Shield Reverse

	VF
1786, IMMUNIS COLUMBIA, eagle reverse.	$15,000.
1786, IMMUNIS COLUMBIA, shield reverse.	10,000.
1786, (No date) Washington obverse.	25,000.
1786, Eagle obverse	17,500.
1786, Washington obverse, eagle reverse (*Unique*)	

VI. COINAGE OF THE STATES

NEW HAMPSHIRE

New Hampshire was the first of the states to consider the subject of coinage following the Declaration of Independence.

NEW HAMPSHIRE

William Moulton was empowered to make a limited quantity of coins of pure copper authorized by the State House of Representatives in 1776.

	VG
1776, New Hampshire copper	$9,000.

MASSACHUSETTS

The coinage of Massachusetts copper cents and half cents in 1787 and 1788 was under the direction of Joshua Witherle. These were the first coins bearing the denomination "Cent" as established by Congress. Many varieties exist, the most valuable being that with arrows in the eagle's right talon.

1787 Half Cent

Good	$35.
Fine	75.
V. Fine	225.
E. Fine	475.
A. Unc.	850.
Unc.	1,600.

	G	F	VF	EF	AU	UNC
1787, Cent, arrows in right talon	$2,000.	$5,500.				
1787, Cent, arrows in left talon	30.	70.	$210.	$450.	$800.	$1,500.

1788 Half Cent

Good	$35.
Fine	75.
V. Fine	225.
E. Fine	475.
A. Unc	850.
Unc	1,600.

1788 Cent

Good	$35.
Fine	75.
V. Fine	225.
E. Fine	475.
A. Unc.	850.
Unc.	1,750.

CONNECTICUT

Authority for establishing a mint near New Haven was granted by the State to Samuel Bishop, Joseph Hopkins, James Hillhouse and John Goodrich in 1785.

1785 Copper
Bust Facing Right

Good	$25.
V. Good	35.
Fine	70.
V. Fine	185.
E. Fine	500.

1785 Copper
Bust Facing Left

Good	$75.
V. Good	130.
Fine	225.
V. Fine	375.
E. Fine	600.

	G	VG	F	VF	EF
1786, Bust Facing Right	$35.	$45.	$75.	$175.	$500.
1787, Copper Mailed Bust Facing Right	40.	60.	150.	375.	600.

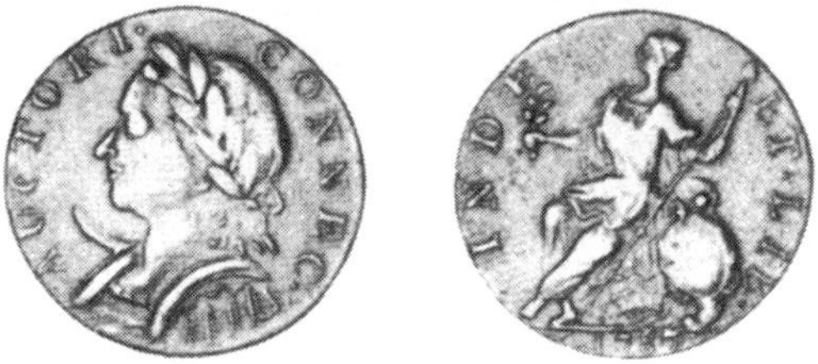

	G	VG	F	VF	EF
1786, Mailed bust facing left	$25.	$35.	$70.	$135.	$350.
1787, Mailed bust facing left	20.	30.	60.	125.	325.
1787, Draped bust facing left	20.	30.	60.	135.	350.
1788, Mailed bust facing right	18.	30.	70.	170.	400.
1788, Mailed bust facing left	18.	28.	65.	150.	375.

	G	VG	F	VF	EF
1788, Draped bust facing left	$18.	$28.	$80.	$185.	$420.

NEW YORK

THE BRASHER DOUBLOON

Perhaps the most famous pieces coined before the establishment of the U.S. Mint at Philadelphia were those produced by a well-known goldsmith and jeweler, Ephraim Brasher.

Brasher produced a gold piece weighing about 408 grains, approximately equal in value to a Spanish doubloon (about $15.00).

The punch-mark EB appears in either of two positions as illustrated. This mark is found on some foreign gold coins as well, and probably was so used by Brasher as evidence of his testing of their value.

1787, New York Gold doubloon, punch on breast (*Unique*) ....

1787, New York doubloon, punch on wing Gold ....

COPPER COINAGE

No coinage was authorized for New York following the Revolutionary War although several propositions were considered. The only coinage laws passed were those regulating coins already in use.

1786

NON VI VIRTUTE VICI

Good	$1,700.
V. Good	2,100.
Fine	3,750.
V. Fine	7,500.

	G	VG	F	VF	EF
1787, EXCELSIOR copper, eagle on globe, facing right	$700.	$1,100.	$2,200.	$4,500.	$10,000.
1787, EXCELSIOR copper, eagle on globe, facing left	700.	1,000.	2,000.	4,200.	9,000.

1787 George Clinton

Good	$3,000.
V. Good	4,000.
Fine	6,500.
V. Fine	13,000.
E. Fine	—

1787
Indian and N.Y. Arms

Good	$2,000.
V. Good	3,000.
Fine	4,250.
V. Fine	8,250.
E. Fine	14,000.

1787
Indian and Eagle on Globe

Good	$3,000.
V. Good	4,200.
Fine	6,500.
V. Fine	12,000.
E. Fine	25,000.

NEW YORK

THE NOVA EBORACS

1787 NOVA EBORAC Reverse Seated Figure Facing Right

Fair	$20.
Good	40.
Fine	150.
V. Fine	400.
E. Fine.	800.
A. Unc.	1,350.

1787 NOVA EBORAC Reverse Seated Figure Facing Left

Fair	$20.
Good	40.
Fine	125.
V. Fine	375.
E. Fine.	750.
A. Unc.	1,200.

NEW JERSEY

On June 1, 1786, the New Jersey Colonial legislature granted to Thomas Goadsby, Albion Cox and Walter Mould authority to coin some three million coppers, no later than June 1788, on condition that they delivered to the Treasurer of the State, "one-tenth part of the full sum they shall strike and coin," in quarterly installments. These coppers were to pass current at 15 to the shilling.

Narrow Shield

Wide Shield

	G	F	VF	EF	AU
1786, Narrow Shield	$20.	$80.	$200.	$550.	$900.
1786, Wide Shield	25.	90.	215.	600.	1,000.

Small Planchet

	G	F	VF	EF	AU
1787, Small planchet, plain shield	25.	85.	200.	550.	900.
1787, Large planchet, plain shield	25.	90.	225.	600.	1,000.

NEW JERSEY

Fox Before Legend

	G	F	VF	EF	AU
1788, Horse's head facing right	$ 20.	$80.	$180.	$500.	$850.
1788, Similar, fox before legend	25.	110.	225.	600.	1,000.
1788, Horse's head facing left	110.	350.	1,000.	2,500.	

VERMONT

Reuben Harmon, Jr., of Rupert, Vermont, was granted permission to coin copper pieces for a period of two years beginning July 1, 1785. The well-known Vermont plow coppers were first produced in that year. The franchise was extended for eight years in 1786.

1785 IMMUNE COLUMBIA

	G	VG	F	VF	EF
1785, IMMUNE COLUMBIA	$1,400.	$2,000.	$2,700.	$6,000.	—

1785-1786 PLOW TYPE

	G	VG	F	VF	EF
1785, VERMONTS	125.	210.	400.	800.	2,500.
1786, VERMONTENSIUM	110.	200.	375.	750.	1,400.

1786 BABY HEAD

	G	VG	F	VF	EF
1786, Baby head	140.	275.	550.	1,400.	2,200.

	1786 Bust left	1787 Bust left
Good	$70.	$1,750.
V. Good	185.	3,000.
Fine	300.	4,500.
V. Fine	700.	11,000.
E. Fine	1,200.	

1787 BRITANNIA

Good	$40.
V. Good	85.
Fine	135.
V. Fine	200.
E. Fine	600.

1787 Bust right

Good	$50.
V. Good	100.
Fine	170.
V. Fine	250.
E. Fine	700.

1788 Bust right

Good	$50.
V. Good	100.
Fine	170.
V. Fine	250.
E. Fine	700.

1788 GEORGIVS III REX*

Good	$165.
V. Good	250.
Fine	800.
V. Fine	1,510.
E. Fine	3,000.

*This piece should not be confused with the common English halfpence with similar design and reverse legend BRITANNIA.

NORTH AMERICAN TOKEN

This piece was struck in Dublin, Ireland. The obverse shows the seated figure of Hibernia facing left.

Copper or Brass
1781

V. Good	$20.
Fine	47.
V. Fine	120.
E. Fine	200.

BAR "COPPER"

The Bar "Copper" is undated and of uncertain origin. It has thirteen parallel and unconnected bars on one side. On the other side is the large Roman letter USA monogram. The design was supposedly copied from a Continental button.

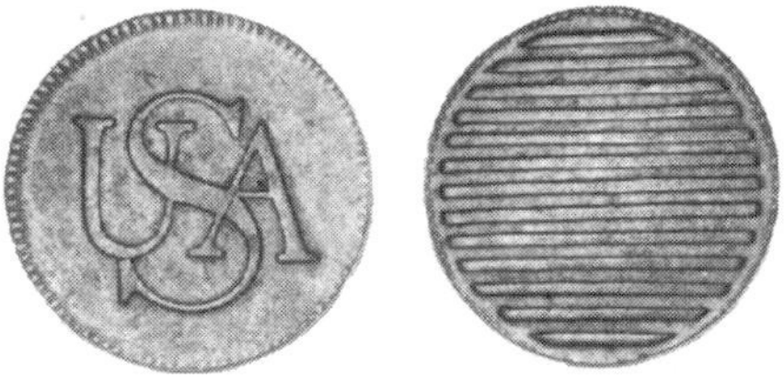

	VG	F	VF	EF	AU
Undated (about 1785) Bar "Copper"	$375.	$600.	$1,300.	$1,850.	$2,300.

AUCTORI PLEBIS TOKEN

This token is sometimes included with the coins of Connecticut as it greatly resembles issues of that state. It was struck in England by an unknown maker, possibly for use in America.

1787
AUCTORI PLEBIS

Good	$30.
V. Good	50.
Fine	100.
V. Fine	220.
E. Fine	400.
A. Unc	1,200.
Unc	2,000.

MOTT TOKEN

This was one of the first tradesman's tokens issued in America. Its exact date of manufacture and origin are unknown. They were distributed by Messrs. Mott of New York probably as a commemorative.

1789
MOTT TOKEN

V. Good	$50.
Fine	100.
V. Fine	190.
E. Fine	375.
A. Unc.	500.
Unc.	1,200.

STANDISH BARRY, BALTIMORE, MARYLAND

Standish Barry, a Baltimore silversmith, circulated a silver threepence in 1790. The tokens were believed to have been an advertising venture at a time when small change was scarce.

	VG	F	VF
1790, Threepence	$875.	$2,375.	$6,000.

KENTUCKY TOKEN

These tokens were struck in England about 1792-94. Each star in the triangle represents a state, identified by its initial letter. These pieces are usually called Kentucky Cents because the letter K (for Kentucky) happens to be at the top.

	VG	VF	EF	AU	UNC
Cent, (1792-94)	$40.	$100.	$175.	$275.	$500.

FRANKLIN PRESS

This piece is an English tradesmans' token but, being associated with Benjamin Franklin, has accordingly been included in American collections.

	VG	VF	EF	AU	UNC
1794, Franklin Press Token	$45.	$110.	$185.	$275.	$500.

TALBOT, ALLUM & LEE CENTS

Talbot, Allum & Lee, engaged in the India trade and located in New York, placed a large quantity of English-made coppers in circulation during 1794 and 1795. ONE CENT appears on the 1794 issue.

1794 Cent with NEW YORK

V. Good	$35.
V. Fine	85.
E. Fine	140.
A. Unc.	210.
Unc.	450.

1794 Cent Without NEW YORK

Good	$100.
V. Good	200.
V. Fine	350.
E. Fine	525.
A. Unc.	1,000.
Unc.	2,000.

1795 Cent

V. Good	$35.
V. Fine	70.
E. Fine	175.
A. Unc.	225.
Unc.	500.

VIII. WASHINGTON PIECES

An interesting series of coins and tokens dated from 1783 to 1795 bear the portrait of George Washington. The likenesses in most instances were faithfully reproduced and were designed to honor Washington. Many of these pieces were of English origin and made later than the dates indicate.

	F	VF	EF	AU	UNC
1783, Large military bust	$35.	$70.	$170.	$425.	$900.

	F	VF	EF	AU	UNC
1783, Draped bust	$40.	$75.	$200.	$400.	$850.

UNITY STATES

V. Good	$40.
V. Fine	120.
E. Fine	185.
A. Unc	450.
Unc	1,000.

Undated Double Head Cent

Fine	$40.
V. Fine	110.
E. Fine	185.
A. Unc	450.
Unc	1,000.

Large Eagle **Small Eagle**

1791, Cent, large eagle (date on obverse)	$170.	$400.	$600.	$1,100.
1791, Cent, small eagle (date on reverse)	170.	400.	600.	1,100.

1791 Liverpool Halfpenny Lettered Edge

Fine	$400.
E. Fine	975.
A. Unc	2,200.

1792 Eagle with Stars

Copper	—
Silver	—
Gold (*Unique*)	—

(1792) Undated Cent
"WASHINGTON BORN VIRGINIA"

	VG	F	VF
Copper	$700.	$1,400.	$2,200.

1792 Cent
"WASHINGTON PRESIDENT"

	VG	F	VF
Plain edge	$800.	$2,300.	$3,000

	VG	F	VF	EF
1792, Small eagle. Copper	$2,000.	$3,500.	—	—

1793 Ship
Halfpenny

Fine	$100.
V. Fine	190.
E. Fine	300.
A. Unc	450.
Unc	1,000.

1795 Halfpenny
Grate Token

	F	VF	EF	AU
1795, lettered edge	$145.	$350.	$425.	$725.
1795, reeded edge	85.	175.	250.	350.

Liberty and Security Tokens

	F	VF	EF	AU	UNC
1795, Half penny, plain edge	$75.	$150.	$275.	$500.	
1795, Half penny, lettered edge	65.	125.	250.	475.	

Liberty and Security Penny

Fine	$125.
V. Fine	200.
E. Fine	375.
Unc.	500.
A. Unc.	1,275.

SUCCESS MEDALS

	F	VF	EF	AU	UNC
Medal, large. Plain or reeded edge	$80.	$175.	$350.	$700.	$1,000.
Medal, small. Plain or reeded edge	100.	220.	375.	800.	1,100.

NORTH WALES HALFPENNY

1795 Halfpenny

Good	$50.
Fine	145.
V. Fine	210.
E. Fine	400.

IX. THE FUGIO CENTS

The first coins issued by authority of the United States were the "Fugio" cents. The legends have been credited to Benjamin Franklin by many, and the coin, as a consequence, has been referred to as the Franklin cent.

1787 With pointed rays

1787 With club rays

	VG	F	VF	EF	AU	UNC
STATES UNITED at sides of circle (illustrated)	$95.	$170.	$275.	$450.	$600.	$1,000.
UNITED STATES at sides of circle	95.	170.	275.	450.	600.	1,000.
Club Rays. Rounded end	135.	240.	600.	1275.		

MODERN PROOF COINS

Proof coins can usually be distinguished by their sharpness of detail, high wire edge, and extremely brilliant, mirrorlike surface. All proofs are originally sold by the mint at a premium.

Proof coins were not struck during 1943-1949 or 1965-67. Sets from 1936 through 1972 include the cent, nickel, dime, quarter and half; from 1973 through 1981 the dollar was also included. Proof sets may be ordered during the year of issue from the United States Mint, Customer Service Center, 10003 Derekwood Lane, Lanham, MD 20706. *Values shown are for original unblemished sets.*

Figures in parentheses represent the total number of full sets minted.

1936	(3,837)	$3,200.00
1937	(5,542)	1,600.00
1938	(8,045)	800.00
1939	(8,795)	650.00
1940	(11,246)	550.00
1941	(15,287)	500.00
1942, Both nickels	(21,120)	550.00
1942, One nickel		475.00
1950	(51,386)	300.00
1951	(57,500)	275.00
1952	(81,980)	150.00
1953	(128,800)	150.00
1954	(233,300)	75.00
1955, Box pack	(378,200)	50.00
1955, Flat pack		60.00
1956	(669,384)	25.00
1957	(1,247,952)	12.00
1958	(875,652)	25.00
1959	(1,149,291)	12.00
1960, with lg. date 1 cent	(1,691,602)	8.00
1960, with sm. date 1 cent		20.00
1961	(3,028,244)	5.00
1962	(3,218,019)	$5.00
1963	(3,075,645)	6.00
1964	(3,950,762)	5.50
1968S	(3,041,506)	3.25
1969S	(2,934,631)	3.25
1970S	(2,632,810)	6.00
1970S, small date 1¢		40.00
1971S	(3,220,733)	2.75
1972S	(3,260,996)	2.00
1973S	(2,760,339)	6.00
1974S	(2,612,568)	5.00
1975S	(2,845,450)	7.50
1976S	(4,149,730)	3.50
1976S, 3-pc. set	(3,998,621)	7.50
1977S	(3,251,152)	4.00
1978S	(3,127,781)	4.50
1979S, filled S	(3,677,175)	5.00
1979S, clear S		48.00
1980S	(3,554,806)	4.00
1981S	(4,063,083)	3.50
1982S	(3,857,479)	2.00
1983S	(3,138,765)	3.00
1983S, Prestige Set	(14061)	35.00

MODERN PROOF COINS

1984S	(2,748,430)	5.00
1984S, Prestige Set	(316,680)	$9.00
1985S	(3,362,821)	2.50
1986S	(2,411,180)	9.00
1986S, Prestige Set	(599,317)	16.00
1987S	(3,792,233)	2.50
1987S, Prestige Set	(435,495)	10.00
1988S	(3,031,287)	5.00
1988S, Prestige Set	(231,661)	13.00
1989S	(3,009,107)	4.00
1989S Prestige Set	(211,087)	15.00
1990S	(2,793,433)	4.50
1990S, with no-S 1 cent proof set	(3,555)	5,000
1990S, with no-S 1 cent Prestige set		5,100
1990S, Prestige Set	(506,126)	12.50
1991S	(2,610,833)	7.00
1991, Prestige Set	(256,954)	28.00
1992S	(26,756,118)	5.00
1992S, Prestige Set	(183,293)	18.00
1992S, Silver	(1,009,586)	8.00
1992S, Silver Premier Set	(308,055)	9.00
1993S	(2,409,394)	8.00
1993S, Prestige Set	(224,045)	22.00
1993S, Silver	(570,213)	17.00
1993S, Silver Premier Set	(191,140)	18.00
1994S	(2,308,701)	9.00
1994S, Prestige Set	(175,893)	25.00
1994S, Silver	(636,009)	17.00
1994S, Silver Premier Set	(149,320)	20.00
1995S	(2,010,384)	30.00
1995S, Prestige Set	(107,112)	90.00
1995S, Silver	(549,878)	40.00
1995S, Silver Premier Set	(130,107)	43.00
1996S	(1,695,244)	$7.00
1996S, Prestige Set	(55,000)	200.00
1996S, Silver	(623,655)	25.00
1996S, Silver Premier Set	(151,366)	25.00
1997S	(1,975,000)	25.00
1997S, Prestige Set	(80,000)	80.00
1997S, Silver	(605,473)	37.00
1997S, Silver Premier Set	(136,205)	38.00
1998S	(2,086,507)	15.00
1998S, Silver	(638,134)	16.00
1998S, Silver Premier Set	(240,658)	17.00
1999S, 9 piece set	(2,543,401)	35.00
1999S, 5 piece quarter set	(1,169,958)	24.00
1999S, Silver 9 piece set	(804,565)	100.00
2000S, 10 piece set	(3,082,483)	10.00
2000S, 5 piece quarter set	(937,600)	8.00
2000S, Silver 10 piece set	(965,421)	18.00
2001S, 10 piece set	(2,294,043)	30.00
2001S, 5 piece quarter set	(799,231)	13.00
2001S, Silver 10 piece set	(889,697)	40.00
2002S, 10 piece set	(2,319,766)	20.00
2002S, 5 piece quarter set	(764,479)	10.00
2002S, Silver 10 piece set	(892,229)	28.00
2003S, Silver 10 piece set		30.00
2003S, 10-piece set		11.00
2003S, Silver 5-piece set		9.00
2003S, 5-piece set		7.00
2004S, 5-piece set		7.00
2004S, Silver 5-piece set		9.00
2004S, 11-piece set		12.00

Original issue prices: 1936 thru 1942, $1.89; 1950 thru 1964, $2.10; 1968 thru 1972S, $5.00; 1973S thru 1976S, $7.00; 1977S thru 1979S, $9.00; 1980S, $10.00; 1981S to 1991S, $11.00; 1992S to 1998S, $12.50.

UNCIRCULATED MINT SETS

Official Mint Sets are specially packaged by the government for sale to collectors. They contain uncirculated specimens of each year's coins for every denomination issued from each mint. Sets from 1947 through 1958 contain two examples of each regular issue coin. No official sets were produced in 1950, 1982 or 1983. Privately assembled sets are valued according to individual coin prices. Only official sets are included in the following list. Unlike the Proof sets, these are normal coins intended for circulation and are not minted with any special consideration for quality. Current year sets may be ordered by telephoning 1-800-USAMINT.

1947, P-D-S	5,000	$600.00
1948, P-D-S	6,000	250.00
1949, P-D-S	5,000	400.00
1951, P-D-S	8,654	375.00
1952, P-D-S	11,499	300.00
1953, P-D-S	15,538	250.00
1954, P-D-S	25,599	150.00
1955, P-D-S	49,656	75.00
1956, P-D	45,475	60.00
1957, P-D	34,324	100.00
1958, P-D	50,314	75.00
1959, P-D	187,000	20.00
1960, P-D	260,485	10.00
1961, P-D	223,704	18.00
1962, P-D	385,285	8.00
1963, P-D	606,612	5.00
1964, P-D	1,008,108	4.00
1965	*2,360,000	5.00
1966	*2,261,583	5.50
1967	*1,863,344	8.00
1968, P-D-S	2,105,128	2.00
1969, P-D-S	1,817,392	3.00
1970, P-D-S	2,038,134	7.00
1971, P-D-S	2,193,396	2.00
1972, P-D-S	2,750,000	2.00
1973, P-D-S	1,767,691	10.00
1974, P-D-S	1,975,981	3.50
1975, P-D-S		$4.00
1776-1976, (3 pieces)	4,908,319	7.00
1976, P-D	1,892,513	5.00
1977, P-D	2,006,869	4.00
1978, P-D	2,162,609	4.00
1979, P-D	2,526,000	4.00
1980, P-D-S	2,815,066	5.00
1981, P-D-S	2,908,145	7.00
1984, P-D	1,832,857	2.50
1985, P-D	1,710,571	3.00
1986, P-D	1,153,536	10.00
1987, P-D	2,890,758	3.50
1988, P-D	1,646,204	3.50
1989, P-D	1,987,915	3.50
1990, P-D	1,809,184	3.00
1991, P-D	1,352,101	5.00
1992, P-D	1,500,143	3.00
1993, P-D	1,297,431	4.25
1994, P-D	1,234,813	4.75
1995, P-D	1,038,787	9.00
1996, P-D plus dime	1,457,949	9.00
1997, P-D	950,473	12.00
1998, P-D	1,187,325	7.00
1999, P-D (18 pieces)	1,243,867	14.00
2000, P-D (20 pieces)	1,416,000	7.00
2001, P-D (20 pieces)	1,113,623	8.00
2002, P-D (20 pieces)	1,139,388	7.00
2003, P-D (20 pieces)		10.00
2004, P-D (22 pieces)		10.00

*Special Mint Sets

HALF CENTS — 1793-1857

The half cent was authorized to be coined April 2, 1792. Originally the weight was to have been 132 grains, but this was changed to 104 grains by the Act of January 14, 1793, before coinage commenced. The weight was again changed to 84 grains January 26, 1796 by presidential proclamation in conformity with the Act of March 3, 1795. Coinage was discontinued by the Act of February 21, 1857. All were coined at the Philadelphia Mint.

LIBERTY CAP TYPE — 1793-1797

AG-3 ABOUT GOOD—*Clear enough to identify.*
G-4 GOOD—*Outline of bust clear, no details. Date readable. Reverse lettering incomplete.*
VG-8 VERY GOOD—*Some hair details. Reverse lettering complete.*
F-12 FINE—*Most of hair detail shows. Leaves worn but all visible.*
VF-20 VERY FINE—*Hair near ear and forehead worn, other areas distinct. Some details in leaves show.*
EF-40 EXTREMELY FINE—*Light wear on highest parts of head and wreath.*
AU-50 ABOUT UNCIRCULATED—*Traces of light wear on only the high points of the design. Half of mint luster is present.*

Head Facing Left 1793

	Mintage	AG-3	G-4	VG-8	F-12	VF-20	EF-40	AU-50
1793	35,334	$425.	$950.	$1,400.	$2,200.	$3,500.	$6,500.	$9,000.

Head Facing Right 1794-1797

1794	81,600	75.	160.	225.	425.	775.	1,800.	2,500.

Pole to Cap

Punctuated Date

No Pole to Cap

		AG-3	G-4	VG-8	F-12	VF-20	EF-40	AU-50
1795, All kinds	139,690							
1795, Lettered edge, with pole		$50.	$150.	$225.	$400.	$650.	$1,600.	$2,000.
1795, Lettered edge,punctuated date		50.	150.	225.	400.	650.	1,600.	2,000.

	Mintage	AG-3	G-4	VG-8	F-12	VF-20	EF-40	AU-50
1795, Plain Edge,Punc.Dt		$45.	$135.	$185.	$375.	$625.	$1,500.	$2,000.
1795, Plain edge,no pole		45.	135.	180.	375.	625.	1,500.	2,000.
1796, With pole	} 1,390	2,200.	3,500.	5,250.	7,750.	14,000.	20,000.	
1796, No pole		5,000.	8,500.	12,000.	20,000.	30,000.	40,000.	

1797 Plain Edge

1797, 1 above 1, Plain Edge

	Mintage	AG-3	G-4	VG-8	F-12	VF-20	EF-40	AU-50
1797, All kinds	127,840							
1797, Lettered edge		130.	425.	750.	1,500.	3,000.	3,500.	
1797, Plain edge		60.	140.	210.	400.	725.	1,700.	2,700.
1797, Gripped edge		2,500.	5,500.	14,000.				
1797, 1 above 1, plain edge		50.	140.	190.	350.	550.	1,500.	

DRAPED BUST TYPE 1800-1808

AG-3 ABOUT GOOD—*Clear enough to identify.*
G-4 GOOD—*Bust outline clear, few details, date readable. Reverse lettering worn and incomplete.*
VG-8 VERY GOOD—*Some drapery shows. Date and legends complete.*
F-12 FINE—*Shoulder drapery and hair over brow worn smooth.*
VF-20 VERY FINE—*Only slight wear in above areas. Slight wear on reverse.*
EF-40 EXTREMELY FINE—*Light wear on highest parts of head and wreath.*
AU-50 ABOUT UNCIRCULATED—*Wear slight on the hair above forehead.*

1st Reverse

2nd Reverse

	Mintage	AG-3	G-4	VG-8	F-12	VF-20	EF-40	AU-50
1800	202,908	$12.	$25.	$30.	$45.	$85.	$175.	$300.
1802, 2 over 0	20,266	100.	275.	500.	1,200.	3,000.	7,250.	
1803	92,000	12.	25.	30.	45.	90.	300.	450.

Plain 4

Crosslet 4

Stemless Wreath

Stems to Wreath

	Mintage	AG-3	G-4	VG-8	F-12	VF-20	EF-40	AU-50
1804, All Kinds	1,055,312							
1804, Plain 4, stems		14.	28.	35.	65.	110.	300.	450.
1804, Plain 4, stemless		12.	25.	30.	42.	55.	110.	220.
1804, Crosslet 4, stemless		12.	25.	30.	42.	55.	110.	220.
1804, Crosslet 4, stems		12.	25.	30.	42.	55.	110.	220.

1804 "Spiked Chin"

Small 5

Large 5

	Mintage	AG-3	G-4	VG-8	F-12	VF-20	EF-40	AU-50
1804, "Spiked chin"	included above	$13.	$25.	$30.	$45.	$70.	$150.	$250.
1805, All Kinds	814,464							
1805, Medium 5, stemless		12.	25.	30.	45.	60.	110.	220.
1805, Small 5, stems		70.	225.	500.	950.	1,900.		
1805, Large 5, stems		10.	22.	27.	40.	55.	110.	220.

Small 6

Large 6

1808, 8 over 7

Normal Date

	Mintage	AG-3	G-4	VG-8	F-12	VF-20	EF-40	AU-50
1806, All Kinds	356,000							
1806, Small 6, stems		25.	85.	150.	250.	400.	950.	2,000.
1806, Small 6, stemless		10.	22.	26.	35.	50.	110.	220.
1806, Large 6, stems		10.	22.	26.	35.	50.	110.	220.
1807	476,000	10.	22.	26.	35.	60.	170.	300.
1808, 8 over 7	} 400,000	25.	50.	100.	200.	400.	1,100.	2,500.
1808		10.	22.	26.	35.	55.	175.	300.

CLASSIC HEAD TYPE 1809-1836

G-4 GOOD—*LIBERTY only partly visible on hair band. Lettering, date, stars, worn but visible.*
VG-8 VERY GOOD—*LIBERTY entirely visible on hair band. Lower curls worn.*
F-12 FINE—*Only part wear on LIBERTY and hair at top worn in spots.*
VF-20 VERY FINE—*Lettering clear-cut. Hair only slightly worn.*
EF-40 EXTREMELY FINE—*Light wear on highest points of hair and leaves*
AU-50 ABOUT UNCIRCULATED—*Sharp hair detail with only a trace of wear on higher points.*
MS-60 UNCIRCULATED—*Typical brown to red surface. No trace of wear.*
MS-63 SELECT UNCIRCULATED—*Well-defined color, brown to red. No traces of wear.*

Brilliant or red uncirculated coins are worth more than prices shown. Spotted, cleaned or discolored pieces are worth less.

	Mintage	AG-3	G-4	VG-8	F-12	VF-20	EF-40	MS-60	PF-60
1809, All kinds	1,154,572	$15.	$20.	$26.	$35.	$50.	$100.	$200.	$300.
1810	215,000	17.	25.	45.	75.	180.	250.	650.	1,000.
1811	63,140	60.	115.	250.	550.	1,300.	1,600.	3,000.	3,700.
1825	63,000	16.	22.	26.	35.	60.	95.	300.	450.
1826	234,000	16.	22.	26.	35.	55.	80.	200.	300.

13 Stars

12 Stars

	Mintage	G-4	VG-8	F-12	VF-20	EF-40	AU-50	MS-60	MS-63	PF-63
1828, 13 stars	606,000	$15.	$20.	$26.	$35.	$45.	$70.	$125.	$180.	
1828, 12 stars		16.	21.	29.	40.	85.	125.	400.	600.	
1829	487,000	15.	20.	26.	35.	50.	75.	135.	180.	
1831, (*Beware of altered date*)	2,200							—	—	4,200
1832 .....(4,500)	51,000	15.	20.	24.	30.	40.	65.	125.	180.	$1,900.
1833 .....(4,500)	103,000	15.	20.	24.	30.	40.	65.	125.	180.	1,900.
1834 .....(4,500)	141,000	15.	20.	24.	30.	40.	65.	125.	180.	1,900.
1835 .....(4,500)	398,000	15.	20.	24.	30.	40.	65.	125.	180.	1,900.
1836, (6,500)									3,000.	

CORONET TYPE 1840-1857

	PF-63
1840, Original .....(4,500)	$2,200.
1840, Restrike .....(4,200)	2,000.
1841, Original ......(4,500)	2,300.
1841, Restrike .....(4,200)	2,200.
1842, Original .....(4,600)	2,500.
1842, Restrike .....(4,200)	2,200.
1843, Original .....(4,500)	2,300.
1843, Restrike .....(4,200)	2,300.
1844, Original .....(5,200)	3,000.
1844, Restrike .....(4,200)	2,300.
1845, Original .....(5,500)	$3,000.
1845, Restrike .....(5,000)	2,800.
1846, Original .....(5,000)	2,800.
1846, Restrike .....(4,200)	2,300.
1847, Original .....(4,500)	2,300.
1847, Restrike .....(4,200)	2,300.
1848, Original .....(4,500)	2,300.
1848, Restrike .....(4,200)	2,300.
1849, Original, SmDt (4,800)	2,600.
1849, Restrike, SmDt(4,800)	2,600.

Brilliant or red uncirculated coins are worth more than prices shown. Spotted, cleaned or discolored pieces are worth less.

VG-8 VERY GOOD—*Beads uniformly distinct. Hairlines show in spots.*
F-12 FINE—*Hairlines above ear worn. Beads sharp.*
VF-20 VERY FINE—*Lowest curl shows wear, hair otherwise distinct.*
EF-40 EXTREMELY FINE—*Light wear on highest points of hair and leaves.*
AU-50 ABOUT UNCIRCULATED—*Traces of light wear on only the high points of the design. Half of mint luster is present.*
MS-60 UNCIRCULATED—*No trace of wear, light blemishes.*
MS-63 SELECT UNCIRCULATED—*Some distracting contact marks or blemishes in prime focal areas. Luster may be impaired.*
PF-65—*Choice Brilliant surfaces with no noticeable blemishes or flaws. May have a few scatered barely noticeable marks or hairlines.*

Small Date

Large Date

	Mintage	VG-8	F-12	VF-20	EF-40	AU-50	MS-60	MS-63	PF-63	PF-65
1849, Large Date	39,864	$17.	$23.	$27.	$32.	$60.	$75.	$150.	$225.	
1850	39,812	17.	23.	27.	32.	60.	75.	150.	250.	
1851	147,672	14.	20.	25.	30.	45.	65.	110.	200.	
1852										2,600.
1853	129,694	14.	20.	25.	30.	45.	65.	110.	200.	
1854	55,358	14.	20.	25.	30.	45.	65.	110.	200.	2,500.
1855	56,500	14.	20.	25.	30.	45.	65.	110.	200.	2,500.
1856	40,430	16.	21.	26.	32.	50.	75.	120.	225.	2,500.
1857	35,180	17.	23.	28.	40.	65.	100.	150.	250.	2,500.

LARGE CENTS — 1793-1857

Cents and half cents were the first coins struck under the authority of the United States government. Coinage began in 1793 with laws specifying that the cent should weigh exactly twice as much as the half cent. Large cents were coined every year from 1793 to 1857 with the exception of 1815, when a lack of copper prevented production. All were coined at the Philadelphia Mint. Varieties listed are those most significant to collectors. Numerous other die varieties may be found because each of the early dies was individually made.

FLOWING HAIR, CHAIN TYPE REVERSE 1793

AG-3 ABOUT GOOD—*Date and devices clear enough to identify.*
G-4 GOOD—*Lettering worn but readable. Bust has no detail.*
VG-8 VERY GOOD—*Date and lettering distinct, some details of head visible.*
F-12 FINE—*About half of hair, etc. details show.*
VF-20 VERY FINE—*Ear visible. Most of details can be seen.*
EF-40 EXTREMELY FINE—*Highest points of hair and back of temple show wear.*

Obverse

AMERI. Reverse

AMERICA Reverse

	Mintage	AG-3	G-4	VG-8	F-12	VF-20	EF-40
1793, Chain	36,103	$800.	$1,900.	$2,950.	$5,500.	$8,500.	$18,000.
1793, AMERI. in legend		800.	1,900.	2,950.	5,500.	8,500.	18,000.
1793, AMERICA		750.	1,800.	2,500.	5,000.	8,000.	16,000.

FLOWING HAIR, WREATH TYPE REVERSE 1793

Wreath Type

Strawberry Leaf Var.

	Mintage	AG-3	G-4	VG-8	F-12	VF-20	EF-40
1793, Wreath	63,353						
1793, Vine/bars edge		$185.	$600.	$850.	$1,600.	$2,700.	$4,500.
1793, Lettered edge		275.	700.	950.	1,700.	2,800.	4,800.
1793, Strawberry leaf	*(4 known)*						

LIBERTY CAP TYPE 1793-1796

1793 Vine and Bar edge
Chain and Wreath Type Only

Lettered edge 1793-1795
ONE HUNDRED FOR A DOLLAR

Beaded Border, 1793 Only

1793-1794

"Head of 1793"
Head is in high
rounded relief

1794 Only

"Head of 1794"
Well defined hair,
hook on lowest curl

1794-1796

"Head of 1795"
Head in low relief,
no hook on lowest curl

	Mintage	AG-3	G-4	VG-8	F-12	VF-20	EF-40
1793, Liberty Cap	11,056	$500.	$1,000.	$2,000.	$3,500.	$8,500.	$20,000.
1794, All kinds	918,521						
1794, "Head of 1793"		140.	375.	750.	1,300.	3,000.	6,000.
1794, "Head of 1794"		30.	85.	150.	300.	500.	1,200.
1794, "Head of 1795"		30.	85.	150.	300.	450.	1,175.
1795, Lettered edge	37,000	30.	85.	150.	300.	500.	1,600.
1795, Plain edge	501,500	25.	70.	110.	225.	425.	1,000.
1796, Liberty Cap	109,825	40.	100.	150.	300.	650.	1,800.

DRAPED BUST TYPE 1796-1807

AG-3 ABOUT GOOD—*Clear enough to identify.*
G-4 GOOD—*Lettering worn, but clear; date clear. Bust lacks details.*
VG-8 VERY GOOD—*Drapery partly visible. Less wear in date and lettering.*
F-12 FINE—*Hair over brow is smooth, some details showing in other parts of hair.*
VF-20 VERY FINE—*Hairlines slightly worn. Hair over brow better defined.*
EF-40 EXTREMELY FINE—*Hair above forehead and left of eye outlined and detailed. Only slight wear on olive leaves.*

LIHERTY error

Gripped Edge

Stems

Stemless

	Mintage	AG-3	G-4	VG-8	F-12	VF-20	EF-40
1796, Draped Bust	363,375	$25.	$55.	$90.	$200.	$500.	$1,200.
1796, LIHERTY error		55.	100.	225.	375.	1,400.	3,250.
1797, All kinds	897,510						
1797, Gripped edge, '96 rev.		20.	42.	90.	200.	285.	1,000.
1797, Plain edge, '96 rev.		25.	45.	95.	210.	310.	1,100.
1797, '97 rev., stems		15.	25.	65.	130.	200.	500.
1797, '97 rev., stemless		20.	45.	100.	190.	400.	1,400.

1798, 8 over 7

1799, 9 over 8

1800 over 1798

1800, 80 over 79

1798, All kinds	1,841,745						
1798, 8 over 7		20.	45.	100.	160.	600.	1,750.
1798		10.	22.	35.	95.	175.	650.
1799, 9 over 8		350.	800.	1,500.	3,200.	9,500.	
1799		300.	750.	1,400.	3,000.	8,500.	
1800, All kinds	2,822,175						
1800 / 1798, Style 1 hair		10.	22.	33.	85.	250.	1,000.
1800, 80 / 79, Style 2 hair		10.	20.	27.	75.	175.	650.
1800		9.	17.	25.	60.	150.	500.

Fraction 1/000

Corrected Fraction

1801 Reverse, 3 Errors

1801, All kinds	1,362,837						
1801		8.	15.	27.	55.	135.	400.
1801, 3 errors: 1/000, one stem & IINITED		20.	45.	75.	250.	600.	2,100.
1801, Fraction 1/000		9.	17.	27.	75.	160.	600.
1801, 1/100 over 1/000		10.	22.	33.	85.	225.	650.
1802, All kinds	3,435,100						
1802		8.	20.	28.	60.	110.	350.
1802, Fraction 1/000		10.	25.	40.	75.	175.	550.
1802, Stemless wreath		8.	20.	28.	60.	110.	375.

1803 Small Date, Blunt 1

1803 Large Date, Pointed 1

Small Fraction

Large Fraction

	Mintage	AG-3	G-4	VG-8	F-12	VF-20	EF-40
1803, All kinds	3,131,691						
1803, Small Date, Small fraction		$8.	$20.	$27.	$55.	$110.	$350.
1803, Small Date, Large fraction		8.	20.	27.	55.	110.	350.
1803, Large Date, Small fraction		800.	2,000.	3,200.	6,000.	9,500.	
1803, Large Date, Large fraction		15.	25.	50.	100.	300.	1,000.
1803, 1 / 100 over 1 / 000		10.	22.	35.	75.	150.	575.
1803, Stemless wreath		10.	22.	35.	75.	150.	575.

1804 With Normal or Broken Dies (broken dies illustrated)

All genuine 1804 cents have a crosslet 4 in the date and a large fraction. The 0 in the date is in line with the O in OF on the reverse of the coin.

	Mintage	AG-3	G-4	VG-8	F-12	VF-20	EF-40
1804	96,500	160.	350.	600.	1,200.	1,700.	3,750.
1805	941,116	8.	20.	28.	60.	140.	375.
1806	348,000	10.	25.	35.	65.	175.	600.

Small 1807, 7 over 6, blunt 1

Large 1807, 7 over 6, pointed 1

	Mintage	AG-3	G-4	VG-8	F-12	VF-20	EF-40
1807, All kinds	829,221						
1807, Small 7/6, Blunt 1		300.	900.	1,800.	3,800.	6,500.	13,000.
1807, Large 7/6		8.	20.	28.	60.	140.	395.
1807, Small fraction		8.	20.	28.	60.	170.	475.
1807, Large fraction		8.	20.	28.	60.	150.	425.

CLASSIC HEAD TYPE 1808-1814

AG-3 ABOUT GOOD—*Details clear enough to identify.*

G-4 GOOD—*Legends, stars, date worn, but plain.*

VG-8 VERY GOOD—*LIBERTY all readable. Ear shows. Details worn but plain.*

F-12 FINE—*Hair on forehead and before ear nearly smooth. Ear and hair under ear sharp.*

VF-20 VERY FINE—*All hairlines show some detail. Leaves on reverse show slight wear.*

EF-40 EXTREMELY FINE—*All hairlines sharp. Very slight wear on high points.*

	Mintage	AG-3	G-4	VG-8	F-12	VF-20	EF-40
1808	1,007,000	$10.	$22.	$45.	$100.	$225.	$575.
1809	222,867	22.	45.	90.	160.	425.	1,200.

1810, 10 over 09

1810 Normal Date

1811, Last 1 over 0

1811 Normal Date

	Mintage	AG-3	G-4	VG-8	F-12	VF-20	EF-40
1810, All kinds	1,458,500						
1810, 10/09		$8.	$20.	$35.	$90.	$250.	$550.
1810		8.	20.	32.	70.	180.	450.
1811, All kinds	218,025						
1811, Last 1/0		15.	30.	55.	175.	450.	1,500.
1811		14.	28.	45.	110.	325.	675.
1812		8.	18.	32.	90.	225.	470.
1813	418,000	11.	22.	40.	100.	250.	550.
1814		8.	18.	32.	90.	225.	475.

CORONET TYPE 1816-1857

G-4 GOOD—*Head details partly visible. Even wear in date and legends.*
VG-8 VERY GOOD—*LIBERTY, date, stars, legends clear. Part of hair cord visible.*
F-12 FINE—*All hairlines show. Hair cords show uniformly.*
VF-20 VERY FINE—*Hair cords only slightly worn. Hairlines only partly worn, all well defined.*
EF-40 EXTREMELY FINE—*Both hair cords stand out sharply. All hairlines sharp.*
AU-50 ABOUT UNCIRCULATED—*Traces of light wear on only the high points of the design. Half of mint luster is present.*
MS-60 UNCIRCULATED—*Typical brown to red surface. No trace of wear.*
MS-63 SELECT UNCIRCULATED—*Some distracting contact marks or blemishes in prime focal areas. Luster may be impaired.*

13 Stars

15 Stars

Brilliant or red uncirculated coins are worth more than prices shown. Spotted, cleaned or discolored pieces are worth less.

	Mintage	G-4	VG-8	F-12	VF-20	EF-40	AU-50	MS-60	MS-63
1816	2,820,982	$8.00	$10.	$15.	$30.	$65.	$90.	$175.	$350.
1817, 13 stars	3,948,400 (1817, 13 stars and 15 stars)	8.00	9.	13.	25.	45.	75.	150.	300.
1817, 15 stars		9.00	11.	15.	40.	175.	275.	750.	—
1818	3,167,000	8.00	9.	13.	25.	45.	75.	150.	300.

1819, 9 over 8

1820, 20 over 19

	Mintage	G-4	VG-8	F-12	VF-20	EF-40	AU-50	MS-60	MS-63
1819, All kinds	2,671,000	$9.	$11.	$13.	$35.	$120.	$150.	$250.	$400.
1819, 9/8		8.	9.	13.	25.	45.	75.	150.	300.
1820, All kinds	4,407,550	6.	8.	12.	30.	50.	75.	150.	300.
1820, 20/19		9.	10.	13.	35.	120.	175.	375.	600.
1821	389,000	12.	22.	45.	140.	350.	700.	2,800.	—
1822	2,072,339	6.	9.	18.	40.	85.	240.	400.	625.

1823, 3 over 2

1824, 4 over 2

1826, 6 over 5

1823, 3/2	Included with 1824	25.	45.	140.	250.	900.	1,500.	2,500.	—
1823		28.	50.	170.	300.	1,200.	1,800.	2,750.	—
1824, 4/2	1,262,000	8.	12.	25.	110.	400.	900.	1,600.	—
1824		6.	8.	12.	60.	175.	250.	650.	1,000.
1825	1,461,100	6.	8.	12.	40.	125.	200.	600.	950.
1826, 6/5	1,517,425	9.	14.	30.	85.	375.	425.	900.	1,750.
1826		6.	8.	10.	32.	85.	150.	335.	550.
1827	2,357,732	6.	8.	10.	32.	60.	110.	225.	400.

This date size appears on cents before 1828.

This date size appears on cents after 1828.

1828, Large narrow date	2,260,624	6.	8.	13.	40.	70.	125.	300.	500.
1828, Small wide date		7.	9.	15.	50.	90.	180.	425.	—
1829		6.	8.	12.	30.	60.	90.	225.	425.
1830		6.	8.	12.	30.	60.	90.	225.	425.
1831	3,359,260	6.	8.	10.	20.	50.	80.	170.	300.
1832		6.	8.	10.	20.	50.	80.	150.	275.
1832, Large letters	2,362,000								
1833	2,739,000	6.	8.	10.	20.	50.	80.	150.	275.
1834, All kinds	1,855,100	6.	8.	10.	20.	60.	90.	175.	300.
1835, All kinds	3,878,400	6.	8.	10.	20.	50.	80.	175.	300.
1836	2,111,000	6.	8.	10.	20.	50.	80.	150.	275.

Young Head 1835-1857

G-4 GOOD—*Considerably worn. LIBERTY readable.*
VG-8 VERY GOOD—*Hairlines smooth but visible, outline of ear clearly defined.*
F-12 FINE—*Hairlines at top of head and behind ear worn but visible. Braid over brow plain, ear clear.*
VF-20 VERY FINE—*All details more sharp. Hair over brow shows only slight wear.*
EF-40 EXTREMELY FINE—*Hair above ear detailed, but slightly worn.*
AU-50 ABOUT UNCIRCULATED—*Traces of light wear on only the high points of the design. Half of mint luster is present.*
MS-60 UNCIRCULATED—*Typical brown to red surface. No trace of wear.*
MS-63 SELECT UNCIRCULATED—*Some distracting contact marks or blemishes in prime focal areas. Luster may be impaired.*

1839 over 1836

Brilliant or red uncirculated coins are worth more than prices shown. Spotted, cleaned or discolored pieces are worth less.

	Mintage	G-4	VG-8	F-12	VF-20	EF-40	AU-50	MS-60	MS-63
1837, All kinds	5,558,300								
1838	6,370,200	$6.	$8.	$10.	$20.	$50.	$80.	$130.	$180.
1839, All kinds	3,128,661	6.	8.	10.	17.	40.	75.	135.	200.
1839, 9/6, plain cords		85.	185.	450.	900.	2,300.	3,500.	—	—
1840, All kinds	2,462,700	6.	8.	10.	15.	38.	55.	135.	200.
1841	1,597,367	6.	8.	10.	15.	30.	50.	135.	250.
1842	2,383,390	6.	8.	10.	15.	28.	50.	120.	150.

"Head of 1840"
Petite Head
1839-1843

"Head of 1844"
Mature Head
1843-1857

Small Letters

Large Letters

	Mintage	G-4	VG-8	F-12	VF-20	EF-40	AU-50	MS-60	MS-63
1843, Petite,SmL.	2,425,342	6.	8.	10.	15.	28.	50.	120.	150.
1843, Petite, LgL.		8.	10.	18.	30.	60.	100.	300.	500.
1843, Mature,LgL		7.	9.	14.	20.	40.	70.	140.	375.
1844	2,398,752	6.	8.	10.	15.	28.	50.	100.	150.
1844, /81 (error)		7.	10.	13.	30.	90.	175.	420.	825.
1845	3,894,804	6.	8.	10.	15.	28.	50.	100.	135.
1846, All kinds	4,120,800	6.	8.	10.	15.	28.	50.	110.	135.
1847	6,183,669	6.	8.	10.	15.	28.	50.	100.	135.
1847, 7/"sm" 7		7.	9.	12.	18.	40.	90.	275.	700.

	Mintage	G-4	VG-8	F-12	VF-20	EF-40	AU-50	MS-60	MS-63
1848	6,415,799	$6.	$8.	$10.	$15.	$28.	$50.	$90.	$125.
1849	4,178,500	6.	8.	10.	15.	28.	50.	90.	140.
1850	4,426,844	6.	8.	10.	15.	28.	50.	90.	125.

1844, 44 over 81

1851, 51 over 81

1847, 7 over "Small" 7

Brilliant or red uncirculated coins are worth more than prices shown. Spotted, cleaned or discolored pieces are worth less.

	Mintage	G-4	VG-8	F-12	VF-20	EF-40	AU-50	MS-60	MS-63
1851	9,889,707 (1851 and 1851, /81)	6.	8.	10.	15.	28.	50.	90.	125.
1851, /81 (error)		7.	9.	12.	25.	50.	90.	200.	350.
1852	5,063,094	6.	8.	10.	15.	28.	50.	90.	125.
1853	6,641,131	6.	8.	10.	15.	28.	50.	90.	125.
1854	4,236,156	6.	8.	10.	15.	28.	50.	90.	125.

1855 Upright 5's

1855 Slanting 5's

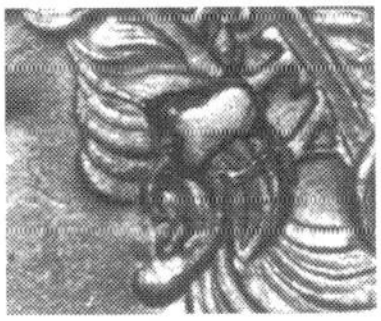

1855 Knob on ear

	Mintage	G-4	VG-8	F-12	VF-20	EF-40	AU-50	MS-60	MS-63
1855, All kinds	1,574,829								
1855, Upright 5's		6.	8.	10.	15.	28.	50.	90.	125.
1855, Slanting 5'S		6.	8.	10.	15.	28.	50.	100.	140.
1855, Slanting 5'S, knob on ear		6.	9.	12.	17.	32.	70.	135.	200.
1856, Upright 5	2,690,463 (1856, both kinds)	6.	8.	10.	15.	28.	50.	90.	125.
1856, Slanting 5		6.	8.	10.	15.	28.	50.	90.	125.

1857 Large Date

1857 Small Date

	Mintage	G-4	VG-8	F-12	VF-20	EF-40	AU-50	MS-60	MS-63
1857, Large Date	333,546 (1857, both dates)	15.	25.	30.	35.	40.	80.	160.	200.
1857, Small Date		16.	27.	32.	38.	42.	85.	180.	240.

SMALL CENTS — 1856 to Date

FLYING EAGLE TYPE 1856-1858

The Act of February 21, 1857 provided for the coinage of the small cent. The 1856 Eagle cent was not an authorized mint issue, as the law governing the new size coin was enacted after the date of issue. It is believed that about 1,500 to 2,500 of these pieces were struck. They are properly referred to as patterns.

G-4 GOOD—*All details worn, but readable.*
VG-8 VERY GOOD—*Feather details and eye of eagle are evident but worn.*
F-12 FINE—*Eagle head details and feather tips sharp.*
VF-20 VERY FINE—*Feathers in right wing and tail show considerable detail.*
EF-40 EXTREMELY FINE—*Slight wear, all details sharp.*
AU-50 ABOUT UNCIRCULATED—*Traces of light wear on only the high points of the design. Half of mint luster is present.*
MS-60 UNCIRCULATED—*No trace of wear. Light blemishes.*
MS-63 SELECT UNCIRCULATED—*Some distracting contact marks or blemishes in prime focal areas. Luster may be impaired.*
PF-63—*Reflective surfaces with only a few blemishes in secondary focal places. No major flaws.*

1858, 8 over 7

1856-1858 Large Letters

1858 Small Letters

Brilliant uncirculated and Proof coins are worth more than prices shown. Spotted, cleaned or discolored pieces are worth less.

	Mintage
1856	est. 2,000
1857 (*485*)	17,450,000
1858, Large. letters (*80*)	24,600,000 (combined)
1858, Small letters (*200*)	

	G-4	VG-8	F-12	VF-20	EF-40	AU-50	MS-60	MS-63	PF-63
1856	$3,200.	$3,750.	$4,000.	$4,500.	$5,000.	$5,300.	$5,600.	$8,500.	$8,500.
1857	9.	10.	14.	20.	65.	85.	150.	275.	3,000.
1858, Large Letter	9.	10.	14.	20.	65.	85.	150.	275.	3,000.
1858, Small Letter	9.	10.	14.	20.	65.	85.	150.	275.	3,000.
1858, 8 over 7		35.	80.	160.	350.	600.	1,000.	3,750.	

SMALL CENTS

INDIAN HEAD TYPE 1859-1909

The small cent was redesigned in 1859, and a representation of an Indian princess was adopted as the obverse device. The 1859 reverse was also changed to represent a laurel wreath. In 1860 the reverse was modified to display an oak wreath with a small shield at the top. From 1859 to 1863 cents were struck in copper-nickel. In 1864 the composition was changed to bronze, although copper-nickel cents were also struck during that year.

G-4 GOOD—*No LIBERTY visible.*
VG-8 VERY GOOD—*At least three letters of LIBERTY readable on head band.*
F-12 FINE—*LIBERTY completely visible.*
VF-20 VERY FINE—*Slight but even wear on LIBERTY.*
EF-40 EXTREMELY FINE—*LIBERTY sharp. All other details sharp. Only slight wear on ribbon end.*
AU-50 ABOUT UNCIRCULATED—*Traces of light wear on only the high points of the design. Half of mint luster is present.*
MS-60 UNCIRCULATED—*No trace of wear. Light blemishes.*
MS-63 SELECT UNCIRCULATED—*Some distracting contact marks or blemishes in prime focal areas. Luster may be impaired.*
PF-63 — *Reflective surfaces with only a few blemishes in secondary focal places. No major flaws.*

Without Shield at Top of Wreath
1859 Only

With Shield on Reverse
1860 to 1909

Brilliant uncirculated and Proof coins are worth more than prices shown. Spotted, cleaned or discolored pieces are worth less.

Copper-nickel, Laurel Wreath Reverse 1859

	Mintage	G-4	VG-8	F-12	VF-20	EF-40	AU-50	MS-60	MS-63	PF-63
1859 . . . . .*(800)*	36,400,000	$5.	$6.	$7.	$20.	$45.	$75.	$110.	$210.	$600.

Copper-nickel, Oak Wreath with Shield Reverse 1860-1864

	Mintage	G-4	VG-8	F-12	VF-20	EF-40	AU-50	MS-60	MS-63	PF-63
1860 . . .*(1,000)*	20,566,000	4.00	5.00	6.	8.	26.	50.	85.	150.	400.
1861 . . .*(1,000)*	10,100,000	8.00	10.00	15.	22.	45.	65.	100.	130.	500.
1862 . . . . .*(550)*	28,075,000	4.00	4.50	5.	7.	15.	30.	50.	75.	380.
1863 . . . . .*(460)*	49,840,000	4.00	4.50	5.	7.	15.	30.	50.	75.	380.
1864 . . . . .*(370)*	13,740,000	6.00	8.00	12.	18.	30.	50.	75.	100.	400.

Bronze 1864-1909

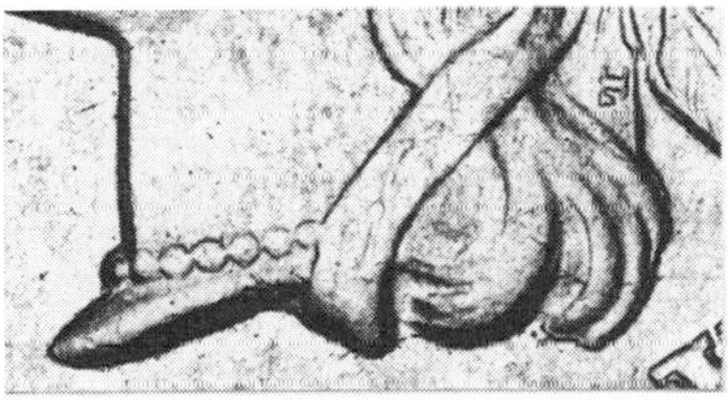

1864 Indian Head Cent with "L"

	Mintage	G-4	VG-8	F-12	VF-20	EF-40	AU-50	MS-60	MS-63	PF-63
1864, All kinds	39,233,714									
1864, No. L . . . .*(150)*		$3.00	$4.50	$7.	$14.	$25.	$35.	$40.	$60.	$400.
1864, L must show . . . .*(20)*		18.00	30.00	45.	75.	125.	160.	185.	300.	
1865 . . . .*(500)*	35,429,286	3.00	4.00	7.	9.	16.	25.	40.	60.	265.
1866 . . . .*(725)*	9,826,500	18.00	20.00	27.	45.	75.	110.	125.	240.	250.
1867 . . . .*(625)*	9,821,000	18.00	20.00	27.	45.	75.	110.	125.	240.	250.
1868 . . . .*(600)*	10,266,500	18.00	20.00	27.	45.	75.	110.	125.	240.	250.
1869 . . . .*(600)*	6,420,000	25.00	30.00	80.	120.	175.	220.	250.	350.	250.
1870 . . . .*(1,000)*	5,275,000	20.00	25.00	75.	110.	150.	220.	250.	400.	250.
1871 . . . .*(960)*	3,929,500	25.00	35.00	110.	130.	175.	240.	300.	450.	275.
1872 . . . .*(950)*	4,042,000	30.00	45.00	120.	150.	200.	275.	325.	500.	285.
1873, All kinds *(1,100)*		8.00	11.00	20.00	25.	60.	80.	90.	175.	175.
1874 . . . .*(700)*	14,187,500	7.00	8.00	11.	20.	40.	70.	80.	125.	160.
1875 . . . .*(700)*	13,528,000	8.00	10.00	17.	22.	40.	55.	80.	125.	160.
1876 . . . .*(1,150)*	7,944,000	12.00	15.00	18.	40.	75.	110.	140.	200.	160.
1877 . . . .*(900)*	852,500	300.00	360.00	450.	675.	900.	1,100.	1,500.	2,000.	1,500.

Brilliant or red uncirculated coins are worth more than prices shown. Spotted, cleaned or discolored pieces are worth less.

	Mintage	G-4	VG-8	F-12	VF-20	EF-40	AU-50	MS-60	MS-63	PF-63
1878 . .(2,350)	5,799,850	$11.00	$14.00	$20.00	$45.00	$80.00	$110.00	$140.	$200.	$150.
1879 . .(3,200)	16,231,200	3.00	4.00	6.00	12.00	25.00	35.00	45.	75.	120.
1880 . .(3,955)	38,964,955	1.25	1.50	2.50	4.50	10.00	18.00	25.	45.	100.
1881 . .(3,575)	39,211,575	1.25	1.50	2.00	3.50	8.00	12.00	20.	35.	100.
1882 . .(3,100)	38,581,100	1.25	1.50	2.00	3.50	8.00	12.00	20.	35.	100.
1883 . .(6,609)	45,598,109	1.25	1.50	2.00	3.50	8.00	12.00	20.	35.	100.
1884 . .(3,942)	23,261,742	1.50	1.75	2.50	5.00	10.00	14.00	25.	35.	100.
1885 . .(3,790)	11,765,384	2.50	2.75	4.50	10.00	25.00	35.00	50.	60.	100.
1886 . .(4,290)	17,654,290	1.25	2.25	6.50	18.00	45.00	60.00	70.	100.	115.
1887 . .(2,960)	45,226,483	0.75	0.85	1.00	1.75	6.00	10.00	20.	35.	100.
1888 . .(4,582)	37,494,414	0.60	0.85	1.10	2.25	6.00	10.00	20.	35.	100.
1889 . .(3,336)	48,869,361	0.60	0.85	1.00	1.75	4.50	9.00	18.	35.	100.
1890 . .(2,740)	57,182,854	0.60	0.85	1.00	1.75	4.00	9.00	18.	35.	100.
1891 . .(2,350)	47,072,350	0.60	0.85	1.00	1.75	4.00	9.00	18.	35.	100.
1892 . .(2,745)	37,649,832	0.60	0.85	1.00	1.75	4.00	10.00	20.	35.	100.
1893 . .(2,195)	46,642,195	0.60	0.85	1.00	1.75	4.00	9.00	18.	35.	100.
1894 . .(2,632)	16,752,132	1.50	1.75	3.50	5.00	15.00	20.00	25.	35.	125.
1895 . .(2,062)	38,343,636	0.60	0.80	0.85	1.50	4.00	9.00	18.	35.	100.
1896 . .(1,862)	39,057,293	0.60	0.80	0.85	1.50	4.00	9.00	18.	35.	100.
1897 . .(1,938)	50,466,330	0.60	0.80	0.85	1.50	4.00	9.00	18.	35.	100.
1898 . .(1,795)	49,823,079	0.60	0.80	0.85	1.50	4.00	9.00	18.	35.	100.
1899 . .(2,031)	53,600,031	0.60	0.80	0.85	1.50	4.00	9.00	18.	35.	100.
1900 . .(2,262)	66,833,764	0.50	0.60	0.75	1.00	3.50	7.50	15.	25.	90.
1901 . .(1,985)	79,611,143	0.50	0.60	0.75	1.00	3.50	7.50	15.	25.	90.
1902 . .(2,018)	87,376,722	0.50	0.60	0.75	1.00	3.50	7.50	15.	25.	90.
1903 . .(1,790)	85,094,493	0.50	0.60	0.75	1.00	3.50	7.50	15.	25.	90.
1904 . .(1,817)	61,328,015	0.50	0.60	0.75	1.00	3.50	7.50	15.	25.	90.
1905 . .(2,152)	80,719,163	0.50	0.60	0.75	1.00	3.50	7.50	15.	25.	90.
1906 . .(1,725)	96,022,255	0.50	0.60	0.75	1.00	3.50	7.50	15.	25.	90.
1907 . .(1,475)	108,138,618	0.50	0.60	0.75	1.00	3.50	7.50	15.	25.	90.

Location of mint mark S on reverse of Indian cent (1908 and 1909 only).

	Mintage	G-4	VG-8	F-12	VF-20	EF-40	AU-50	MS-60	MS-63	PF-63
1908 . .(1,620)	32,327,987	0.50	0.60	0.75	1.00	3.50	7.50	16.	25.	100.
1908S	1,115,000	25.00	35.00	40.00	45.00	60.00	75.00	125.	200.	
1909 . .(2,175)	14,370,645	1.25	1.50	1.50	1.75	6.00	9.00	16.	25.	100.
1909S	309,000	150.00	175.00	190.00	220.00	275.00	300.00	350.	500.	

LINCOLN TYPE, WHEAT EARS REVERSE 1909-1958

Victor D. Brenner designed this cent which was issued to commemorate the hundredth anniversary of Lincoln's birth. The designer's initials V.D.B. appear on the reverse of a limited quantity of cents of 1909. Later in the year they were removed from the dies but restored in 1918 as very small incuse letters beneath the shoulder. The Lincoln type was the first cent to have the motto IN GOD WE TRUST.

G-4 GOOD—*Date worn but apparent. Lines in wheat heads missing. Full rims.*
VG-8 VERY GOOD—*Half of lines show in upper wheat heads.*
F-12 FINE—*Wheat lines worn but visible.*
VF-20 VERY FINE—*Cheek and jaw bones worn but separated. No worn spots on wheat heads.*
EF-40 EXTREMELY FINE—*Slight wear. All details sharp.*
AU-50 ABOUT UNCIRCULATED—*Traces of light wear on only the high points of the design. Half of mint luster is present.*
MS-60 UNCIRCULATED—*No trace of wear. Light blemishes or discoloration.*
MS-63 SELECT UNCIRCULATED—*No trace of wear. Slight blemishes.*
PF-63—*Reflective surfaces with only a few blemishes in secondary focal places. No major flaws.*

Location of mint mark S or D on obverse of Lincoln cent.

Location of designer's initials V.D.B. on 1909 only.

No V.D.B. on reverse 1909-1958.

Bronze 1909-1942

Brilliant uncirculated coins are worth more than prices shown. Spotted, cleaned or discolored pieces are worth less.

	Mintage	G-4	VG-8	F-12	VF-20	EF-40	AU-50	MS-60	MS-63
1909, V.D.B.	27,995,000	$1.75	$2.00	$2.25	$2.50	$2.75	$4.00	$5.50	$7.00
1909, V.D.B., Matte Pf	(1,194)								750.00
1909S, V.D.B.	484,000	275.00	320.00	350.00	400.00	500.00	550.00	600.00	700.00
1909	72,702,618	.40	.60	.75	1.25	1.75	3.00	7.00	10.00
1909, Matte Pf	(2,352)								160.00
1909S	1,825,000	30.00	35.00	40.00	60.00	80.00	90.00	100.00	150.00
1910	146,801,218	.05	.10	.15	.20	.75	2.50	7.00	11.00
1910, Matte Pf	(4,083)								140.00
1910S	6,045,000	3.25	4.00	4.50	6.00	11.00	20.00	35.00	40.00
1911	101,177,787	.05	.10	.25	.40	1.00	3.00	9.00	21.00
1911, Matte Pf	(2,411)								150.00
1911D	12,672,000	1.75	2.25	3.50	6.00	16.00	28.00	40.00	60.00
1911S	4,026,000	8.00	9.00	10.00	12.00	20.00	35.00	75.00	120.00
1912	68,153,060	.10	.25	.50	1.50	2.50	7.00	15.00	20.00
1912, Matte Pf	(2,145)								130.00
1912D	10,411,000	2.50	2.75	3.50	7.50	22.00	30.00	65.00	90.00
1912S	4,431,000	5.00	6.50	7.50	9.00	22.00	30.00	55.00	75.00
1913	76,532,352	.10	.20	.40	1.25	6.00	8.00	12.00	18.00
1913, Matte Pf	(2,848)								130.00
1913D	15,804,000	.75	1.00	1.50	3.50	12.00	17.00	45.00	70.00
1913S	6,101,000	2.50	3.00	3.50	5.50	15.00	25.00	65.00	100.00
1914	75,238,432	.10	.25	.50	1.50	5.00	13.00	20.00	27.00
1914, Matte Pf	(1,365)								160.00
1914D*	1,193,000	60.00	70.00	95.00	135.00	275.00	400.00	600.00	1000.00
1914S	4,137,000	4.50	5.00	6.00	10.00	20.00	55.00	120.00	200.00
1915	29,092,120	.30	.50	1.35	3.50	16.00	23.00	37.00	45.00
1915, Matte Pf	(1,150)								250.00
1915D	22,050,000	.35	.50	.65	1.25	5.00	14.00	30.00	47.00
1915S	4,833,000	3.00	3.50	4.00	6.00	17.00	50.00	80.00	110.00
1916	131,833,677	.03	.05	.10	.30	1.00	3.00	6.00	12.00
1916, Matte Pf	(1,050)								300.00
1916D	35,956,000	.08	.13	.40	.75	3.00	8.00	27.00	40.00
1916S	22,510,000	.30	.40	.75	1.35	4.50	12.00	32.00	60.00
1917	196,429,785	.03	.05	.10	.25	.60	2.00	6.00	12.00
1917D	55,120,000	.08	.10	.25	.75	3.00	9.00	27.00	35.00
1917S	32,620,000	.08	.10	.25	.50	2.75	8.00	28.00	45.00

*Beware of altered date or mint mark. No V.D.B. on shoulder of genuine 1914D cent.

SMALL CENTS

Brilliant uncirculated coins before 1934 are worth more than prices shown. Spotted, cleaned or discolored pieces are worth less

Designer's initials restored starting 1918.

	Mintage	G-4	VG-8	F-12	VF-20	EF-40	AU-50	MS-60	MS-63
1918	288,104,634	$.03	$.05	$.10	$.20	$1.00	$2.00	$6.00	$12.00
1918D	47,830,000	.08	.13	.35	.80	3.00	6.00	26.00	50.00
1918S	34,680,000	.08	.13	.35	.80	3.00	12.00	30.00	60.00
1919	392,021,000	.03	.04	.05	.15	.75	1.50	4.00	10.00
1919D	57,154,000	.04	.06	.10	.40	2.00	12.00	22.00	40.00
1919S	139,760,000	.04	.06	.10	.30	1.35	4.50	17.00	32.00
1920	310,165,000	.03	.04	.05	.15	.50	1.50	4.00	9.00
1920D	49,280,000	.04	.06	.10	.30	3.00	9.00	27.00	40.00
1920S	46,220,000	.04	.06	.10	.30	2.00	12.00	35.00	80.00
1921	39,157,000	.05	.08	.15	.35	1.50	5.00	18.00	30.00
1921S	15,274,000	.35	.50	.70	1.25	8.00	25.00	45.00	75.00
1922D }	7,160,000	3.50	4.50	5.00	7.00	12.00	18.00	35.00	50.00
1922 † }		180.00	235.00	285.00	350.00	850.00	1250.00	3000.00	8000.00
1923	74,723,000	.03	.04	.05	.15	1.00	2.50	5.00	10.00
1923S	8,700,000	.50	.60	.75	2.00	10.00	27.00	85.00	150.00
1924	75,178,000	.03	.04	.06	.15	1.50	3.50	11.00	20.00
1924D	2,520,000	5.00	6.00	8.00	14.00	33.00	60.00	125.00	150.00
1924S	11,696,000	.35	.45	.70	1.00	5.00	22.00	50.00	90.00
1925	139,949,000	.03	.04	.05	.15	.50	2.00	4.00	9.00
1925D	22,580,000	.04	.06	.10	.30	3.00	10.00	25.00	35.00
1925S	26,380,000	.04	.06	.10	.25	3.00	10.00	30.00	65.00
1926	157,088,000	.03	.04	.05	.15	.50	2.00	4.00	7.00
1926D	28,020,000	.04	.06	.10	.30	2.50	8.00	25.00	35.00
1926S	4,550,000	.85	1.25	2.00	2.50	6.00	18.00	52.00	90.00
1927	144,440,000	.03	.04	.05	.20	.50	1.00	4.00	8.00
1927D	27,170,000	.04	.06	.10	.25	1.00	4.00	21.00	35.00
1927S	14,276,000	.25	.30	.50	1.00	4.00	10.00	33.00	60.00
1928	134,116,000	.03	.04	.05	.15	.50	1.00	4.00	8.00
1928D	31,170,000	.04	.06	.10	.25	.85	4.00	12.00	30.00
1928S	17,266,000	.06	.10	.25	.50	1.50	5.00	28.00	50.00
1929	185,262,000	.03	.04	.05	.15	.35	1.50	3.00	5.00
1929	41,730,000	.04	.06	.10	.25	1.00	2.00	8.00	11.00
1929S	50,148,000	.03	.05	.10	.15	.60	1.75	6.00	9.00
1930	157,415,000	.03	.04	.05	.15	.25	.75	2.00	3.50
1930D	40,100,000	.04	.06	.10	.25	.60	1.00	5.00	9.00
1930S	24,286,000	.03	.05	.10	.15	.40	2.00	3.50	5.00
1931	19,396,000	.15	.20	.30	.40	.60	2.00	8.00	12.00
1931D	4,480,000	1.00	1.25	1.50	2.00	4.00	10.00	25.00	35.00
1931S	866,000	24.00	26.00	30.00	35.00	38.00	40.00	45.00	50.00
1932	9,062,000	.40	.50	.60	1.00	1.25	3.50	9.00	11.00
1932D	10,500,000	.25	.35	.40	.50	.85	3.00	8.00	12.00
1933	14,360,000	.25	.35	.45	.60	1.10	3.50	9.00	12.00
1933D	6,200,000	.60	.75	1.00	1.25	1.75	4.00	10.00	11.00
1934	219,080,000	.03	.03	.03	.03	.10	1.00	3.00	4.00
1934D	28,446,000	.04	.06	.08	.10	.25	1.25	7.00	12.00
1935	245,388,000	.03	.03	.03	.04	.06	.20	2.00	3.00
1935D	47,000,000	.03	.03	.03	.04	.20	.50	3.00	4.00
1935S	38,702,000	.03	.04	.04	.04	.12	1.25	4.00	6.00
1936	309,637,569	.03	.03	.03	.04	.06	.25	1.00	3.00
1936 Proof -63	(5,569)								80.00
1936D	40,620,000	.03	.03	.03	.04	.08	.20	1.00	3.00
1936S	29,130,000	.03	.03	.03	.04	.10	.20	1.00	3.00

†The 1922 without D was caused by a defective die. Beware of removed mint mark. Those with weak D are worth considerably less.

	Mintage	G-4	VG-8	F-12	VF-20	EF-40	MS-60	MS-63	MS-65	PF-63
1937	309,179,320	$.02	$.02	$.02	$.03	$.05	$.20	$.50	$2.00	
1937 Proof-63	(9,320)									30.00
1937D	50,430,000	.02	.02	.02	.03	.06	.30	.75	3.00	
1937S	34,500,000	.03	.03	.03	.04	.06	.30	.80	3.00	
1938	156,696,734	.02	.02	.02	.03	.05	.30	.75	2.00	
1938, Proof-63	(14,734)									22.00
1938D	20,010,000	.02	.03	.04	.06	.15	.50	1.00	4.00	
1938S	15,180,000	.06	.08	.10	.12	.15	.30	1.00	3.50	
1939	316,479,520	.02	.02	.02	.03	.05	.20	.30	2.00	
1939, Proof-63	(13,520)									20.00
1939D	15,160,000	.06	.08	.10	.12	.15	.35	1.00	3.00	
1939S	52,070,000	.03	.03	.03	.04	.10	.30	.70	3.00	
1940	586,825,872	.02	.02	.02	.03	.03	.20	.30	2.00	
1940, Proof-63	(15,872)									15.00
1940D	81,390,000	.02	.02	.02	.03	.03	.20	.40	2.00	
1940S	112,940,000	.02	.02	.02	.03	.04	.20	.40	2.75	
1941	887,039,100	.02	.02	.02	.03	.03	.20	.30	2.00	
1941, Proof-63	(21,100)									14.00
1941D	128,700,000	.02	.02	.02	.03	.03	.40	.80	3.00	
1941S	92,360,000	.02	.02	.02	.03	.04	.35	.80	4.00	
1942	657,828,600	.02	.02	.02	.03	.03	.10	.15	1.00	
1942, Proof-63	(32,600)									14.00
1942D	206,698,000	.02	.02	.02	.03	.03	.10	.15	1.50	
1942S	85,590,000	.02	.02	.02	.03	.10	1.00	2.00	7.50	

Zinc-coated Steel 1943 Only

	Mintage	G-4	VG-8	F-12	VF-20	EF-40	MS-60	MS-63	MS-65
1943	684,628,670			.05	.10	.15	.30	.70	2.00
1943D	217,660,000			.05	.10	.15	.35	1.25	2.50
1943S	191,550,000			.06	.12	.20	.60	1.50	4.00

Bronze Resumed 1944-1958

	Mintage	VF-20	EF-40	MS-63	MS-65
1944	1,435,400,000	$.02	$.03	$.15	$.50
1944D	} 430,578,000	.02	.03	.20	.50
1944D, D/S		50.00	65.00	180.00	500.00
1944S	282,760,000	.02	.03	.15	1.50
1945	1,040,515,000	.02	.03	.20	.50
1945D	266,268,000	.02	.03	.15	.50
1945S	181,770,000	.02	.03	.10	2.00
1946	991,655,000	.02	.03	.10	.50
1946D	315,690,000	.02	.03	.15	1.00
1946S	198,100,000	.02	.03	.15	1.25
1947	190,555,000	.02	.03	.25	.50
1947D	194,750,000	.02	.02	.12	.50

1944D, D over S

1955 Doubled Die Error

	Mintage	VF-20	EF-40	MS-63	MS-65
1947S	99,000,000	.02	.03	.15	1.50
1948	317,570,000	.02	.02	.15	.50
1948D	172,637,500	.02	.02	.12	.60
1948S	81,735,000	.02	.03	.20	1.50
1949	217,775,000	.02	.02	.30	.75
1949D	153,132,500	.02	.02	.20	.75

	Mintage	VF-20	EF-40	MS-63	MS-65	PF-65
1949S	64,290,000	$.03	$.05	$.50	$2.00	
1950 (51,386)	272,686,386	.02	.02	.25	.50	$25.00
1950D	334,950,000	.02	.02	.10	.50	
1950S	118,505,000	.02	.03	.25	.80	
1951 (57,500)	284,633,500	.02	.02	.25	.80	30.00
1951D	625,355,000	.02	.02	.10	.50	
1951S	136,010,000	.02	.03	.30	.60	
1952 (81,980)	186,856,980	.02	.02	.15	.60	20.00
1952D	746,130,000	.02	.02	.15	.60	
1952S	137,800,004	.02	.03	.50	1.25	
1953 (128,800)	256,883,800	.02	.03	.10	.50	20.00
1953D	700,515,000	.02	.02	.10	.50	
1953S	181,835,000	.02	.03	.12	.50	
1954 (233,300)	7,173,350	.03	.05	.10	.50	10.00
1954D	251,552,500	.02	.02	.05	.30	
1954S	96,190,000	.02	.03	.05	.30	
1955, Double Die Obverse	330,958,200	350.00	450.00	*850.00	1000.00	
1955 (378,200)		.02	.02	.06	.25	9.00
1955D	563,257,500	.02	.02	.05	.20	
1955S	44,610,000	.10	.15	.15	.50	
1956 (669,384)	421,414,384	.02	.02	.05	.20	1.50
1956D	1,098,201,100	.02	.02	.05	.20	
1957 (1,247,952)	283,787,952	.02	.02	.05	.20	1.50
1957D	1,051,342,000	.02	.02	.03	.20	
1958 (875,652)	253,400,652	.02	.02	.03	.20	1.75
1958D	800,953,300	.02	.02	.03	.20	

*Value for MS-60 Uncirculated is $600.00.

LINCOLN TYPE, MEMORIAL REVERSE 1959 TO DATE

Small Date

Large Date

	Mintage	MS-63	MS-65	PF-65
1959 (1,149,291)	610,864,291	$.01	$.10	$1.00
1959D	1,279,760,000	.01	.10	
1960, Large Date (1,691,602)	588,096,602	.01	.10	.50
1960, Small Date		1.00	2.50	8.00
1960D, Large Date	1,580,884,000	.01	.10	
1960D, Small Date		.02	.10	
1961 (3,028,244)	756,373,244	.01	.10	.50
1961D	1,753,266,700	.01	.10	
1962 (3,218,019)	609,263,019	.01	.10	.50
1962D	1,793,148,140	.01	.10	
1963 (3,075,645)	757,185,645	.01	.10	.50
1963D	1,774,020,400	.01	.10	
1964 (3,950,762)	2,652,525,762	.01	.10	.50
1964D	3,799,071,500	.01	.10	
1965	1,497,224,900	.02	.12	
1966	2,188,147,783	.04	.12	
1967	3,048,667,100	.03	.12	
1968	1,707,880,970	.02	.12	
1968D	2,886,269,600	.01	.10	
1968S (3,041,506)	261,311,507	.02	.10	.50
1969	1,136,910,000	.05	.20	
1969D	4,002,832,200	.03	.10	
1969S (2,934,631)	547,309,631	.03	.10	.50
1969S, Double Die Obverse		—	—	

Small Date Numbers aligned at top

Large Date Low 7 in date

Enlarged Detail of 1972 Doubled Die Error

1969S Doubled Die Error

	Mintage	MS-63	MS-65	PF-65
1970	1,898,438,900	$.05	$.10	
1970D	2,891,438,900	.02	.10	
1970S, Small Date (high 7)		12.00	20.00	$25.00
1970S, Large Date (low 7)		.03	.10	.25
1971	1,919,490,000	.05	.20	
1971D	2,911,045,600	.03	.20	
1971S	(3,220,733) 528,354,192	.03	.20	.25
1972, DblDieObv.		150.00	225.00	
1972	2,933,255,000	.01	.05	
1972D	2,665,071,400	.02	.10	
1972S	(3,260,996) 380,200,104	.02	.10	.25
1973	3,728,245,000	.01	.10	
1973D	3,549,576,588	.01	.10	
1973S	(2,760,339) 319,937,634	.02	.10	.25
1974	4,232,140,523	.01	.10	
1974D	4,235,098,000	.01	.10	
1974S	(2,612,568) 412,039,228	.03	.10	.25
1975	5,451,476,142	.01	.10	
1975D	4,505,275,300	.01	.10	
1975S, Pf	(2,845,450)			1.10

	Mintage	MS-63	MS-65	PF-65
1976	4,674,292,426	$.01	$.10	
1976D	4,221,592,455	.02	.10	
1976S, Pf	(4,149,730)			$1.00
1977	4,469,930,000	.01	.10	
1977D	4,194,062,300	.01	.10	
1977S, Pf	(3,251,152)			.80
1978	5,558,605,000	.01	.10	
1978D	4,280,233,400	.01	.10	
1978S, Pf	(3,127,781)			.80
1979	6,018,515,000	.01	.10	
1979D	4,139,357,254	.01	.10	
1979S, Pf, Filled S				1.50
1979S, Pf, Clear S				1.75
1980	7,414,705,000	.01	.10	
1980D	5,140,098,660	.01	.10	
1980S, Pf	(3,554,806)			.80
1981	7,491,750,000	.01	.10	
1981D	5,373,235,677	.01	.10	
1981S, Filled S Pf				1.50
1981S, Clear S Pf				1.75
1982, Large Date		.01	.10	
1982, Small Date		.02	.12	
1982D, Large Date		.01	.10	
1982S, Pf	(3,857,479)			.80

Large Date

Small Date

1995 Double Die showing strong doubling on word "LIBERTY"

Copper Plated Zinc

	Mintage	MS-63	MS-65	PF-65
1982, Large Date	Incl. above	$.01	$.05	
1982, Small Date	Incl. above	.01	.05	
1982D, Large Date	Incl. above	.05	.50	
1982D, Small Date	Incl. above	.01	.05	
1983	7,752,355,000	.01	.05	
1983D	6,467,199,428	.01	.05	
1983S, Pf	(3,279,126)	.01	.05	$1.10
1984	8,151,079,000	.01	.05	
1984, Doubled ear				
1984D	5,569,238,906	.01	.05	
1984S, Pf	(3,065,110)			1.10
1985	5,648,489,887	.01	.05	
1985D	5,287,339,926	.01	.05	

	Mintage	MS-63	MS-65	PF-65
1985S, Pf	(3,362,821)			$1.25
1986	4,491,395,493	$.01	$.05	
1986D	4,442,866,698	.01	.05	
1986S, Pf	(3,010,497)			2.00
1987	4,682,466,931	.01	.05	
1987D	4,879,389,514	.01	.05	
1987S, Pf	(4,227,728)			1.10
1988	6,092,810,000	.01	.05	
1988D	5,253,740,443	.01	.05	
1988S, Pf	(3,262,948)			3.25
1989	7,261,535,000	.01	.05	
1989D	5,345,467,111	.01	.05	

SMALL CENTS

	Mintage	MS-63	MS-65	PF-63
1989S, Pf	(3,220,194)			$3.00
1990	6,851,765,000	$.01	$.05	
1990D	4,922,894,533	.01	.05	
1990S, Pf	(3,299,559)			2.00
1990, Pf w/o S				
1991	5,165,940,000	.01	.05	
1991D	4,158,446,076	.01	.05	
1991S, Pf	(2,867,787)			10.00
1992	4,648,905,000	.01	.05	

	Mintage	MS-63	MS-65	PF-65
1992D	4,448,673,300	$.01	$.05	
1992D, Close AM				
1992S, Pf	(4,176,560)			$1.10
1993	5,684,705,000	.01	.05	
1993D	6,426,650,571	.01	.05	
1993S, Pf	(3,394,792)			2.00
1994	6,500,850,000	.01	.05	
1994D	7,131,765,000	.01	.05	
1994S, Pf	(3,269,923)			2.00

SMALL CENTS

	Mintage	MS-63	MS-65	PF-63
1995	6,411,440,000	$.01	$.05	
1995, DblDieObv.			10.00	
1995D	7,128,560,000	.01	.05	
1995S, Pf	(2,797,481)			$2.00
1996	6,612,465,000	.01	.05	
1996D	6,510,795,000	.01	.05	
1996S, Pf	(2,525,265)			1.25
1997	4,622,800,000	.01	.05	
1997D	4,576,555,000	.01	.05	
1997S, Pf	(2,796,678)			2.00
1998	5,032,155,000	.01	.05	
1998, Wide AM*			6.00	
1998D	5,225,353,500	.01	.05	
1998S, Pf	(2,086,507)			2.00
1999	5,237,600,000	.01	.05	
1999 Wide AM*			6.00	
1999D	6,360,065,000	.01	.05	
1999S, Pf	(2,543,401)			1.00

	Mintage	MS-63	MS-65	PF-65
2000	5,503,200,000	$.01	$.05	
2000, Wide AM*		7.00		
2000D	8,774,220,000	.01	.05	
2000S, Pf	(3,082,483)			$1.00
2001	4,959,600,000	.01	.05	
2001D	5,374,990,000	.01	.05	
2001S, Pf	(2,294,043)			1.00
2002	3,260,800,000	.01	.05	
2002D	4,028,055,000	.01	.05	
2002S, Pf	(2,277,720)			$1.00
2003		.01	.05	
2003D		.01	.05	
2003S, Pf				1.00
2004		.01	.05	
2004D		.01	.05	
2004S, Pf				1.00

*Varieties were made using Proof dies that have a wide space between AM in AMERICA. The letters nearly touch on other uncirculated cents.

TWO-CENT PIECES — 1864-1873

The Act of April 22, 1864, which changed the weight and composition of the cent, included a provision for the bronze two-cent piece. The weight was specified as 96 grains, the alloy being the same as for the cent. There are two varieties for the first year of issue, 1864: the small motto and the large motto. The differences are explained in the illustrations below.

1864 Small Motto

1864 Large Motto

On the obverse the D in GOD is narrow on the large motto. The stem to the leaf shows plainly on the small motto variety.

G-4 GOOD—*At least IN GOD visible.*
VG-8 VERY GOOD—*WE weakly visible.*
F-12 FINE—*Complete motto visible. WE weak.*
VF-20—*Shows moderate wear on high points of design. All major details are clear.*
EF-40 EXTREMELY FINE—*WE is bold.*
AU-50 ABOUT UNCIRCULATED—*Traces of light wear on only the high points of the design. Half of mint luster is present.*
MS-60 UNCIRCULATED—*No trace of wear. Light blemishes.*
MS-63 SELECT UNCIRCULATED—*Some distracting contact marks or blemishes in prime focal areas. Luster may be impaired.*
PF-63—*Reflective surfaces with only a few blemishes in secondary focal places. No major flaws.*

Brilliant red choice uncirculated and proof coins are worth more than prices shown. Cleaned or discolored pieces are worth less.

	Mintage	G-4	VG-8	F-12	VF-20	EF-40	AU-50	MS-60	MS-63	PF-63
1864, Small motto	19,847,500	$40.	$50.	$70.	$160.	$250.	$300.	$400.	$500.	$8,000.
1864, Large motto *(100+)*		6.	7.	9.	12.	18.	26.	45.	75.	250.
1865 *(500+)*	13,640,000	6.	7.	9.	12.	18.	26.	45.	75.	225.
1866 *(725+)*	3,177,000	6.	7.	9.	12.	18.	26.	45.	75.	225.
1867 *(625+)*	2,938,750	6.	7.	9.	12.	18.	26.	50.	85.	225.
1868 *(600+)*	2,803,750	6.	7.	9.	12.	20.	30.	55.	85.	225.
1869 *(600+)*	1,546,500	7.	8.	10.	14.	25.	50.	100.	125.	275.
1870 *(1,000+)*	861,250	9.	11.	16.	20.	50.	70.	135.	185.	300.
1871 *(960+)*	721,250	10.	12.	18.	22.	55.	75.	150.	195.	350.
1872 *(950+)*	65,000	90.	120.	150.	200.	300.	325.	425.	500.	500.
1873 *(1,000+)*										850.

SILVER THREE-CENT PIECES 1851-1873

This smallest of United States silver coins was authorized by Congress March 3, 1851. The first three-cent silver pieces had no lines bordering the six-pointed star. From 1854 through 1858 there were three lines, while issues of the last fifteen years show only two lines. Issues from 1854 through 1873 have an olive sprig over the III and a bundle of three arrows beneath.

G-4 GOOD—*Star worn smooth. Legend and date readable.*
VG-8 VERY GOOD—*Outline of shield defined. Legend and date clear.*
F-12 FINE—*Only star points worn smooth.*
VF-20 VERY FINE—*Only partial wear on star ridges.*
EF-40 EXTREMELY FINE—*Ridges on star points show.*
AU-50 ABOUT UNCIRCULATED—*Traces of light wear on only the high points of the design. Half of mint luster is present.*
MS-60 UNCIRCULATED—*No trace of wear. Light blemishes.*
MS-63 SELECT UNCIRCULATED—*Some distracting contact marks or blemishes in prime focal areas. Luster may be impaired.*
PF-63—*Reflective surfaces with only a few blemishes in secondary focal places. No major flaws.*

Mint Mark
← O

No outline around star.

Well-struck specimens command higher prices.

	Mintage	G-4	VG-8	F-12	VF-20	EF-40	AU-50	MS-60	MS-63	PF-63
1851	5,447,400	$10.	$12.	$14.	$18.	$27.	$60.	$75.	$110.	
1851O	720,000	12.	15.	18.	32.	65.	90.	165.	200.	
1852	18,663,500	10.	12.	14.	18.	27.	60.	75.	110.	
1853	11,400,000	10.	12.	14.	18.	27.	60.	75.	110.	

Three outlines to star, large date.

	Mintage	G-4	VG-8	F-12	VF-20	EF-40	AU-50	MS-60	MS-63	PF-63
1854	671,000	11.	13.	15.	22.	45.	90.	100.	275.	
1855	139,000	12.	17.	25.	42.	75.	110.	275.	400.	$1,800.
1856	1,458,000	10.	12.	15.	22.	42.	80.	140.	275.	1,700.
1857	1,042,000	10.	12.	15.	22.	42.	80.	140.	275.	1,500.
1858 (300+)	1,604,000	10.	12.	15.	22.	42.	80.	140.	275.	1,100.

Two outlines to star, small date.

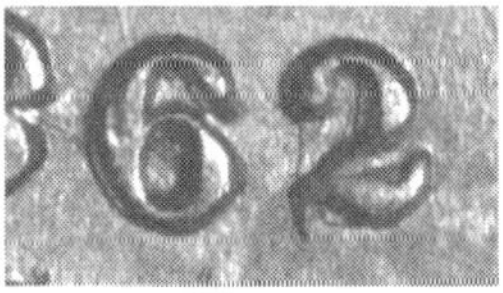

1862 2 over 1

	Mintage	G-4	VG-8	F-12	VF-20	EF-40	AU-50	MS-60	MS-63	PF-63
1859 (800)	365,000	10.	12.	14.	19.	32.	60.	75.	120.	250.
1860 (1,000)	287,000	10.	12.	14.	19.	32.	60.	75.	120.	250.
1861 (1,000)	498,000	10.	12.	14.	19.	32.	60.	75.	120.	250.
1862, 2/1	} 343,550	11.	14.	16.	20.	35.	70.	100.	160.	
1862 (550)		10.	11.	14.	19.	32.	60.	75.	120.	225.
1863 (460)	21,460				125.	150.	200.	285.	425.	275.
1864 (470)	12,470				125.	150.	200.	285.	425.	275.
1865 (500)	8,500				150.	175.	200.	285.	430.	285.
1866 (725)	22,725				125.	150.	200.	285.	425.	285.
1867 (625)	4,625				150.	175.	200.	285.	430.	285.
1868 (600)	4,100				150.	175.	200.	285.	500.	285.
1869 (600)	5,100				150.	175.	200.	285.	425.	285.
1870 (1,000)	4,000				150.	175.	200.	285.	425.	300.
1871 (960)	4,360				150.	175.	200.	285.	425.	300.
1872 (950)	1,950				170.	200.	225.	300.	500.	300.
1873 (600)			(Proof only)							500.

THREE-CENT PIECES (NICKEL)
ISSUED 1865-1889

The three-cent pieces struck in nickel composition were designed to replace the silver three-cent coins. Composition is 75% copper and 25% nickel. All were coined at Philadelphia and have plain edges.

Brilliant choice uncirculated and proof coins are worth more than prices shown. Spotted, cleaned or discolored pieces are worth less.

G-4 GOOD—*Date and legends complete though worn. III smooth.*
VG-8 VERY GOOD—*III is half worn. Rims complete.*
F-12 FINE—*Hair curls well defined.*
VF-20—*Shows moderate wear on high points of design. All major details are clear.*
EF-40 EXTREMELY FINE—*Slight, even wear.*
AU-50 ABOUT UNCIRCULATED—*Traces of light wear on only the high points of the design. Half of mint luster is present.*
MS-60 UNCIRCULATED—*No trace of wear. Light blemishes.*
MS-63 SELECT UNCIRCULATED—*Some distracting contact marks or blemishes in prime focal areas. Luster may be impaired.*
PF-63—*Reflective surfaces with only a few blemishes in secondary focal places. No major flaws.*

	Mintage	G-4	VG-8	F-12	VF-20	EF-40	AU-50	MS-60	MS-63	PF-63
1865 ....(*500+*)	11,382,000	$5.50	$7.	$8.	$10.	$12.	$20.	$40.	$70.	$600.
1866 ....(*725+*)	4,801,000	5.50	7.	8.	10.	12.	20.	40.	70.	140.
1867 ....(*625+*)	3,915,000	5.50	7.	8.	10.	12.	20.	40.	70.	140.
1868 ....(*600+*)	3,252,000	5.50	7.	8.	10.	12.	20.	40.	70.	140.
1869 ....(*600+*)	1,604,000	5.50	7.	8.	10.	12.	22.	45.	75.	140.
1870 ....(*1,000+*)	1,335,000	5.50	7.	8.	10.	12.	22.	45.	75.	140.
1871 ....(*960+*)	604,000	5.50	7.	8.	10.	12.	22.	45.	75.	140.
1872 ....(*950+*)	862,000	5.50	7.	8.	10.	12.	22.	45.	75.	140.
1873		5.50	7.	8.	10.	12.	22.	45.	75.	140.
1874 ....(*700+*)	790,000	6.00	8.	9.	11.	15.	25.	47.	80.	140.
1875 ....(*700+*)	228,000	7.00	9.	10.	12.	18.	28.	80.	90.	140.
1876 ....(*1,150+*)	162,000	7.00	9.	11.	13.	20.	32.	90.	100.	150.
1877, PfS only .(*510+*)	510				450.		525.			700.
1878, PfS only .(2,350)	2,350				275.		300.			325.
1879 ....(3,200)	41,200	26.00	30.	32.	37.	45.	50.	125.	175.	175.
1880 ....(3,955)	24,955	30.00	40.	50.	55.	65.	70.	140.	160.	175.
1881 ....(3,575)	1,080,575	5.50	7.	8.	10.	12.	20.	40.	70.	140.
1882 ....(3,100)	25,300	27.00	36.	40.	45.	55.	70.	140.	175.	175.
1883 ....(6,609)	10,609	60.00	70.	90.	110.	125.	150.	200.	300.	185.
1884 ....(3,942)	5,642	125.00	150.	175.	200.	225.	250.	400.	500.	250.
1885 ....(3,790)	4,790	150.00	175.	200.	250.	275.	300.	425.	525.	250.
1886, PfS only .(4,290)	4,290				125.	175.				210.
1887 All kinds } (2,960)	7,961	95.00	110.	135.	150.	175.	190.	225.	250.	210.
1887, 7/6 }	7,961				150.	185.				250.
1888 ....(4,582)	41,083	18.00	20.	25.	30.	38.	50.	125.	150.	160.
1889 ....(3,436)	21,561	27.00	35.	45.	50.	55.	60.	130.	160.	160.

NICKEL FIVE-CENT PIECES — 1866 to Date
SHIELD TYPE 1866-1883

The shield type nickel was made possible by the Act of May 16, 1866. Its weight was set at 77-16/100 grains with the same composition as the nickel three-cent piece which was authorized in 1865.

Rays Between Stars 1866-1867

G-4 GOOD—*All letters in motto readable.*
VG-8 VERY GOOD—*Motto stands out clearly. Rims worn slightly but even. Part of shield lines visible.*
F-12 FINE—*Half of each olive leaf is smooth.*
EF-40 EXTREMELY FINE—*Leaf tips show slight wear. Cross over shield slightly worn.*
AU-50 ABOUT UNCIRCULATED—*Traces of light wear on only the high points of the design. Half of mint luster is present.*
MS-60 UNCIRCULATED—*No trace of wear. Light blemishes.*
MS 63 SELECT UNCIRCULATED—*Some distracting contact marks or blemishes in prime focal areas. Luster may be impaired.*
PF-63—*Reflective surfaces with only a few blemishes in secondary focal places. No major flaws.*

NICKEL FIVE-CENT PIECES

Brilliant choice uncirculated and proof coins are worth more than prices shown. Spotted, cleaned or discolored pieces are worth less.

	Mintage	G-4	VG-8	F-12	EF-40	AU-50	MS-60	MS-63	PF-63
1866, Rays . . . . .(*200+*)	14,742,500	$10.	$15.	$18.	$60.	$80.	$110.	$160.	$1,100.
1867, Rays . . . . . .(*25+*)	2,019,000	12.	16.	20.	70.	100.	200.	250.	10,000.
1867, No rays . . .(*600+*)	28,890,500	8.	9.	10.	18.	22.	60.	100.	175.

Without Rays 1867-1883

Typical example of 1883, 3 over 2. Other varieties exist.

	Mintage	G-4	VG-8	F-12	EF-40	AU-50	MS-60	MS-63	PF-63
1868 . . . .(*600+*)	28,817,000	8.	9.	10.	18.	22.	60.	100.	175.
1869 . . . .(*600+*)	16,395,000	8.	9.	10.	18.	22.	60.	100.	175.
1870 . . . .(*1,000+*)	4,806,000	8.	9.	10.	20.	24.	65.	100.	175.
1871 . . . .(*960+*)	561,000	20.	25.	35.	80.	100.	125.	150.	200.
1872 . . . .(*950+*)	6,036,000	8.	9.	10.	20.	24.	60.	100.	175.
1873, Cl 3 . . . .(*1,100+*)	436,050	8.	9.	10.	24.	30.	70.	100.	175.
1873, Op 3	4,113,950	8.	9.	10.	20.	24.	65.	100.	
1874 . . . .(*700+*)	3,538,000	9.	10.	12.	24.	30.	65.	100.	175.
1875 . . . .(*700+*)	2,097,000	8.	12.	18.	30.	40.	85.	100.	175.
1876 . . . .(*1,150+*)	2,530,000	10.	11.	16.	27.	33.	65.	100.	175.
1877, PfS only . .(*510+*)	510			400.	750.				1,000.
1878, PfS only . .(2,350)	2,350			275.	400.				425.
1879 . . . .(3,200)	29,100	145.	200.	230.	300.	325.	350.	400	350.
1880 . . . .(3,955)	19,955	100.	225.	240.	325	350.	425.	475.	425.
1881 . . . .(3,575)	72,375	100.	120.	150.	210.	240.	300.	350.	300.
1882 . . . .(3,100)	11,476,000	7.	8.	9.	18.	22.	60.	175.	150.
1883 . . . .(5,419)	} 1,456,919	7.	8.	9.	18.	22.	60.	175.	150.
1883, 3/2			50.	60	125	175	275	400	

LIBERTY HEAD TYPE 1883-1913

In 1883 the design was changed to the familiar "Liberty head." This type first appeared without the word CENTS on the coin, merely a large letter "V." These "centless" coins were goldplated and passed for five dollars. Later in that year the word CENTS was added.

Without CENTS 1883 Only

G-4 GOOD—*No details in head. LIBERTY obliterated.*
VG-8 VERY GOOD—*At least 3 letters in LIBERTY readable.*
F-12 FINE—*All letters in LIBERTY show.*
VF-20 VERY FINE—*LIBERTY bold, including letter I*
EF-40 EXTREMELY FINE—*LIBERTY sharp. Corn grains at bottom of wreath show, on reverse.*
AU-50 ABOUT UNCIRCULATED—*Traces of light wear on only the high points of the design. Half of mint luster is present.*
MS-60 UNCIRCULATED—*No trace of wear. Light blemishes.*
MS-63 SELECT UNCIRCULATED—*Some distracting contact marks or blemishes in prime focal areas. Luster may be impaired.*
PF-63—*Reflective surfaces with only a few blemishes in secondary focal places. No major flaws.*

Brilliant choice uncirculated and proof coins are worth more than prices shown. Spotted, cleaned or discolored pieces are worth less.

	Mintage	G-4	VG-8	F-12	VF-20	EF-40	AU-50	MS-60	MS-63	PF-63
1883, w/o CENTS . . . .(5,219)	.5,479,519	$2.25	$2.50	$3.00	$3.50	$4.50	$5.	$14.	$20.	$160.

NICKEL FIVE-CENT PIECES
With CENTS 1883-1913

Location of mint mark

	Mintage	G-4	VG-8	F-12	VF-20	EF-40	AU-50	MS-60	MS-63	PF-63
1883, w/ CENTS ....(6,783)	16,032,983	$4.00	$5.00	$7.00	$11.00	$25.	$35.	$55.	$70.	$135.
1884 ...(3,942)	11,273,942	6.00	10.00	12.00	14.00	30.	40.	75.	100.	140.
1885 ...(3,790)	1,476,490	185.00	220.00	300.00	375.00	400.	450.	650.	750.	600.
1886 ...(4,290)	3,330,290	70.00	100.00	150.00	200.00	250.	300.	350.	400.	350.
1887 ...(2,960)	15,263,652	3.50	6.00	10.00	14.00	30.	35.	60.	100.	120.
1888 ...(4,582)	10,172,483	8.00	10.00	15.00	30.00	35.	40.	100.	150.	120.
1889 ...(3,336)	15,881,361	2.50	4.00	8.00	12.00	20.	25.	60.	100.	110.
1890 ...(2,740)	16,259,272	2.50	4.00	8.00	12.00	20.	25.	65.	100.	110.
1891 ...(2,350)	16,834,350	2.50	4.00	7.00	10.00	20.	25.	60.	100.	110.
1892 ...(2,745)	11,699,642	2.50	4.00	7.00	10.00	20.	25.	55.	100.	110.
1893 ...(2,195)	13,370,195	2.50	4.00	7.00	10.00	20.	25.	55.	100.	110.
1894 ...(2,632)	5,413,132	4.00	7.00	30.00	45.00	80.	120.	110.	125.	120.
1895 ...(2,062)	9,979,884	1.50	2.50	7.00	10.00	20.	25.	55.	110.	110.
1896 ...(1,862)	8,842,920	2.00	5.00	9.00	12.00	22.	25.	55.	115.	110.
1897 ...(1,938)	20,428,735	.75	1.00	3.00	6.00	14.	20.	40.	100.	110.
1898 ...(1,795)	12,532,087	.75	1.00	3.00	6.00	14.	20.	40.	100.	110.
1899 ...(2,031)	26,029,031	.75	1.00	3.00	6.00	14.	20.	40.	90.	110.
1900 ...(2,262)	27,255,995	.60	.75	2.00	4.00	11.	18.	35.	90.	100.
1901 ...(1,985)	26,480,213	.60	.75	2.00	4.00	11.	18.	35.	70.	100.
1902 ...(2,018)	31,489,579	.60	.75	2.00	4.00	11.	18.	35.	70.	100.
1903 ...(1,790)	28,006,725	.60	.75	2.00	4.00	11.	18.	35.	70.	100.
1904 ...(1,817)	21,404,984	.60	.75	2.00	4.00	11.	18.	35.	70.	100.
1905 ...(2,152)	29,827,276	.60	.75	2.00	4.00	11.	18.	35.	70.	100.
1906 ...(1,725)	38,613,725	.60	.75	2.00	4.00	11.	18.	35.	70.	100.
1907 ...(1,475)	39,214,800	.60	.75	2.00	4.00	11.	18.	35.	70.	100.
1908 ...(1,620)	22,686,177	.60	.75	2.00	4.00	11.	18.	35.	70.	100.
1909 ...(4,763)	11,590,526	.60	.75	2.00	4.00	11.	18.	40.	70.	100.
1910 ...(2,405)	30,169,353	.60	.75	2.00	4.00	11.	18.	31.	70.	100.
1911 ...(1,733)	39,559,372	.60	.75	2.00	4.00	11.	18.	35.	70.	100.
1912 ...(2,145)	26,236,714	.60	.75	2.00	4.00	11.	18.	35.	70.	100.
1912D	8,474,000	.75	.85	4.00	10.00	27.	65.	110.	120.	
1912S	238,000	50.00	65.00	90.00	140.00	300.	450.	500.	600.	
1913, Liberty Head (*5 known*)										1,500,000.

INDIAN HEAD or BUFFALO TYPE 1913-1938

The Buffalo nickel was designed by James E. Fraser, whose initial F is below the date. He modeled the bison after Black Diamond in the New York Central Park Zoo.

Variety 1 — FIVE CENTS on Raised Ground

G-4 GOOD—*Legends and date readable. Horn worn off.*
VG-8 VERY GOOD—*Half horn shows.*
F-12 FINE—*Three-quarters of horn shows. Obv. rim intact.*
VF-20 VERY FINE—*Full horn shows. Indian's cheekbone worn.*
EF-40 EXTREMELY FINE—*Full horn. Slight wear on Indian's hair ribbon.*
AU-50 ABOUT UNCIRCULATED—*Traces of light wear on only the high points of the design. Half of mint luster is present.*
MS-60 UNCIRCULATED—*No trace of wear. Light blemishes. Attractive mint luster.*
MS-63 SELECT UNCIRCULATED—*Some distracting contact marks or blemishes in prime focal areas. Luster may be impaired.*
PF-63—*Reflective surfaces with only a few blemishes in secondary focal places. No major flaws.*

Brilliant choice uncirculated coins are worth more than prices shown. Spotted, cleaned, weakly struck or discolored pieces are worth less.

	Mintage	G-4	VG-8	F-12	VF-20	EF-40	AU-50	MS-60	MS-63	Matte PF-63
1913, Var. 1 .(1,520)	30,993,520	$2.50	$3.00	$4.00	$5.00	$8.00	$9.	$15.	$20.	$600.
1913D, Var. 1	5,337,000	5.00	6.00	7.00	9.00	12.00	15.	28.	35.	
1913S, Var. 1	2,105,000	12.00	14.00	18.00	22.00	30.00	40.	50.	65.	

Mint mark below FIVE CENTS

1916 Doubled Die Obverse

1918D, 8 over 7

Variety 2 — FIVE CENTS in Recess

	Mintage	G-4	VG-8	F-12	VF-20	EF-40	AU-50	MS-60	MS-63	Matte PF-63
1913, Var. 2 (1,514)	29,858,700	$3.00	$4.00	$4.50	$5.00	$8.00	$10.	$17.	$25.	$500.
1913D, Var. 2	4,156,000	30.00	40.00	45.00	50.00	70.00	85.	100	125.	
1913S, Var. 2	1,209,000	80.00	100.00	135.00	160.00	200.00	225.	275.	325.	
1914 ....(1,275)	20,665,738	6.00	7.00	8.00	9.00	10.00	15.	28.	35.	500.
1914D	3,912,000	25.00	30.00	35.00	45.00	90.00	120.	140.	225.	
1914S	3,470,000	8.00	10.00	12.00	16.00	28.00	65.	70.	200.	
1915 ....(1,050)	20,987,270	1.50	1.75	2.25	3.50	9.00	20.	32.	35.	550.
1915D	7,569,000	6.00	7.00	12.00	20.00	40.00	60.	100.	140.	
1915S	1,505,000	12.00	18.00	30.00	55.00	100.00	150.	200.	300.	
1916 ....(600)	63,498,066	1.50	1.75	2.00	2.25	3.50	6.	20.	25.	800.
1916, Double Die Obverse		750.00	1600.00	3000.00	4000.00	6000.00	10,000.	29,000.	50,000.	
1916D	13,333,000	4.50	6.00	7.00	13.00	32.00	35.	70.	90.	
1916S	11,860,000	2.00	3.00	6.00	12.00	25.00	40.	80.	100.	
1917	51,424,019	1.50	2.00	2.50	3.00	5.00	10.	22.	45.	
1917D	9,910,000	5.00	7.00	12.00	30.00	55.00	80.	135.	250.	
1917S	4,193,000	8.00	12.00	18.00	36.00	65.00	100.	160.	425.	
1918	32,086,314	1.25	1.50	2.00	4.00	12.00	16.	40.	100.	
1918D, 8/7 ....}	8,362,000	350.00	475.00	800.00	1800.00	3600.00	4,000	10,000.	22,500.	
1918D ....}		5.00	9.00	12.00	45.00	85.00	120.	190.	450.	
1918S	4,882,000	4.00	10.00	14.00	35.00	70.00	100.	170.	1,100.	
1919	60,868,000	.45	.50	.75	1.75	5.00	10.	25.	35.	
1919D	8,006,000	4.00	8.00	18.00	45.00	100.00	130.	245.	600.	
1919S	7,521,000	3.00	7.00	12.00	45.00	100.00	125.	250.	650.	
1920	63,093,000	.40	.50	1.00	2.00	5.00	10.	27.	45.	
1920D	9,418,000	2.50	4.50	10.00	40.00	120.00	120.	240.	650.	
1920S	968,900	1.25	2.25	8.00	35.00	80.00	100.	190.	600.	
1921	10,663,000	.75	1.00	1.50	7.00	18.00	25.	50.	100.	
1921S	1,557,000	22.00	37.00	60.00	225.00	375.00	400.	675.	800.	
1923	35,715,000	.40	.50	.75	1.50	4.50	12.	24.	50.	
1923S	6,142,000	2.00	2.50	4.00	45.00	120.00	130.	175.	325.	
1924	21,620,000	.35	.50	.60	2.00	6.00	15.	30.	50.	
1924D	5,258,000	1.75	2.50	7.00	30.00	90.00	110.	160.	350.	
1924S	1,437,000	5.00	10.00	25.00	195.00	650.00	650.	1,000.	1,500.	

†Uncirculated pieces with full sharp details are worth considerably more.

NICKEL FIVE-CENT PIECES

Brilliant choice uncirculated coins are worth more than prices shown. Spotted, cleaned, weakly struck or discolored pieces are worth less.

1937 D "3-Legged" Variety

1938 D, D over S

	Mintage	G-4	VG-8	F-12	VF-20	EF-40	AU-50	MS-60	MS-63	PF-63
1925	35,565,100	$.50	$.75	$1.00	$2.00	$5.00	$10.00	$20.	$35.	
1925D	4,450,000	2.75	6.00	14.00	35.00	70.00	90.00	200.	240.	
1925S	6,256,000	1.50	3.50	6.00	33.00	75.00	90.00	200.	750.	
1926	44,693,000	.30	.40	.50	1.00	3.00	7.00	18.	25.	
1926D†	5,638,000	1.75	4.00	8.00	35.00	65.00	100.00	110.	200.	
1926S	970,000	6.00	12.00	24.00	175.00	400.00	1000.00	1650.	2500.	
1927	37,981,000	.30	.40	.50	1.00	3.00	7.00	16.	25.	
1927D	5,730,000	.75	1.75	2.00	11.00	30.00	40.00	70.	100.	
1927S	3,430,000	.50	.80	1.50	14.00	35.00	60.00	200.	850.	
1928	23,411,000	.35	.40	.50	1.00	3.00	8.00	16.	22.	
1928D	6,436,000	.40	.75	1.50	5.00	16.00	18.00	21.	35.	
1928S	6,936,000	.50	.60	1.00	4.00	12.00	40.00	80.	220.	
1929	36,446,000	.30	.35	.50	1.00	3.00	7.00	14.	22.	
1929D	8,370,000	.40	.50	.75	2.50	13.00	15.00	26.	45.	
1929S	7,754,000	.35	.50	.65	.80	4.50	9.00	18.	30.	
1930	22,849,000	.35	.40	.60	.75	3.00	7.00	13.	25.	
1930S	5,435,000	.35	.40	.60	.75	4.50	10.00	18.	40.	
1931S	1,200,000	5.00	6.00	7.50	8.50	10.00	15.00	24.	30.	
1934	20,213,003	.30	.40	.50	.65	2.00	7.00	13.	20.	
1934D	7,480,000	.30	.40	.50	1.00	5.00	15.00	20.	35.	
1935	58,264,000	.30	.40	.50	.65	1.00	3.00	8.	15.	
1935D	12,092,000	.30	.40	.50	.65	2.50	15.00	18.	30.	
1935S	10,300,000	.30	.40	.50	.65	1.50	6.00	14.	25.	
1936	119,001,420	.30	.40	.50	.65	1.00	3.00	8.	15.	
1936 Pf	(4,420)									$500.
1936D All kinds	24,814,000	.30	.40	.50	.65	1.25	4.00	12.00	14.	
1936S	14,930,000	.30	.40	.50	.65	1.00	3.50	9.	14.	
1937 ....(5,769)	79,485,769	.30	.40	.50	.65	1.00	2.50	12.	14.	
1937D	17,826,000	.30	.40	.50	.65	1.00	3.00	9.	14.	
1937D, 3-Legged*			100.00	200.00	220.00	250.00	300.00	400.00	750.	1800.
1937S	5,635,000	.30	.40	.50	.65	1.00	3.00	9.	15.	
1938D	7,020,000	.30	.40	.50	.65	1.00	3.00	9.	12.	
1938D, D/S				3.00	3.50	6.00	10.00	18.	25.	

†Uncirculated pieces with full sharp details are worth considerably more. *Beware of removed leg.

JEFFERSON TYPE 1938 to Date

This nickel was designed by Felix Schlag. He won an award of $1,000 in a competition with some 390 artists. It established the definite public approval of portrait and pictorial rather than symbolic devices on our coinage. On October 8, 1942, the wartime five-cent piece composed of copper (56%), silver (35%) and manganese (9%) was introduced to eliminate nickel, a critical war material. A larger mint mark was placed above the dome. Letter P (Philadelphia) was used for the first time, indicating the change of alloy. The designer's initials FS were added below the bust starting in 1966. Mint mark position was moved to the obverse starting in 1968.

VG-8 VERY GOOD—*Second porch pillar from right nearly gone, other three still visible but weak.*
F-12 FINE—*Cheekbone worn flat. Hairlines and eyebrow faint. Second pillar weak, especially at bottom.*
VF-20 VERY FINE—*Second pillar plain and complete on both sides.*
EF-40 EXTREMELY FINE—*Cheekbone, hairlines, eyebrow slightly worn but well defined. Base of triangle above pillars visible but weak.*
MS-63 SELECT UNCIRCULATED—*No trace of wear. Slight blemishes.*
MS-65—CHOICE UNCIRCULATED—*Only light scattered contact marks that are not distracting. Strong luster, good eye appeal.*
PF-65—*Choice Brilliant surfaces with no noticeable blemishes or flaws. May have a few scatered barely noticeable marks or hairlines.*

NICKEL FIVE-CENT PIECES

Uncirculated pieces with fully-struck steps are valued higher.

Mint mark located at right of building

Wartime Silver

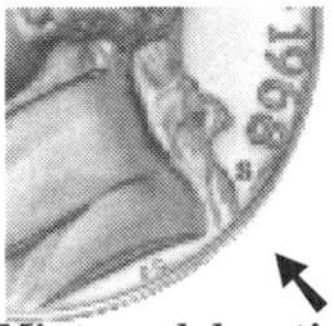

Mint mark location starting 1968

	Mintage	VG-8	F-12	VF-20	EF-40	MS-63	MS-65	PF-65
1938 . . . . .(19,365)	19,515,365	.07	.10	$.20	$.25	$1.00	$5.00	$40.
1938D	5,376,000	.25	.35	.50	.75	1.50	6.00	
1938S	4,105,000	.40	.60	.85	1.50	2.00	7.00	
1939 . . . . .(12,535)	120,627,535	.08	.10	.12	.25	1.00	2.00	38.
1939D	3,514,000	1.20	1.60	2.25	3.50	25.00	40.00	
1939S	6,630,000	.25	.30	.35	1.25	12.00	16.00	
1940 . . . . .(14,158)	176,499,158			.05	.10	1.00	2.00	36.
1940D	43,540,000			.05	.10	1.25	3.00	
1940S	39,690,000			.05	.10	1.25	3.00	
1941 . . . . .(18,720)	203,283,720			.05	.10	.50	2.00	36.
1941D	53,432,000			.05	.10	1.25	3.00	
1941S	43,445,000			.05	.10	1.50	3.50	
1942 . . . . .(29,600)	49,818,600			.05	.10	1.25	3.00	36.
1942D	13,938,000	.10	.15	.25	.50	10.00	20.00	

Wartime Silver Five-Cent Pieces 1942-1945

	Mintage	VG-8	F-12	VF-20	EF-40	MS-63	MS-65	PF-65
1942P . . . .(27,600)	57,900,600	$.20	$.20	$.25	$.35	$4.	$8.	$65.
1942S	32,900,000	.20	.20	.25	.35	4.	8.	
1943P, 3/2	271,165,000 (both)		15.00	20.00	30.00	125.	300.	
1943P		.20	.20	.25	.35	3.	6.	
1943D	15,294,000	.20	.30	.35	.50	5.	7.	
1943S	104,060,000	.20	.20	.25	.35	3.	6.	
1944P	119,150,000	.20	.30	.25	.35	5.	8.	
1944D	32,309,000	.20	.20	.25	.35	5.	8.	
1944S	21,640,000	.20	.20	.25	.35	4.	9.	
1945P	119,408,100	.20	.20	.25	.35	3.	8.	
1945D	37,158,000	.20	.20	.25	.35	3.	7.	
1945S	58,939,000	.25	.20	.25	.35	3.	7.	

Prewar composition and mint mark style resumed 1946-1967

	Mintage	VF-20	EF-40	MS-63	MS-65	PF-65
1946	161,116,000	$.05	$.05	$.25	$2.00	
1946D	45,292,200	.05	.05	.25	2.00	
1946S	13,560,000	.05	.06	.15	1.50	
1947	95,000,000	.05	.05	.25	2.00	
1947D	37,822,000	.05	.05	.25	2.00	
1947S	24,720,000	.05	.06	.20	1.75	
1948	89,348,000	.05	.05	.20	1.75	
1948D	44,734,000	.05	.06	.25	2.00	
1948S	11,300,000	.05	.06	.20	1.75	
1949	60,652,000	.05	.05	.50	2.50	
1949D	36,498,000 (both)	.05	.05	.25	2.00	
1949D, D/S		18.00	30.00	120.00	150.00	
1949S	9,716,000	.05	.10	.35	1.75	
1950 . . . . .(51,386)	9,847,386	.05	.10	.50	2.50	$20.
1950D	2,630,030	2.00	2.25	3.00	4.00	
1951 . . . . .(57,500)	28,609,500	.05	.05	.50	2.50	18.
1951D	20,460,000	.05	.05	.75	3.00	
1951S	7,776,000	.05	.10	.50	2.50	
1952 . . . . .(81,980)	64,069,980	.05	.05	.20	1.75	10.

	Mintage	VF-20	EF-40	MS-63	MS-65	PF-65
1952D	30,638,000	$.05	$.05	$2.00	$3.00	
1952S	20,572,000	.05	.05	.50	1.00	
1953 (128,800)	46,772,800	.05	.05	.10	.25	$15.00
1953D	59,878,600	.05	.05	.10	.25	
1953S	19,210,900	.05	.05	.20	.25	
1954 (233,300)	47,917,350	.05	.05	.15	.25	7.50
1954D	117,183,060	.05	.05	.15	.25	
1954S }	29,384,000	.05	.05	.25	.25	
1954S, S/D }		2.50	5.00	20.00	35.00	
1955 (378,200)	8,266,200	.06	.08	.40	.50	5.00

1943, 3 over 2

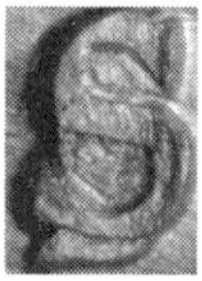

1954S, S over D

1955D, D over S*

	Mintage	VF-20	EF-40	MS-63	MS-65	PF-65
1955D }	74,464,100	.05	.05	.10	.40	
1955D, D/S* }		3.00	5.00	30.00	35.00	
1956 (669,384)	35,885,384		.05	.10	.50	1.00
1956D	67,222,940		.05	.10	.50	
1957 (1,247,952)	39,655,952		.05	.10	.50	1.00
1957D	136,828,900		.05	.10	.50	
1958 (875,652)	17,963,652		.05	.10	.60	1.50
1958D	168,249,120		.05	.10	.50	
1959 (1,149,291)	28,397,291		.05	.10	.50	.75
1959D	160,738,240		.05	.10	.20	
1960 (1,691,602)	57,107,602		.05	.10	.20	.75
1960D	192,582,180		.05	.10	.20	
1961 (3,028,144)	76,668,244		.05	.10	.20	.75
1961D	229,342,760		.05	.10	.20	
1962 (3,218,019)	100,602,019		.05	.10	.20	.75
1962D	280,195,720		.05	.10	.25	
1963 (3,075,645)	178,851,645		.05	.10	.20	.75
1963D	276,829,460			.10	.20	
1964 (3,950,762)	1,028,622,762			.10	.20	.75
1964D	1,787,297,160			.10	.20	
1965	136,131,380			.10	.20	
1966	156,208,283			.10	.20	
1967	107,325,800			.10	.20	
1968D	91,227,880			.10	.20	
1968S (3,041,506)	103,437,510			.10	.20	
1969D	202,807,500			.10	.20	
1969S (2,934,631)	123,099,631			.10	.20	
1970D	515,485,380			.10	.20	
1970S (2,632,810)	241,464,814			.10	.20	
1971	106,884,000			.25	.35	
1971D	316,144,800			.10	.20	
1971S, Pf (3,220,733)						1.00
1972	202,036,000			.10	.20	
1972D	351,694,600			.10	.20	
1972S, Pf (3,260,996)						1.00
1973	384,396,000			.10	.20	
1973D	261,405,000			.10	.20	
1973S, Pf (2,760,339)						1.00
1974	601,752,000			.10	.20	
1974D	277,373,000			.10	.20	

*Varieties exist. Value is for that illustrated.

NICKEL FIVE-CENT PIECES

	Mintage	MS-65	PF-65
1974S, Pf	(2,612,568)		$.75
1975	181,772,000	$.20	
1975D	401,875,300	.20	
1975S, Pf	(2,845,450)		.75
1976	367,124,00)	.20	
1976D	563,964,147	.20	
1976S, Pf	(4,149,730)		.75
1977	585,376,000	.20	
1977D	297,313,422	.50	
1977S, Pf	(3,251,152)		.75
1978	391,308,000	.20	
1978D	313,092,780	.20	
1978S, Pf	(3,127,781)		.75
1979	463,188,000	.20	
1979D	325,867,672	.20	
1979S, Pf, Filled S			.75
1979S, Pf, Clear S			1.00
1980P	593,004,000	.20	
1980D	502,323,448	.20	
1980S, Pf	(3,554,806)		.75
1981P	657,504,000	.20	
1981D	364,801,843	.20	
1981S, Pf	(4,063,083)		.75
1982P	292,355,000	1.75	
1982D	373,726,544	1.25	
1982S, Pf	(3,857,479)		1.00
1983P	561,615,000	1.50	
1983D	536,726,276	1.00	
1983S, Pf	(3,279,126)		1.00
1984P	746,769,000	1.00	
1984D	517,675,146	.20	
1984S, Pf	(3,065,110)		1.50
1985P	647,114,962	.20	
1985D	459,747,446	.20	
1985S, Pf	(3,362,821)		1.25
1986P	536,883,483	.25	
1986D	361,819,140	.60	
1986S, Pf	(3,010,497)		2.00
1987P	371,499,481	.20	
1987D	410,590,604	.20	
1987S, Pf	(4,227,728)		1.00
1988P	771,360,000	.20	
1988D	663,771,652	.20	
1988S, Pf	(3,262,948)		2.00
1989P	898,812,000	.20	
1989D	570,842,474	.20	
1989S, Pf	(3,220,194)		$1.50
1990P	661,636,000	$.20	
1990D	663,938,503	.20	
1990S, Pf	(3,299,559)		1.75
1991P	614,104,000	.20	
1991D	436,496,678	.20	
1991S, Pf	(2,867,787)		2.00
1992P	399,552,000	1.00	
1992D	450,565,113	.20	
1992S, Pf	(4,176,560)		1.50
1993P	412,076,000	.20	
1993D	406,084,135	.20	
1993S, Pf	(3,394,792)		1.50
1994P	722,160,000	.20	
1994D	715,762,110	.20	
1994S, Pf	(3,269,923)		1.50
1995P	774,156,000	.40	
1995D	888,112,000	.20	
1995S, Pf	(2,797,481)		1.75
1996P	829,332,000	.20	
1996D	817,736,000	.20	
1996S, Pf	(2,525,265)		1.00
1997P	470,972,000	.20	
1997D	466,640,000	.20	
1997S, Pf	(2,796,678)		2.00
1998P	688,272,000	.20	
1998D	635,360,000	.20	
1998S, Pf	(2,086,507)		2.00
1999P	1,212,000,000	.20	
1999D	1,066,720,000	.20	
1999S, Pf	(2,543,401)		1.00
2000P	846,240,000	.20	
2000D	1,509,520,000	.20	
2000S, Pf	(3,082,483)		1.00
2001P	675,704,000	.20	
2001D	627,680,000	.20	
2001S, Pf	(2,294,043)		1.00
2002P	539,280,000	.20	
2002D	691,200,000	.20	
2002S, Pf	(2,277,720)		1.00
2003 P		.20	
2003 D		.20	
2003S, Pf			1.00

NICKEL FIVE-CENT PIECES

PEACE MEDAL

The "Peace Medal" nickel design for 2004 commemorates the bicentennials of the Louisiana Purchase and the Lewis and Clark expedition. The reverse side of the new nickel is a depiction of the original Jefferson Peace Medal designed in 1801. Lewis and Clark gave these medals as tokens to Native Americans they met during their journey. The second nickel design of 2004 features the keelboat that transported Lewis and Clark.

PEACE MEDAL

	Mintage	MS-65	PF-65
2004P, Louisiana Purchase / Peace Medal	361,440,000	$.05	
2004D, Louisiana Purchase / Peace Medal	372,000,000	.05	
2004S, Pf, Louisiana Purchase / Peace Medal			$.05
2004P, Lewis and Clark / Keelboat		.05	
2004D, Lewis and Clark / Keelboat		.05	
2004S, Pf, Lewis and Clark / Keelboat			.05

HALF DIMES 1794-1873

The half dime types present the same general characteristics as larger United States silver coins. Authorized by the Act of April 2, 1792, they were not coined until February, 1795, although dated 1794. At first the weight was 20.8 grains, and fineness 892.4. By the Act of January 18, 1837, the weight was slightly reduced to 20 5/8 grains and the fineness changed to .900. Finally the weight was reduced to 19.2 grains by the Act of February 21, 1853.

FLOWING HAIR TYPE 1794-1795

AG-3 ABOUT GOOD—*Details clear enough to identify.*
G-4 GOOD—*Eagle, wreath, bust outlined but lack details.*
VG-8 VERY GOOD—*Some details remain on face. All lettering readable.*
F-12 FINE—*Hair ends show. Hair at top smooth.*
VF-20 VERY FINE—*Hairlines at top show. Hair about ear defined.*
EF-40 EXTREMELY FINE—*Hair above forehead and at neck well defined but shows some wear.*
AU-50 ABOUT UNCIRCULATED—*Traces of light wear on only the high points of the design. Half of mint luster is present.*
MS-60 UNCIRCULATED—*No trace of wear. Light blemishes.*
MS-63 SELECT UNCIRCULATED—*Some distracting contact marks or blemishes in prime focal areas. Luster may be impaired.*

Weakly-struck uncirculated coins are worth less than values shown.

	Mintage	AG-3	G-4	VG-8	F-12	VF-20	EF-40	AU-50	MS-60	MS-63
1794	} 86,416	$200.	$400.	$525.	$750.	$1,200.	$2,100.	$3,500.	$6,000.	$8,000.
1795		150.	350.	475.	600.	900.	1,600.	2,500.	4,000.	5,500.

DRAPED BUST TYPE, SMALL EAGLE REVERSE 1796-1797

AG-3 ABOUT GOOD—*Details clear enough to identify.*
G-4 GOOD—*Date, stars, LIBERTY readable. Bust outlined but no details.*
VG-8 VERY GOOD—*Some details show.*
F-12 FINE—*Hair and drapery lines worn, but visible.*
VF-20 VERY FINE—*Only left of drapery indistinct.*
EF-40 EXTREMELY FINE—*All hairlines show details.*
AU-50 ABOUT UNCIRCULATED—*Traces of light wear on only the high points of the design. Half of mint luster is present.*
MS-60 UNCIRCULATED—*No trace of wear. Light blemishes.*
MS-63 SELECT UNCIRCULATED—*Some distracting contact marks or blemishes in prime focal areas. Luster may be impaired.*

HALF DIMES

	Mintage	AG-3	G-4	VG-8	F-12	VF-20	EF-40	AU-50	MS-60	MS-63
1796, 6/5		$250.	$450.	$525.	$900.	$1,500.	$2,500.	$4,000.	$9,000.	$15,000.
1796	10,230	200.	425.	500.	800.	1,300.	2,000.	3,500.	4,750.	10,000.
1796, LIKERTY		200.	425.	500.	800.	1,300.	2,000.	3,500.	5,000.	12,000.
1797, 15 stars		175.	400.	500.	700.	1,200.	2,000.	3,500.	4,500.	10,000.
1797, 16 stars	44,527	175.	400.	500.	700.	1,200.	2,000.	3,500.	4,500.	10,000.
1797, 13 stars		250.	450.	600.	950.	1,500.	3,000.	4,500.	10,000.	15,000.

1800 LIBEKTY

DRAPED BUST TYPE, HERALDIC EAGLE REVERSE 1800-1805

	Mintage	AG-3	G-4	VG-8	F-12	VF-20	EF-40	AU-50	MS-60	MS-63
1800	24,000	$110.	$250.	$300.	$500.	$750.	$1,500.	$2,500.	$3,500.	$5,000.
1800, LIBEKTY	16,000	110.	250.	300.	500.	750.	1,500.	2,500.	3,500.	5,000.
1801	27,760	120.	250.	350.	550.	800.	1,500.	2,500.	5,000.	6,500.
1802	3,060	3,000.	8,000.	10,000.	16,000.	27,000.	40,000.	—	—	—
1803	37,850	120.	300.	400.	550.	800.	1,500.	2,500.	3,750.	5,500.
1805	15,600	150.	350.	450.	575.	900.	1,900.	4,000.	—	—

CAPPED BUST TYPE 1829-1837

G-4 GOOD—*Bust outlined, no detail. Date and legend readable.*
VG-8 VERY GOOD—*Complete legend and date plain. At least 3 letters of LIBERTY show clearly.*
F-12 FINE—*All letters in LIBERTY show.*
VF-20 VERY FINE—*Full rims. Ear and shoulder clasp show plainly.*
EF-40 EXTREMELY FINE—*Ear very distinct, eyebrow and hair well defined.*
AU-50 ABOUT UNCIRCULATED—*Traces of light wear on only the high points of the design. Half of mint luster is present.*
MS-60 UNCIRCULATED—*No trace of wear. Light blemishes.*
MS-63 SELECT UNCIRCULATED—*Some distracting contact marks or blemishes in prime focal areas. Luster may be impaired.*

	Mintage	G-4	VG-8	F-12	VF-20	EF-40	AU-50	MS-60	MS-63
1829	1,230,000	$10.	$14.	$18.	$30.	$60.	$90.	$150.	$300.
1830	1,240,000	10.	14.	18.	30.	60.	90.	150.	300.
1831	1,242,700	10.	14.	18.	30.	60.	90.	150.	300.
1832	965,000	10.	14.	18.	30.	60.	90.	150.	300.
1833	1,370,000	10.	14.	18.	30.	60.	90.	150.	300.
1834	1,480,000	10.	14.	18.	30.	60.	90.	150.	300.
1835 All kinds	2,760,000	10.	14.	18.	30.	60.	90.	150.	300.
1836	1,900,000	10.	14.	18.	30.	60.	90.	150.	300.
1837, Small 5C	871,000	12.	16.	25.	45.	85.	150.	450.	800.
1837, Large 5C		10.	14.	18.	30.	60.	90.	150.	300.

HALF DIMES

LIBERTY SEATED TYPE 1837-1873

No Stars on Obverse 1837-1838

G-4 GOOD—*LIBERTY On shield smooth. Date and letters readable.*
VG-8 VERY GOOD—*At least 3 letters in LIBERTY are visible.*
F-12 FINE—*Entire LIBERTY visible, weak spots.*
VF-20 VERY FINE—*Entire LIBERTY strong and even.*
EF-40 EXTREMELY FINE—*LIBERTY and scroll edges distinct.*
AU-50 ABOUT UNCIRCULATED—*Traces of light wear on only the high points of the design. Half of mint luster is present.*
MS-60 UNCIRCULATED—*No trace of wear. Light blemishes.*
MS-63 SELECT UNCIRCULATED—*Some distracting contact marks or blemishes in prime focal areas. Luster may be impaired.*
PF-63—*Reflective surfaces with only a few blemishes in secondary focal places. No major flaws.*

	Mintage	G-4	VG-8	F-12	VF-20	EF-40	AU-50	MS-60	MS-63
1837	1,405,000	$12.	$19.	$26.	$50.	$90.	$150.	$300.	$400.
1838O, No stars	70,000	32.	50.	80.	170.	300.	450.	800.	3,000.

Stars on Obverse 1838-1853

From 1838 through 1859 the mint mark is located above bow on reverse. Large, medium, or small mint mark varieties occur for several dates.

	Mintage	G-4	VG-8	F-12	VF-20	EF-40	AU-50	MS-60	MS-63
1838	2,255,000	5.	6.	9.	12.	27.	60.	160.	175.
1839O	1,034,039	5.	6.	9.	12.	27.	60.	160.	175.
1840	1,344,085	5.	6.	9.	12.	27.	60.	160.	175.
1841	1,150,000	5.	6.	9.	12.	27.	60.	100.	125.
1841O	815,000	6.	8.	13.	20.	40.	110.	350.	600.
1842	815,000	5.	6.	9.	12.	27.	60.	90.	125.
1842O	350,000	11.	14.	25.	70.	200.	300.	525.	800.
1843	1,165,000	5.	6.	9.	12.	27.	60.	90.	125.
1844	430,000	5.	6.	9.	12.	27.	60.	90.	125.
1844O	220,000	27.	40.	65.	200.	450.	1,000.	2,000.	5,000.
1845	1,564,000	5.	6.	9.	12.	27.	60.	90.	125.
1846	27,000	80.	125.	250.	300.	900.	1,500.	3,000.	
1847	1,274,000	5.	6.	9.	12.	27.	65.	100.	200.
1848	668,000	5.	6.	9.	12.	27.	65.	100.	125.
1848O	600,000	7.	9.	13.	23.	40.	100.	190.	250.
1849, 9/6	}	8.	10.	15.	23.	40.	90.	200.	550.
1849, 9/8	} 1,309,000	8.	11.	19.	25.	50.	110.	250.	700.
1849	}	5.	6.	9.	12.	27.	60.	90.	200.
1849O	140,000	11.	17.	33.	90.	200.	400.	800.	1,750.
1850	955,000	5.	6.	9.	12.	27.	60.	90.	125.
1850O	690,000	6.	8.	10.	20.	45.	125.	325.	650.
1851	781,000	5.	6.	9.	12.	27.	60.	90.	125.
1851O	860,000	6.	8.	10.	17.	45.	100.	225.	350.
1852	1,000,500	5.	6.	9.	12.	27.	60.	90.	125.
1852O	260,000	11.	16.	26.	50.	110.	200.	375.	750.
1853, No arrows	135,000	12.	17.	26.	50.	100.	175.	300.	450.
1853O, No arrows	160,000	75.	125.	150.	250.	500.	1,000.	2,200.	5,000.

Arrows at Date 1853-1855

As on the dimes, quarters and halves, arrows were placed at the sides of the date for a short period starting in 1853 to denote reduction of weight.

	Mintage	G-4	VG-8	F-12	VF-20	EF-40	AU-50	MS-60	MS-63	PF-63
1853	13,210,020	$6.	$7.	$9.	$12.	$25.	$50.	$100.	$120.	
1853O	2,200,000	7.	8.	11.	18.	30.	70.	125.	400.	
1854	5,740,000	6.	7.	9.	12.	25.	60.	110.	125.	$4,000.
1854O	1,560,000	7.	8.	11.	18.	30.	70.	135.	350.	
1855	1,750,000	6.	7.	9.	12.	25.	50.	110.	120.	3,500.
1855O	600,000	6.	9.	12.	24.	70.	100.	275.	450.	

No Arrows at Date 1856-1859

	Mintage	G-4	VG-8	F-12	VF-20	EF-40	AU-50	MS-60	MS-63	PF-63
1856	4,880,000	$6.	$7.	$9.	$12.	$25.	$50.	$80.	$120.	$2,000.
1856O	1,100,000	6.	7.	10.	20.	40.	100.	210.	450.	
1857	7,280,000	6.	7.	9.	12.	25.	50.	80.	120.	1,500.
1857O	1,380,000	6.	7.	10.	16.	30.	80.	175.	210.	

1858 over Inverted Date

	Mintage	G-4	VG-8	F-12	VF-20	EF-40	AU-50	MS-60	MS-63	PF-63
1858	3,500,000	$6.	$7.	$9.	$12.	$25.	$50.	$80.	$120.	$700.
1858, / inverted date		15.	20.	30.	50.	95.	150.	275.	550.	
1858O	1,660,000	6.	7.	10.	18.	28.	60.	125.	180.	
1859	340,000	7.	8.	12.	20.	50.	90.	130.	150.	600.
1859O	560,000	7.	8.	12.	20.	50.	90.	150.	150.	

Legend on Obverse 1860-1873

	Mintage	G-4	VG-8	F-12	VF-20	EF-40	AU-50	MS-60	MS-63	PF-63
1860 (1,000)	799,000	$6.00	$7.	$9.	$11.	$18.	$30.	$70.	$100.	$300.
1860O	1,060,000	6.00	7.	9.	11.	18.	35.	100.	135.	
1861 (1,000)	3,361,000	6.00	7.	9.	11.	18.	30.	70.	100.	300.
1862 (550)	1,492,550	8.00	10.	17.	20.	25.	40.	110.	125.	300.
1863 (460)	18,460	60.00	70.	95.	125.	200.	270.	300.	400.	350.
1863S	100,000	10.00	14.	17.	21.	60.	160.	350.	450.	
1864 (470)	48,470	110.00	170.	200.	275.	400.	500.	550.	600.	350.
1864S	90,000	18.00	20.	35.	50.	110.	180.	310.	700.	
1865 (500)	13,500	100.00	125.	180.	210.	275.	300.	400.	600.	350.
1865S	120,000	10.00	14.	17.	22.	60.	200.	450.	800.	
1866 (725)	10,725	100.00	115.	150.	200.	300.	320.	375.	600.	300.
1866S	120,000	10.00	14.	17.	22.	60.	180.	200.	400.	
1867 (625)	8,625	175.00	200.	250.	300.	350.	400.	450.	620.	350.
1867S	120,000	6.50	12.	17.	25.	60.	140.	210.	500.	
1868 (600)	89,200	20.00	25.	40.	70.	120.	200.	300.	400.	350.
1868S	280,000	6.00	8.	10.	12.	19.	40.	125.	250.	
1869 (600)	208,600	6.00	8.	10.	12.	19.	60.	120.	150.	300.
1869S	230,000	6.00	8.	10.	12.	19.	50.	150.	350.	
1870 (1,000)	536,000	6.00	8.	9.	10.	19.	30.	70.	120.	300.
1870S (*Unique*)										
1871 (960)	1,873,960	6.00	8.	9.	10.	19.	30.	70.	120.	300.
1871S	161,000	7.00	10.	15.	25.	40.	70.	125.	200.	
1872 (950)	2,947,950	6.00	8.	9.	10.	19.	30.	70.	120.	300.
1872S	837,000	6.00	8.	9.	10.	19.	30.	70.	120.	
1873 (600)	712,6000	6.00	8.	9.	10.	19.	30.	70.	120.	300.
1873S	324,000	6.00	8.	9.	10.	19.	30.	70.	120.	

DIMES — 1796 to Date

The designs of the dimes, first coined in 1796, follow closely those of the half dimes up through the Liberty seated type. The dimes in each instance weigh twice as much as the half dimes.

DRAPED BUST TYPE, SMALL EAGLE REVERSE 1796-1797

AG-3 ABOUT GOOD—*Details clear enough to identify.*
G-4 GOOD—*Date readable. Bust outlined, but no detail.*
VG-8 VERY GOOD—*All but deepest drapery folds worn smooth. Hairlines nearly gone and curls lack detail.*
F-12 FINE—*All drapery lines visible. Hair partly worn.*
VF-20 VERY FINE—*Only left side of drapery is indistinct.*
EF-40 EXTREMELY FINE—*Hair well outlined and shows details.*
AU-50 ABOUT UNCIRCULATED—*Traces of light wear on only the high points of the design. Half of mint luster is present.*
MS-60 UNCIRCULATED—*No trace of wear. Light blemishes.*
MS-63 SELECT UNCIRCULATED—*Some distracting contact marks or blemishes in prime focal areas. Luster may be impaired.*

1797, 16 Stars

1797, 13 Stars

	Mintage	AG-3	G-4	VG-8	F-12	VF-20	EF-40	AU-50	MS-60	MS-63
1796	22,135	$250.	$500.	$850.	$1,000.	$1,600.	$3,000.	$3,500.	$5,200.	$9,500.
1797, 16 stars	} 25,261	250.	550.	850.	1,000.	1,700.	3,200.	4,000.	5,500.	10,000.
1797, 13 stars		250.	550.	850.	1,000.	1,700.	3,200.	4,000.	5,500.	10,000.

DRAPED BUST TYPE, HERALDIC EAGLE REVERSE 1798-1807

	Mintage	AG-3	G-4	VG-8	F-12	VF-20	EF-40	AU-50	MS-60	MS-63
1798 All Kinds	27,550									
1798, /97,16 stars on rev.		125.	250.	350.	450.	650.	1,100.	2,000.	3,000.	5,000.
1798, /97,13 stars		250.	800.	1,000.	1,500.	3,000.	4,000.	—	—	
1798		125.	210.	250.	425.	550.	1,000.	1,500.	2,500.	5,000.
1800	21,760	125.	210.	250.	425.	550.	1,100.	1,600.	2,700.	4,500.
1801	34,640	125.	210.	275.	500.	900.	1,800.	3,200.	5,000.	7,000.
1802	10,975	150.	325.	450.	650.	1,200.	2,500.	4,000.	9,000.	
1803	33,040	100.	225.	300.	400.	600.	1,500.	3,500.	5,000.	
1804 All kinds	8,265	250.	500.	700.	1,200.	2,000.	5,000.	12,000.	17,000.	
1805	120,780	85.	175.	225.	325.	450.	900.	1,100.	2,800.	4,200.
1807	165,000	85.	175.	225.	325.	450.	800.	1,000.	2,100.	4,000.

CAPPED BUST TYPE 1809-1837

G-4 GOOD—*Date, letters and stars discernible. Bust outlined, no details.*
VG-8 VERY GOOD—*Legends and date plain. Minimum of 3 letters in LIBERTY.*
F-12 FINE—*Full LIBERTY. Ear and shoulder clasp visible. Part of rim shows both sides.*
VF-20 VERY FINE—*LIBERTY distinct. Full rim. Ear and clasp plain and distinct.*
EF-40 EXTREMELY FINE—*LIBERTY sharp. Ear distinct. Hair above eye well defined.*
AU-50 ABOUT UNCIRCULATED—*Traces of light wear on only the high points of the design. Half of mint luster is present.*
MS-60 UNCIRCULATED—*No trace of wear. Light blemishes.*
MS-63 SELECT UNCIRCULATED—*Some distracting contact marks or blemishes in prime focal areas. Luster may be impaired.*

Wide Border 1809-1828

	Mintage	G-4	VG-8	F-12	VF-20	EF-40	AU-50	MS-60	MS-63
1809	51,065	$45.	$70.	$125.	$200.	$425.	$700.	$1,700.	$2,100.
1811/9	65,180	30.	50.	100.	185.	400.	650.	1,500.	2,200.
1814	421,500	13.	15.	25.	70.	175.	250.	450.	900.
1820	942,587	10.	12.	20.	45.	170.	250.	450.	900.
1821	1,186,512	10.	12.	20.	45.	170.	250.	500.	900.
1822	100,000	150.	275.	400.	600.	1,200.	2,000.	4,000.	7,000.
1823, 3/2 All kinds	440,000								
1823, 3/2,Small E's		10.	12.	20.	45.	170.	250.	500.	1,000.
1823, 3/2,Large E's		10.	12.	20.	45.	170.	250.	500.	1,000.

1823, 3 over 2

1824, 4 over 2

1828 Large Date

1828 Small Date

	Mintage	G-4	VG-8	F-12	VF-20	EF-40	AU-50	MS-60	MS-63
1824, 4/2	510,000 (combined)	12.	18.	40.	125.	275.	550.	900.	1,700.
1825	510,000 (combined)	10.	12.	20.	45.	150.	275.	450.	1,000.
1827	1,215,000	10.	12.	20.	45.	150.	275.	450.	1,000.
1828, Large Date, curl base 2		20.	35.	50.	125.	275.	700.	1,000.	1,700.

Modified Design 1828-1837

1829 Small 10c

Large 10c

1830, 30 over 29

	Mintage	G-4	VG-8	F-12	VF-20	EF-40	AU-50	MS-60	MS-63
1828, Small Date, sq.base 2		12.	17.	30.	50.	175.	300.	600.	1,000.
1829, Small 10c		10.	12.	14.	30.	110.	150.	400.	700.
1829, Medium 10c		10.	12.	14.	30.	110.	150.	325.	625.
1829, Large 10c		10.	15.	21.	40.	125.	200.	400.	625.
1830, 30/29		16.	25.	45.	85.	225.	250.	500.	900.
1830, Large 10C		10.	12.	14.	30.	110.	140.	325.	600.
1830, Small 10C		10.	12.	14.	30.	110.	140.	325.	600.
1831	771,350	10.	12.	14.	30.	110.	140.	325.	600.
1832	522,500	10.	12.	14.	30.	110.	140.	325.	600.
1833	485,000	10.	12.	14.	30.	110.	140.	325.	600.
1834	635,000	10.	12.	14.	30.	110.	140.	325.	600.
1835	1,410,000	10.	12.	14.	30.	110.	140.	325.	600.
1836	1,190,000	10.	12.	14.	30.	110.	140.	325.	600.
1837	359,500	10.	12.	14.	30.	110.	140.	325.	600.

LIBERTY SEATED TYPE 1837-1891

No Stars on Obverse 1837-1838

G-4 GOOD—*LIBERTY on shield smooth. Date and letters readable.*
F-12 FINE—*Entire LIBERTY visible, weak spots.*
VF-20 VERY FINE—*Entire LIBERTY strong and even.*
EF-40 EXTREMELY FINE—*LIBERTY and scroll edges distinct.*
AU-50 ABOUT UNCIRCULATED—*Traces of light wear on only the high points of the design. Half of mint luster is present.*
MS-60 UNCIRCULATED—*No trace of wear. Light blemishes.*
MS-63 SELECT UNCIRCULATED—*Some distracting contact marks or blemishes in prime focal areas. Luster may be impaired.*

No Drapery from Elbow
No Stars on Obverse

Mint marks on Liberty seated dimes are placed on the reverse, within or below the wreath.

	Mintage	G-4	F-12	VF-20	EF-40	AU-50	MS-60	MS-63
1837	682,500	$13.	$32.	$110.	$220.	$325.	$600.	$800.
1838O	406,034	16.	50.	150.	285.	500.	1,200.	2,500.

Stars on Obverse 1838-1853

1838 Small Stars

No Drapery from Elbow
Tilted Shield

1838 Large Stars

	Mintage	G-4	F-12	VF-20	EF-40	AU-50	MS-60	MS-63
1838, Small S	1,992,500 (all three)	$8.	$18.	$35.	$70.	$175.	$400.	$600.
1838, Large S		6.	10.	13.	40.	100.	150.	350.
1838, Part Drapery		8.	18.	35.	70.	200.	400.	900.
1839	1,053,115	6.	10.	13.	40.	100.	150.	350.
1839O	1,323,000	7.	12.	15.	45.	120.	175.	500.
1840	981,500	6.	10.	13.	40.	100.	150.	350.
1840O	1,175,000	7.	12.	18.	50.	120.	475.	900.

Drapery from Elbow
Upright Shield

	Mintage	G-4	F-12	VF-20	EF-40	AU-50	MS-60	MS-63	PF-63
1840	377,500	$12.	$30.	$55.	$125.	$170.	$425.	$2,000.	
1841	1,622,500	6.	9.	12.	20.	50.	135.	250.	
1841O	2,007,500	7.	12.	15.	28.	90.	425.	900.	
1842	1,887,500	6.	9.	12.	20.	50.	135.	250.	
1842O	2,020,000	7.	12.	15.	70.	450.	1,200.	2,500.	
1843	1,370,000	6.	9.	12.	20.	50.	135.	250.	
1843O	150,000	13.	45.	100.	250.	425.	1,000.		
1844	72,500	90.	200.	300.	500.	700.	1,000.	3,000.	

	Mintage	G-4	F-12	VF-20	EF-40	AU-50	MS-60	MS-63	PF-63
1845	1,755,000	$6.	$9.	$12.	$20.	$50.	$135.	$275.	
1845O	230,000	8.	20.	80.	175.	400.	1,000.		
1846	31,300	30.	70.	150.	400.	900.	1,900.	4,000.	
1847	245,000	7.	15.	27.	55.	120.	400.	1,000.	
1848	451,500	6.	10.	15.	35.	60.	210.	400.	
1849	839,000	6.	9.	12.	20.	50.	150.	425.	
1849O	300,000	7.	15.	50.	110.	300.	1,000.	2,000.	
1850	1,931,500	6.	9.	12.	20.	50.	125.	300.	
1850O	510,000	7.	12.	33.	65.	150.	425.	900.	
1851	1,026,500	6.	9.	12.	20.	50.	160.	325.	
1851O	400,000	7.	15.	30.	75.	150.	900.	1,200.	
1852	1,535,500	6.	9.	12.	20.	50.	150.	300.	
1852O	430,000	8.	17.	45.	100.	150.	850.	1,200.	
1853, No arrows	95,000	20.	40.	75.	135.	175.	350.	400.	

Arrows at Date 1853-1855

1853-1855
Arrows at Date

1856-1860
Small Date, Arrows Removed

	Mintage	G-4	F-12	VF-20	EF-40	AU-50	MS-60	MS-63	PF-63
1853, w/ arrows	12,078,010	6.	7.	10.	21.	50.	150.	300.	
1853O	1,100,000	6.	7.	15.	40.	100.	325.	1,100.	
1854	4,470,000	6.	7.	10.	21.	50.	150.	300.	5,000.
1854O	1,770,000	6.	7.	12.	35.	60.	285.	500.	
1855	2,075,000	6.	7.	10.	21.	50.	175.	400.	5,000.

No Arrows at Date 1856-1860

	Mintage	G-4	F-12	VF-20	EF-40	AU-50	MS-60	MS-63	PF-63
1856, Large Date	5,780,000	6.	7.	10.	17.	40.	140.	250.	
1856, Small Date		6.	7.	10.	17.	40.	140.	250.	1,750.
1856O	1,180,000	6.	7.	10.	22.	90.	300.	600.	
1856S	70,000	30.	120.	200.	375.	600.	1,000.	—	
1857	5,580,000	6.	7.	9.	17.	40.	135.	250.	1,750.
1857O	1,540,000	6.	7.	10.	17.	70.	190.	250.	
1858 (*300+*)	1,540,000	6.	7.	9.	17.	40.	135.	250.	800.
1858O	290,000	7.	15.	35.	75.	125.	300.	450.	
1858S	60,000	35.	75.	150.	300.	500.	1,000.		
1859((*800+*)	430,000	6.	7.	10.	25.	50.	135.	250.	650.
1859O	480,000	6.	8.	17.	37.	100.	180.	325.	
1859S	60,000	35.	110.	175.	450.	850.	2,000.		
1860S	140,000	10.	20.	50.	125.	350.	900.	1,750.	

Legend on Obverse 1860-1873

	Mintage	G-4	F-12	VF-20	EF-40	AU-50	MS-60	MS-63	PF-63
1860 ....(1,000)	607,000	$6.00	$7.00	$9.	$17.	$40.	$135.	$250.	$375.
1860O	40,000	150.00	350.00	600.	1,200.	2,000.	5,000.	—	
1861 ....(1,000)	1,884,000	6.00	7.00	9.	17.	40.	100.	180.	375.
1861S	172,500	12.00	40.00	75.	125.	200.	550.	1,750.	
1862 ....(550)	847,550	5.00	6.00	8.	13.	25.	100.	120.	300.
1862S	180,750	9.00	21.00	50.	100.	125.	600.	1,000.	
1863 ....(460)	14,460	100.00	200.00	300.	350.	400.	550.	600.	375.
1863S	157,500	8.50	20.00	40.	70.	125.	450.	1,200.	
1864 ....(470)	11,470	70.00	150.00	200.	350.	425.	550.	600.	375.
1864S	230,000	7.00	16.00	32.	60.	110.	500.	550.	
1865 ....(500)	10,500	75.00	200.00	250.	310.	375.	525.	600.	375.
1865S	175,000	7.00	16.00	32.	100.	250.	800.	1,900.	
1866 ....(725)	8,725	120.00	235.00	375.	400.	600.	700.	800.	375.
1866S	135,000	10.00	20.00	40.	100.	135.	550.	1,100.	
1867 ....(625)	6,625	175.00	275.00	400.	475.	550.	675.	800.	400.
1867S	140,000	8.00	20.00	40.	100.	220.	600.	900.	
1868 ....(600)	464,600	5.50	6.50	15.	31.	60.	175.	375.	275.
1868S	260,000	6.00	12.00	30.	50.	75.	185.	450.	
1869 ....(600)	256,600	6.00	12.00	25.	40.	70.	185.	400.	275.
1869S	450,000	6.00	10.00	15.	35.	65.	185.	375.	
1870 ....(1,000)	471,500	5.00	7.00	9.	18.	40.	110.	200.	275.
1870S	50,000	100.00	150.00	200.	180.	350.	750.	1,000.	
1871 ....(960)	907,710	5.00	7.00	9.	15.	65.	140.	180.	275.
1871CC	20,100	350.00	900.00	1,500.	2,750.	4,000.	—	—	
1871S	320,000	6.00	20.00	28.	65.	120.	275.	650.	
1872 ....(950)	2,396,450	5.00	6.00	9.	13.	30.	75.	110.	275.
1872CC	35,480	170.00	375.00	900.	2,100.	4,500.	—	—	
1872S	190,000	7.50	30.00	45.	95.	175.	500.	1,000.	
1873, Cl 3 .....(1,100)	1,508,000	5.00	6.00	9.	13.	30.	100.	125.	275.
1873, Op 3	60,000	8.00	20.00	30.	60.	90.	195.	550.	
1873CC .....(*Unique*)	12,400								

Arrows at Date 1873-1874

In 1873 the dime was increased in weight to 2.50 grams. Arrows at date in 1873 and 1874 indicate this change.

	Mintage	G-4	F-12	VF-20	EF-40	AU-50	MS-60	MS-63	PF-63
1873 .....(800)	2,378,500	$6.	$9.	$20.	$50.	$100.	$275.	$425.	$700.
1873CC	18,791	400.	1,200.	2,750.	4,000.	7,000.	—		
1873S	455,000	7.	15.	28.	65.	150.	450.	900.	
1874 .....(700)	2,940,000	6.	9.	20.	50.	125.	285.	425.	700.
1874CC	10,817	1,000.	2,000.	4,000.	7,000.	10,000.	—		
1874S	240,000	9.	25.	45.	90.	200.	400.	900.	

No Arrows at Date 1875-1891

	Mintage	G-4	F-12	VF-20	EF-40	AU-50	MS-60	MS-63	PF-63
1875 .....(700)	10,350,700	5.	6.	8.	12.	30.	75.	110.	250.
1875CC	4,645,000	5.	6.	8.	15.	32.	125.	170.	
1875S	9,070,000	5.	6.	8.	12.	30.	75.	110.	
1876 ...(1,150)	1,146,150	5.	6.	8.	12.	30.	75.	110.	250.
1876CC	8,270,000	5.	6.	8.	15.	32.	100.	150.	
1876S	10,420,000	5.	6.	8.	12.	30.	75.	110.	
1877 .....(510)	7,310,510	5.	6.	8.	12.	30.	75.	110.	275.
1877CC	7,700,000	5.	6.	8.	12.	30.	100.	150.	
1877S	2,340,000	5.	6.	8.	12.	30.	75.	110.	

	Mintage	G-4	F-12	VF-20	EF-40	AU-50	MS-60	MS-63	PF-63
1878 .....(800)	1,678,000	$5.	$6.	$8.	$12.	$30.	$80.	$110.	$250.
1878CC	200,000	19.	45.	70.	135.	200.	400.	650.	
1879 ...(1,100)	15,100	70.	120.	180.	210.	275.	325.	350.	250.
1880 ...(1,355)	37,355	50.	100.	125.	175.	225.	275.	350.	250.
1881 .....(975)	24,975	50.	100.	125.	175.	225.	300.	350.	250.
1882 ...(1,100)	3,911,100	5.	6.	8.	12.	30.	75.	110.	250.
1883 ...(1,039)	7,675,712	5.	6.	8.	12.	30.	75.	110.	250.
1884 .....(875)	3,366,380	5.	6.	8.	12.	30.	75.	110.	250.
1884S	564,969	8.	12.	20.	35.	100.	325.	500.	
1885 .....(930)	2,533,427	5.	6.	8.	12.	30.	75.	110.	250.
1885S	43,690	150.	325.	600.	950.	1,600.	2,500.	2,800.	
1886 .....(886)	6,377,570	5.	6.	8.	12.	30.	75.	110.	250.
1886S	206,524	9.	20.	30.	50.	90.	275.	500.	
1887 .....(710)	11,283,939	5.	6.	8.	12.	30.	75.	110.	250.
1887S	4,454,450	5.	6.	8.	12.	30.	75.	110.	
1888 .....(832)	5,496,487	5.	6.	8.	12.	30.	75.	110.	250.
1888S	1,720,000	5.	6.	8.	13.	40.	120.	300.	
1889 .....(711)	7,380,711	5.	6.	8.	12.	30.	75.	110.	250.
1889S	972,678	6.	10.	20.	35.	60.	200.	400.	
1890 .....(590)	9,911,541	5.	6.	8.	12.	30.	75.	110.	250.
1890S	1,423,076	6.	8.	17.	30.	60.	135.	275.	
1891 .....(600)	15,310,600	5.	6.	8.	12.	30.	75.	110.	250.
1891O	4,540,000	5.	6.	8.	15.	40.	100.	150.	
1891S	3,196,116	5.	6.	8.	13.	35.	100.	125.	

BARBER or LIBERTY HEAD TYPE 1892-1916

This type was designed by Charles E. Barber, Chief Engraver of the Mint. His initial B is at the truncation of the neck. He also designed quarters and half dollars of the same period.

G-4 GOOD—*Date and letters plain. LIBERTY Is obliterated.*
VG-8 VERY GOOD—*At least 3 letters visible in LIBERTY.*
F-12 FINE—*All letters in LIBERTY visible, though some are weak.*
VF-20 VERY FINE—*All letters of LIBERTY evenly plain.*
EF-40 EXTREMELY FINE—*All letters in LIBERTY are sharp, distinct. Headband edges are distinct.*
AU-50 ABOUT UNCIRCULATED—*Traces of light wear on only the high points of the design. Half of mint luster is present.*
MS-60 UNCIRCULATED—*No trace of wear. Light blemishes.*
MS-63 SELECT UNCIRCULATED—*Some distracting contact marks or blemishes in prime focal areas. Luster may be impaired.*
PF-63—*Reflective surfaces with only a few blemishes in secondary focal places. No major flaws.*

Mint mark location is on the reverse below the wreath.

	Mintage	G-4	VG-8	F-12	VF-20	EF-40	AU-50	MS-60	MS-63	PF-63
1892 ...(1,245)	12,121,245	$1.50	$2.	$6.	$10.	$12.	$25.	$60.	$75.	$200.
1892O	3,841,700	2.50	5.	10.	15.	25.	30.	75.	135.	
1892S	990,710	18.00	30.	65.	75.	100.	110.	180.	250.	
1893, 3/2	} 3,340,732					75.	100.	250.	750.	450.
1893 .....(792)		3.00	4.	7.	10.	15.	25.	75.	100.	200.
1893O	1,760,000	9.00	12.	40.	50.	60.	75.	140.	275.	
1893S	2,491,401	4.00	8.	10.	18.	25.	40.	125.	300.	
1894 .....(972)	1,330,972	5.00	10.	35.	50.	60.	75.	125.	250.	200.
1894O	720,000	20.00	35.	80.	100.	160.	250.	575.	850.	
1894S	24							300,000.		
1895 .....(880)	690,880	35.00	40.	50.	175.	200.	210.	310.	425.	250.
1895O	440,000	125.00	150.	310.	500.	800.	900.	2,000.	2,500.	
1895S	1,120,000	10.00	15.	50.	65.	75.	90.	200.	425.	
1896 .....(762)	2,000,762	3.00	7.	15.	20.	30.	40.	80.	175.	200.
1896O	610,000	25.00	40.	90.	120.	175.	200.	450.	950.	
1896S	575,056	25.00	40.	90.	110.	160.	190.	375.	625.	

	Mintage	G-4	VG-8	F-12	VF-20	EF-40	AU-50	MS-60	MS-63	PF-63
1897 ....(731)	10,869,264	$.75	$1.00	$2.00	$3.50	$10.	$18.	$65.	$75.	$200.
1897O	666,000	24.00	35.00	100.00	140.00	175.	200.	400.	600.	
1897S	1,342,844	4.00	8.00	30.00	35.00	50.	75.	180.	350.	
1898 ....(735)	16,320,735	.75	1.00	2.00	4.00	11.	15.	50.	75.	200.
1898O	2,130,000	2.00	5.00	25.00	40.00	60.	75.	210.	450.	
1898S	1,702,507	1.50	4.00	10.00	15.00	25.	50.	130.	450.	
1899 ....(846)	19,580,846	.75	1.00	2.00	4.00	11.	15.	50.	75.	200.
1899O	2,650,000	.75	4.00	22.00	36.00	50.	75.	175.	325.	
1899S	1,867,493	.75	3.00	6.00	12.00	16.	35.	120.	300.	
1900 ....(912)	17,600,912	.75	1.00	2.00	4.00	11.	15.	50.	75.	200.
1900O	2,010,000	3.00	14.00	30.00	36.00	80.	115.	260.	325.	
1900S	5,168,270	1.50	1.75	3.00	4.50	12.	25.	90.	150.	
1901 ....(813)	18,860,478	.75	1.00	2.00	4.00	11.	22.	60.	75.	200.
1901O	5,620,000	1.00	1.50	3.00	7.00	22.	35.	180.	300.	
1901S	593,022	25.00	40.00	140.00	175.00	225.	250.	450.	525.	
1902 ....(777)	21,380,777	.75	.85	1.50	3.50	11.	20.	60.	75.	200.
1902O	4,500,000	1.00	1.50	4.00	10.00	20.	40.	160.	375.	
1902S	2,070,000	2.50	4.00	16.00	25.00	40.	65.	160.	375.	
1903 ....(755)	19,500,755	.75	.85	1.50	3.50	11.	20.	60.	75.	200.
1903O	8,180,000	1.00	1.50	4.00	6.00	15.	32.	135.	250.	
1903S	613,300	25.00	40.00	150.00	200.00	350.	400.	600.	750.	
1904 ....(670)	14,601,027	.75	.85	1.50	3.50	11.	20.	60.	75.	200.
1904S	800,000	15.00	25.00	60.00	75.00	120.	175.	350.	650.	
1905 ....(727)	14,552,350	.75	.85	1.50	3.50	11.	20.	60.	75.	200.
1905O	3,400,000	.80	1.50	12.00	18.00	25.	40.	125.	200.	
1905S	6,855,199	.80	1.50	3.00	5.00	15.	25.	120.	175.	
1906 ....(675)	19,958,406	.75	.85	1.50	3.50	11.	20.	60.	75.	200.
1906D	4,060,000	.80	1.50	3.00	6.00	12.	25.	80.	140.	
1906O	2,610,000	1.00	3.00	18.00	25.00	32.	50.	115.	150.	
1906S	3,136,640	1.00	1.50	4.00	8.00	15.	35.	110.	130.	
1907 ....(575)	22,220,575	.75	.85	1.50	3.50	11.	20.	60.	75.	200.
1907D	4,080,000	.80	2.00	3.00	6.00	14.	35.	125.	410.	
1907O	5,058,000	.80	3.00	9.00	12.00	20.	30.	100.	165.	
1907S	3,178,470	1.00	2.00	5.00	9.00	16.	35.	175.	300.	
1908 ....(545)	10,600,545	.75	.85	1.50	3.50	11.	20.	60.	75.	200.
1908D	7,490,000	.80	1.20	3.00	4.00	12.	25.	65.	140.	
1908O	1,789,000	1.00	4.00	18.00	25.00	35.	60.	140.	250.	
1908S	3,220,000	.80	2.00	4.00	6.00	14.	60.	140.	260.	
1909 ....(650)	10,240,650	.75	.85	1.50	3.00	11.	20.	60.	75.	200.
1909D	954,000	2.00	7.00	25.00	35.00	50.	80.	200.	425.	
1909O	2,287,000	1.00	2.00	4.00	8.00	16.	40.	95.	240.	
1909S	1,000,000	2.00	6.00	30.00	40.00	70.	130.	220.	500.	
1910 ....(551)	11,520,551	.75	.85	1.50	3.00	11.	20.	60.	75.	200.
1910D	3,490,000	.80	2.00	3.00	5.00	15.	35.	110.	200.	
1910S	1,240,000	.80	3.00	20.00	30.00	40.	60.	170.	325.	
1911 ....(543)	18,870,543	.75	.85	1.50	3.00	11.	20.	60.	75.	200.
1911D	11,209,000	.80	.85	1.50	3.00	11.	20.	60.	75.	
1911S	3,520,000	.80	2.00	4.00	6.00	13.	35.	90.	170.	
1912 ....(700)	19,350,000	.75	.85	1.50	3.00	11.	20.	60.	75.	200.
1912D	11,760,000	.80	.85	1.50	3.00	11.	20.	60.	75.	
1912S	3,420,000	.80	2.00	3.00	6.00	13.	40.	85.	150.	
1913 ....(622)	19,760,622	.75	.85	1.50	3.00	11.	20.	60.	75.	200.
1913S	510,000	5.00	10.00	32.00	45.00	75.	140.	225.	325.	
1914 ....(425)	17,360,655	.75	.85	1.50	3.00	11.	20.	60.	75.	200.
1914D	11,908,000	.80	.85	1.50	3.00	11.	20.	60.	75.	
1914S	2,100,000	.80	2.00	4.00	6.00	11.	20.	75.	160.	
1915 ....(450)	5,620,450	.75	.85	1.50	3.00	11.	20.	60.	75.	200.
1915S	960,000	.80	2.00	15.00	18.00	25.	60.	120.	240.	
1916	18,490,000	.75	.85	1.50	3.00	11.	20.	60.	75.	
1916S	5,820,000	.80	.90	1.50	3.00	11.	20.	60.	75.	

WINGED LIBERTY HEAD or "MERCURY" TYPE 1916-1945

Although this coin is commonly called the "Mercury Dime," the main device is in fact a representation of Liberty. The wings crowning her cap are intended to symbolize liberty of thought. The designer's monogram AW is right of neck.

Mint mark location is on reverse left of fasces.

G-4 GOOD—*Letters and date clear. Lines and bands in fasces are obliterated.*
VG-8 VERY GOOD—*One-half of sticks discernible in fasces.*
F-12 FINE—*All sticks in fasces are defined. Diagonal bands worn nearly flat.*
VF-20 VERY FINE—*The two crossing diagonal bands must show.*
EF-40 EXTREMELY FINE—*Diagonal bands show only slight wear. Braids and hair before ear show clearly.*
AU-50 ABOUT UNCIRCULATED—*Traces of light wear on only the high points of the design. Half of mint luster is present.*
MS-60 UNCIRCULATED—*No trace of wear. Light blemishes.*
MS-63 SELECT UNCIRCULATED—*No trace of wear. Slight blemishes.*
MS-65—CHOICE UNCIRCULATED—*Only light scattered marks that are not distracting. Strong luster, good eye appeal.*
PF-63 Proof—*Reflective surfaces with only a few blemishes in secondary focal places. No major flaws.*

Uncirculated values shown are for average pieces with minimum blemishes, those with sharp strikes and split bands on reverse are worth much more.

	Mintage	G-4	VG-8	F-12	VF-20	EF-40	MS-60	MS-63	MS-65
1916	22,180,080	$1.00	$2.00	$3.00	$4.00	$5.00	$16.	$22.	$40.
1916D	264,000	300.00	450.00	800.00	1,000.00	1,700.00	2,750.	3,600.	8,500.
1916S	10,450,000	2.00	3.00	4.00	5.00	8.00	16.	28.	85.
1917	55,230,000	.50	.75	1.00	1.50	3.00	12.	24.	65.
1917D	9,402,000	2.00	3.00	4.00	6.00	18.00	60.	175.	500.
1917S	27,330,000	.50	.85	1.00	2.50	5.00	28.	80.	200.
1918	26,680,000	.50	.75	1.10	5.00	12.00	35.	75.	180.
1918D	22,674,800	.50	.75	1.00	5.00	11.00	50.	125.	300.
1918S	19,300,000	.50	.75	1.00	4.00	7.00	40.	125.	300.
1919	35,740,000	.50	.75	1.00	2.50	4.00	25.	60.	150.
1919D	9,939,000	.50	.85	2.00	9.00	18.00	75.	225.	650.
1919S	8,850,000	.50	.75	1.50	6.50	16.00	80.	250.	500.
1920	59,030,000	.50	.75	1.00	3.00	3.50	20.	35.	120.
1920D	19,171,000	.50	.75	1.00	4.50	10.00	50.	175.	350.
1920S	13,820,000	.50	.75	1.00	4.25	9.00	40.	130.	575.
1921	1,230,000	20.00	30.00	50.00	135.00	250.00	550.	850.	1,600.
1921D	1,080,000	27.00	50.00	75.00	150.00	280.00	575.	950.	1,600.
1923	50,130,000	.50	.75	1.00	2.50	3.00	12.	22.	60.
1923S	6,440,000	.50	.75	2.00	3.50	25.00	65.	170.	450.
1924	24,010,000	.50	.75	1.00	2.50	4.00	18.	40.	80.
1924D	6,810,000	.50	.75	2.00	3.50	10.00	85.	200.	500.
1924S	7,120,000	.50	.75	2.00	3.25	10.00	80.	260.	500.
1925	25,610,000	.50	.75	1.00	2.50	5.00	22.	35.	80.
1925D	5,117,000	2.00	3.00	5.00	18.00	45.00	125.	300.	750.
1925S	5,850,000	.50	.75	2.00	3.50	15.00	75.	200.	675.
1926	32,160,000	.50	.75	1.00	2.50	6.00	20.	25.	100.
1926D	6,828,000	.50	.75	1.00	4.00	16.00	45.	80.	210.
1926S	1,520,000	2.50	3.50	8.00	20.00	110.00	375.	750.	1,600.
1927	28,080,000	.50	.75	1.00	2.50	5.00	8.	20.	65.
1927D	4,812,000	.50	.75	2.00	8.00	25.00	85.	180.	650.
1927S	4,770,000	.50	.75	1.00	2.50	16.00	100.	250.	700.
1928	19,480,000	.50	.75	1.00	2.50	5.00	20.	40.	65.
1928D	4,161,000	.50	.75	3.00	8.00	18.00	75.	160.	420.

	Mintage	G-4	VG-8	F-12	VF-20	EF-40	MS-60	MS-63	MS-65
1928S	7,400,000	$.50	$.75	$1.00	$1.50	$7.00	$28.	$110.	$180.
1929	25,970,000	.50	.75	1.00	1.50	2.50	8.	15.	28.
1929D	5,034,000	.50	.75	1.00	2.00	4.00	12.	18.	30.
1929S	4,730,000	.50	.75	1.00	1.50	3.00	14.	20.	45.
1930	6,770,000	.50	.75	1.00	1.50	3.00	10.	20.	45.
1930S	1,843,000	.60	1.25	1.50	1.75	3.75	25.	50.	85.
1931	3,150,000	.50	.75	1.00	1.50	4.50	14.	32.	65.
1931D	1,260,000	3.00	3.50	4.50	8.00	15.00	42.	55.	100.
1931S	1,800,000	1.00	1.50	2.00	3.00	6.00	30.	42.	90.

1942, 2 over 1

1942D, 2 over 1

	Mintage	VG-8	F-12	VF-20	EF-40	MS-60	MS-63	MS-65	PF-63
1934	24,080,000	$.30	$.40	$.50	$.60	$7.	$10.	$20.	
1934D	6,772,000	.30	.40	.50	.60	16.	20.	30.	
1935	58,830,000	.30	.40	.50	.60	6.	8.	13.	
1935D	10,477,000	.30	.40	.50	.60	17.	20.	35.	
1935S	15,840,000	.30	.40	.50	.60	10.	14.	20.	
1936 (4,130)	87,504,130	.30	.40	.50	.60	7.	10.	12.	750.
1936D	16,132,000	.30	.40	.50	.60	12.	14.	20.	
1936S	9,210,000	.30	.40	.50	.60	9.	12.	15.	
1937 (5,756)	56,865,756	.30	.40	.50	.60	5.	8.	10.	250.
1937D	14,146,000	.30	.40	.50	.60	12.	14.	20.	
1937S	9,740,000	.30	.40	.50	.60	9.	12.	16.	
1938 (8,728)	22,198,728	.30	.40	.50	.60	5.	8.	10.	150.
1938D	5,537,000	.30	.40	.50	.60	8.	9.	12.	
1938S	8,090,000	.30	.40	.50	.60	7.	8.	10.	
1939 (9,321)	67,749,321	.30	.40	.50	.60	4.	6.	8.	150.
1939D	24,394,000	.30	.40	.50	.60	4.	6.	9.	
1939S	10,540,000	.30	.40	.50	.60	10.	14.	22.	
1940 (11,827)	65,361,827	.30	.40	.50	.60	4.	5.	10.	125.
1940D	21,198,000	.30	.40	.50	.60	4.	7.	12.	
1940S	21,560,000	.30	.40	.50	.60	4.	6.	11.	
1941 (16,557)	175,106,557	.30	.40	.50	.60	4.	5.	10.	110.
1941D	45,634,000	.30	.40	.50	.60	4.	7.	12.	
1941S	43,090,000	.30	.40	.50	.60	4.	6.	11.	
1942, 2/1	205,432,329	150.00	200.00	250.00	300.00	900.	1,800.	5,000.	
1942 (22,329)		.30	.40	.50	.60	4.	5.	10.	110.
1942D, 2/1	60,740,000	160.00	200.00	250.00	300.00	850.	1,600.	4,000.	
1942D		.30	.40	.50	.60	5.	7.	11.	
1942S	4,930,000	.30	.40	.50	.60	6.	8.	12.	
1943	191,710,000	.30	.40	.50	.60	4.	5.	10.	
1943D	71,949,000	.30	.40	.50	.60	5.	6.	11.	
1943S	60,400,000	.30	.40	.50	.60	5.	6.	11.	
1944	231,410,000	.30	.40	.50	.60	4.	5.	10.	
1944D	62,224,000	.30	.40	.50	.60	4.	5.	10.	
1944S	49,490,000	.30	.40	.50	.60	4.	5.	10.	
1945	159,130,000	.30	.40	.50	.60	4.	5.	10.	

	Mintage	VG-8	F-12	VF-20	EF-40	MS-60	MS-63	MS-65	PF-63
1945D	40,245,000	$.30	$.40	$.50	$.60	$4.	$5.	$12.	
1945S	41,920,000	.30	.40	.50	.60	4.	6.	12.	
1945S, Micro S		.30	.40	.50	.60	8.	14.	40.	

ROOSEVELT TYPE 1946 to Date

John R. Sinnock (whose initials JS are at the truncation of the neck) designed this dime showing a portrait of Franklin D. Roosevelt. The design has heavier lettering and a more modernistic character than preceding types.

VF-20 VERY FINE—*Hair above ear slightly worn. All vertical lines on torch plain.*
EF-40 EXTREMELY FINE—*All lines of torch, flame and hair very plain.*
MS-63 SELECT UNCIRCULATED—*No trace of wear. Slight blemishes.*
MS-65—CHOICE UNCIRCULATED—*Only light scattered contact marks that are not distracting. Strong luster, good eye appeal.*
PF-65—*Choice Brilliant surfaces with no noticeable blemishes or flaws. May have a few scatered barely noticeable marks or hairlines.*

SILVER COINAGE — 1946-1964

Mint mark on reverse 1946-1964.

	Mintage	VF-20	EF-40	MS-63	MS-65	PF-65
1946	255,250,000	$.30	$.40	$.09	$1.50	
1946D	61,043,500	.30	.40	.65	1.40	
1946S	27,900,000	.30	.40	2.00	3.00	
1947	121,520,000	.30	.40	1.50	2.50	
1947D	46,835,000	.30	.40	2.50	3.50	
1947S	34,840,000	.30	.40	2.00	3.00	
1948	74,950,000	.30	.40	1.50	3.00	
1948D	52,841,000	.30	.40	1.50	3.00	
1948S	35,520,000	.30	.40	2.00	4.00	
1949	30,940,000	.30	.40	10.00	14.00	
1949D	26,034,000	.30	.40	4.25	7.00	
1949S	13,510,000	.30	.40	16.00	22.00	
1950 (51,386)	50,181,500	.30	.40	2.50	3.50	$15.00
1950D	46,803,000	.30	.40	2.00	3.00	
1950S	20,440,000	.30	.40	12.00	15.00	
1951 (57,500)	103,937,602	.30	.40	.60	1.50	18.00
1951D	56,529,000	.30	.40	.60	1.50	
1951S	31,630,000	.30	.40	4.00	9.00	
1952 (81,980)	99,122,073	.30	.40	.60	1.50	12.00
1952D	122,100,000	.30	.40	.60	1.50	
1952S	44,419,500	.30	.40	2.00	5.00	
1953 (128,800)	53,618,920	.30	.40	.85	2.00	12.00
1953D	136,433,000	.30	.40	.85	2.00	
1953S	39,180,000	.30	.40	1.00	1.50	
1954 (233,300)	114,243,503	.30	.40	.75	1.35	8.00
1954D	106,397,000	.30	.40	.75	1.35	
1954S	22,860,000	.30	.40	.75	1.35	
1955 (378,200)	12,828,381	.30	.40	1.00	2.00	8.00
1955D	13,959,000	.30	.40	.75	1.35	
1955S	18,510,000	.30	.40	.75	1.35	
1956 (669,384)	109,309,384	.30	.40	.75	1.35	1.00
1956D	108,015,100	.30	.40	.75	1.35	
1957 (1,247,952)	161,407,952	.30	.40	.75	1.35	1.00
1957D	113,354,330	.30	.40	.75	1.35	

DIMES

	Mintage	VF-20	EF-40	MS-63	MS-65	PF-65
1958 . . . .(875,652)	32,785,652	$.30	$.40	$.60	$1.25	$1.00
1958D	136,564,600	.30	.40	.60	1.25	
1959 . . . .(1,149,291)	86,929,291	.30	.40	.60	1.25	1.00
1959D	164,919,790	.30	.40	.60	1.25	
1960 . . . .(1,691,602)	72,081,602	.30	.40	.60	1.25	1.00
1960D	200,160,400	.30	.40	.60	1.25	
1961 . . . .(3,028,244)	96,758,244	.30	.40	.60	1.25	1.00
1961D	209,146,550	.30	.40	.60	1.25	
1962 . . . .(3,218,019)	75,668,019	.30	.40	.60	1.25	1.00
1962D	334,948,380	.30	.40	.60	1.25	
1963 . . . .(3,075,645)	126,725,645	.30	.40	.60	1.25	1.00
1963D	421,476,530	.30	.40	.60	1.25	
1964 . . . .(3,950,762)	933,310,762	.30	.40	.60	1.25	1.00
1964D	1,357,517,180	.30	.40	.60	1.25	

Clad Coinage

Mint mark on obverse starting 1968

	Mintage	MS-63	MS-65	PF-65
1965	1,652,140,570	$.15	$.25	$.25
1966	1,382,734,540	.15	.25	.25
1967	2,244,007,320	.15	.25	.25
1968	424,470,400	.15	.20	.20
1968D	480,748,280	.15	.20	.20
1968S, Pf	. . .(3,041,506)			.50
1969	145,790,000	.25	.50	.50
1969D	563,323,870	.15	.20	.20
1969S, Pf	. . .(2,394,631)			.50
1970	345,570,000	.15	.25	.25
1970D	754,942,100	.15	.25	.25
1970S, Pf	. . .(2,632,810)			.50
1971	162,690,000	.18	.30	.30
1971D	377,914,240	.16	.20	.30
1971S, Pf	. . .(3,220,733)			.50
1972	431,540,000	.15	.25	.25
1972D	330,290,000	.15	.25	.25
1972S, Pf	. . .(3,260,996)			.50
1973	315,670,000	.15	.25	.25
1973D	455,032,426	.15	.25	.25
1973S, Pf	. . .(2,760,339)			.50
1974	470,248,000	.15	.25	.25
1974D	571,083,000	.15	.25	.25
1974S, Pf	. . .(2,612,568)			.50
1975	585,673,900	.15	.25	.25
1975D	313,705,300	.15	.25	.25
1975S, Pf	. . .(2,845,450)			.60
1976	568,760,000	1.50	.25	.25
1976D	695,222,774		.15	.25
1976S, Pf	. . .(4,149,730)			.50
1977	796,930,000	.15	.25	.25
1977D	376,607,228	.15	.25	.25
1977S, Pf	. . .(3,251,152)			.50

	Mintage	MS-63	MS-65	PF-65
1978	663,980,000		$.15	$.25
1978D	 282,847,540		.15	.25
1978S, Pf	. . .(3,127,781)			.40
1979	315,440,000	.15	.25	.25
1979D	390,921,184	.15	.25	.25
1979S, Pf, Filled S	. . . . .			.50
1979S, Pf, Clear S	. . . . .			.75
1980P	735,170,000	.15	.25	.25
1980D	719,354,321	.15	.25	.25
1980S, Pf	. . .(3,554,806)			.40
1981P	676,650,000	.15	.25	.25
1981D	712,284,143	.15	.25	.25
1981S, Pf	. . .(4,063,083)			.40
1982, (no mint mark)	. . .	75.00	100.00	100.00
1982P	519,475,000	1.50	2.00	2.00
1982D	542,713,584	.60	1.10	1.10
1982S, Pf	. . .(3,857,479)			.60
1983P	647,025,000	1.25	1.50	1.50
1983D	730,129,224	.35	.60	.60
1983S, Pf	. . .(3,279,126)			.50
1984P	856,669,000	.15	.25	.25
1984D	704,803,976	.20	.35	.35
1984S, Pf	. . .(3,065,110)			.75
1985P	 705,200,962	.15	.25	.25
1985D	587,979,970	.15	.25	.25
1985S, Pf	. . .(3,362,821)			.50
1986P	682,649,693	.25	.35	.35
1986D	473,326,970	.25	.35	.35
1986S, Pf	. . .(3,010,497)			1.00
1987P	762,709,481	.15	.35	.25
1987D	653,203,402	.15	.35	.25
1987S, Pf	. . .(4,227,728)			.60

	Mintage	MS-63	MS-65	PF-65
1988P	1,030,550,000	$.12	$.20	
1988D	962,385,489	.12	.20	
1988S, Pf	(3,262,948)			$1.00
1989P	1,298,400,000	.10	.20	
1989D	896,535,597	.10	.20	
1989S, Pf	(3,220,194)			1.00
1990P	1,034,340,000	.10	.20	
1990D	839,995,824	.10	.20	
1990S, Pf	(3,299,559)			1.00
1991P	927,220,000	.10	.20	
1991D	601,241,114	.12	.20	
1991S, Pf	(2,867,787)			1.20
1992P	593,500,000	.10	.15	
1992D	616,273,932	.10	.15	
1992S, Pf	(2,858,981)			2.00
1992S, Silver Pf	1,317,579			3.00
1993P	766,180,000	.10	.15	
1993D	750,110,166	.10	.15	
1993S, Pf	(2,633,439)			2.00
1993S, Silver Pf	(761,353)			2.50
1994P	1,189,000,000	.10	.15	
1994D	1,303,268,110	.10	.15	
1994S, Pf	(2,484,594)			2.00
1994S, Silver Pf	(785,329)			2.50
1995P	1,125,500,000	.10	.20	
1995D	1,274,890,000	.15	.25	
1995S, Pf	(2,117,496)			3.00
1995S, Silver Pf	(679,985) . .67			4.00
1996P	1,421,163,000	.10	.20	
1996D	1,400,300,000	.10	.20	
1996W	1,457,000	8.00	8.00	
1996S, Pf	(1,750,244)			2.00
1996S, Silver Pf	(775,021)			3.00
1997P	991,640,000	$.10	$.15	
1997D	979,810,000	.10	.15	
1997S Pf	(2,055,000)			$3.00
1997S Silver Pf	(741,678)			8.50
1998P	1,163,000,000	.10	.15	
1998D	1,172,250,000	.10	.15	
1998S Pf	(2,086,507)			2.00
1998S Silver Pf	(878,792)			3.00
1999P	2,164,000,000	.10	.15	
1999D	1,397,750,000	.10	.15	
1999S Pf	(2,543,401)			1.00
1999S Silver Pf	(800,000)			3.00
2000P	1,842,500,000	.10	.15	
2000D	1,818,700,000	.10	.15	
2000S Pf	(3,082,483)			1.00
2000S Silver Pf	(856,400)			2.00
2001P	1,369,590,000	.10	.15	
2001D	1,412,800,000	.10	.15	
2001S Pf	(2,294,043)			.50
2001S Silver Pf	(889,697)			2.00
2002P	1,187,500,000	.10	.15	
2002D	1,379,500,000	.10	.15	
2002S Pf	(2,277,720)			.75
2002S Silver Pf	(888,826)			1.50
2003P		.10	.15	
2003D		.10	.15	
2003S Pf				.50
2003S Silver Pf				1.50
2004P		.10		
2004D		.10		
2004S Pf				.50
2004S Silver Pf				.50

TWENTY-CENT PIECES — 1875-1878

This short-lived coin was authorized by the Act of March 3, 1875. The edge of the coin is plain. Most of the 1876CC coins were melted at the Mint and never released. Mint mark is on the reverse below the eagle.

G-4 GOOD—*LIBERTY on shield obliterated. Letters and date legible.*
VG-8 VERY GOOD—*One or two letters in LIBERTY may show. Other details will be bold.*
F-12 FINE—*At least 3 letters of LIBERTY show.*
VF-20 VERY FINE—*LIBERTY completely readable, but partly weak.*
EF-40 EXTREMELY FINE—*LIBERTY sharp. Only slight wear on high points of coin.*
AU-50 ABOUT UNCIRCULATED—*Traces of light wear on only the high points of the design. Half of mint luster is present.*
MS-60 UNCIRCULATED—*No trace of wear. Light blemishes.*
MS-63 SELECT UNCIRCULATED—*Some distracting contact marks or blemishes in prime focal areas. Luster may be impaired.*
PF-63—*Reflective surfaces with only a few blemishes in secondary focal places. No major flaws.*

	Mintage	G-4	VG-8	F-12	VF-20	EF-40	AU-50	MS-60	MS-63	PF-63
1875 . . . .(2,790)	39,700	$35.	$40.	$50.	$75.	$125.	$175.	$300.	$450.	$1,000.
1875CC	133,290	45.	55.	90.	120.	175.	200.	400.	800.	
1875S	1,155,000	35.	40.	50.	70.	100.	150.	250.	450.	—
1876 . . . .(1,260)	15,900	45.	55.	85.	120.	175.	200.	425.	500.	1,100.
1876CC	10,000							35,000.		
1877 . . . . . .(350)	350				700.	800.				1,500.
1878 . . . . . .(600)	600				600.	750.				1,300.

QUARTER DOLLARS — 1796 to Date

Authorized in 1792, this denomination was not issued until four years later. The first type weighed 104 grains which remained standard until modified to 103 1/8 grains by the Act of January 18, 1837. As with the dime and half dime, the weight was reduced and arrows placed at the date in 1853. Rays were placed in the field of the reverse during that year only.

DRAPED BUST TYPE, SMALL EAGLE REVERSE 1796

AG-3 ABOUT GOOD—*Details clear enough to identify.*
G-4 GOOD—*Date readable. Bust outlined, but no detail.*
VG-8 VERY GOOD—*All but deepest drapery folds worn smooth. Hairlines nearly gone and curls lack detail.*
F-12 FINE—*All drapery lines visible. Hair partly worn.*
VF-20 VERY FINE—*Only left side of drapery is indistinct.*
EF-40 EXTREMELY FINE—*Hair well outlined and detailed.*
AU-50 ABOUT UNCIRCULATED—*Traces of light wear on only the high points of the design. Half of mint luster is present.*
MS-60 UNCIRCULATED—*No trace of wear. Light blemishes.*
MS-63 SELECT UNCIRCULATED—*Some distracting contact marks or blemishes in prime focal areas. Luster may be impaired.*

	Mintage	AG-3	G-4	VG-8	F-12	VF-20	EF-40	AU-50	MS-60	MS-63
1796	6,146	$1,200.	$2,250.	$3,200.	$5,000.	$7,500.	$9,500.	$12,000.	$18,000.	$25,000.

DRAPED BUST TYPE, HERALDIC EAGLE REVERSE 1804-1807

	Mintage	AG-3	G-4	VG-8	F-12	VF-20	EF-40	AU-50	MS-60	MS-63
1804	6,738	$300.	$750.	$950.	$1,500.	$2,100.	$4,500.	$8,000.	—	
1805	121,394	45.	90.	130.	200.	400.	800.	1,300.	$2,600.	$3,500.
1806, 6/5	206,124 (both)	45.	90.	130.	200.	400.	900.	1,400.	2,850.	6,000.
1806		45.	90.	130.	200.	400.	800.	1,300.	2,600.	3,500.
1807	220,643	45.	90.	130.	200.	400.	800.	1,300.	2,600.	3,500.

CAPPED BUST TYPE 1815-1838
Large Size 1815-1828

AG-3 ABOUT GOOD—*Details clear enough to identify.*
G-4 GOOD—*Date, letters and stars readable. Hair under headband smooth. Cap lines worn smooth.*
VG-8 VERY GOOD—*Rim well defined. Main details visible. Full LIBERTY on cap. Hair above eye nearly smooth.*
F-12 FINE—*All hairlines show but drapery has only part details. Shoulder clasp distinct.*
VF-20 VERY FINE—*All details show, but some wear. Clasp and ear sharp.*
EF-40 EXTREMELY FINE—*All details show distinctly. Hair well outlined.*
AU-50 ABOUT UNCIRCULATED—*Traces of light wear on only the high points of the design. Half of mint luster is present.*
MS-60 UNCIRCULATED—*No trace of wear. Light blemishes.*
MS-63 SELECT UNCIRCULATED—*Some distracting contact marks or blemishes in prime focal areas. Luster may be impaired.*

	Mintage	AG-3	G-4	VG-8	F-12	VF-20	EF-40	AU-50	MS-60	MS-63
1815	89,235	$13.	$25.	$35.	$55.	$150.	$450.	$550.	$1,100.	$2,000.
1818, 8/5	361,174	13.	25.	35.	55.	150.	425.	550.	1,300.	2,200.
1818 ..		13.	25.	30.	50.	135.	375.	500.	1,000.	2,000.
1819	144,000	13.	25.	30.	50.	135.	375.	500.	1,000.	2,000.
1820	127,444	13.	25.	30.	50.	135.	375.	500.	1,000.	2,000.
1821	216,851	13.	25.	30.	50.	135.	375.	500.	1,000.	2,000.
1822, All kinds	604,080	13.	25.	35.	60.	150.	400.	550.	1,200.	2,200.
1822, 25/50c		250.	600.	1,200.	1,700.	2,500.	4,200.	6,000.	8,000.	
1823, 3/2	17,800	1,600.	3,750.	6,000.	9,500.	14,000.	19,000.			
1824, 4/2	168,000	15.	30.	40.	90.	225.	600.	1,200.	2,200.	
1825 ...		13.	25.	28.	45.	125.	385.	500.	1,100.	2,000.
1827, Orginal (Curl base 2 in 25c)	4,000									50,000.
1827, Restrike (Square base 2 in 25c)										20,000.
1828, All kinds	102,000	13.	25.	28.	45.	125.	285.	500.	1,200.	2,200.
1828, 25/50c		25.	50.	100.	175.	350.	650.	1,200.	2,750.	

Reduced Size, No Motto on Reverse 1831-1838

G-4 GOOD—*Bust well defined. Hair under headband smooth. Date, letters, stars readable. Scant rims.*
VG-8 VERY GOOD—*Details apparent but worn on high spots. Rims strong. Full LIBERTY.*
F-12 FINE—*All hairlines visible. Drapery partly worn. Shoulder clasp distinct.*
VF-20 VERY FINE—*Only top spots worn. Clasp sharp. Ear distinct.*
EF-40 EXTREMELY FINE—*Hair details and clasp are bold and clear.*
AU-50 ABOUT UNCIRCULATED—*Traces of light wear on only the high points of the design. Half of mint luster is present.*
MS-60 UNCIRCULATED—*No trace of wear. Light blemishes.*
MS-63 SELECT UNCIRCULATED—*Some distracting contact marks or blemishes in prime focal areas. Luster may be impaired.*

	Mintage	G-4	VG-8	F-12	VF-20	EF-40	AU-50	MS-60	MS-63
1831	398,000	$20.	$24.	$30.	$50.	$120.	$250.	$450.	$1,000.
1832	320,000	20.	24.	30.	50.	120.	250.	450.	1,000.
1833	156,000	22.	27.	35.	60.	150.	275.	600.	1,250.
1834	286,000	20.	24.	30.	50.	120.	250.	450.	1,000.
1835	1,952,000	20.	24.	30.	50.	120.	250.	450.	1,000.
1836	472,000	20.	24.	30.	50.	120.	250.	450.	1,000.
1837	252,400	20.	24.	30.	50.	120.	250.	450.	1,000.
1838	366,000	20.	24.	30.	50.	120.	250.	450.	1,000.

QUARTER DOLLARS

LIBERTY SEATED TYPE 1838-1891

No Motto Above Eagle 1838-1853

G-4 GOOD—*Scant rim. LIBERTY on shield worn off. Date and letters readable.*
VG-8 VERY GOOD—*Rim fairly defined, at least 3 letters in LIBERTY evident.*
F-12 FINE—*LIBERTY complete, but partly weak.*
VF-20 VERY FINE—*LIBERTY strong.*
EF-40 EXTREMELY FINE—*Complete LIBERTY and edges of scroll. Clasp shows plainly.*
AU-50 ABOUT UNCIRCULATED—*Traces of light wear on only the high points of the design. Half of mint luster is present.*
MS-60 UNCIRCULATED—*No trace of wear. Light blemishes.*
MS-63 SELECT UNCIRCULATED—*Some distracting contact marks or blemishes in prime focal areas. Luster may be impaired.*

Mint mark location is on the reverse below the eagle.

	Mintage	G-4	VG-8	F-12	VF-20	EF-40	AU-50	MS-60	MS-63
1838	466,000	$8.	$10.	$16.	$30.	$100.	$200.	$600.	$1,500.
1839	491,146	8.	10.	16.	30.	100.	200.	550.	1,500.
1840	188,127	9.	12.	21.	35.	70.	110.	550.	1,000.
1840O	425,200	9.	12.	21.	35.	70.	110.	550.	1,000.
1841	120,000	16.	25.	42.	60.	110.	125.	425.	600.
1841O	452,000	7.	9.	15.	27.	80.	120.	425.	600.

Small Date

Large Date

	Mintage	G-4	VG-8	F-12	VF-20	EF-40	AU-50	MS-60	MS-63
1842,Small Date PfS only									$12,000.
1842, Large Date	88,000	$30.	$40.	$75.	$130.	$175.	$225.	$800.	1,200.
1842O, Small Date }	769,000	130.	225.	400.	650.	1,300.	2,500.	—	
1842O, Large Date }		9.	10.	16.	30.	70.	125.	650.	1,800.
1843	645,600	7.	9.	15.	20.	40.	60.	275.	600.
1843O	968,000	9.	13.	20.	40.	100.	275.	700.	1,300.
1844	421,200	7.	9.	15.	20.	40.	60.	225.	600.
1844O	740,000	7.	9.	17.	30.	80.	110.	550.	1,000.
1845	922,000	7.	9.	15.	20.	40.	60.	225.	600.
1846	510,000	7.	9.	15.	20.	40.	60.	225.	600.
1847	734,000	7.	9.	15.	20.	40.	60.	225.	600.
1847O	368,000	10.	15.	27.	50.	100.	275.	800.	2,000.
1848	146,000	12.	16.	28.	50.	80.	100.	450.	1,000.
1849	340,000	8.	10.	18.	26.	70.	90.	400.	600.
1849O, included below			140.	230.	410.	800.	1,400.	1,900.	
1850	190,800	13.	16.	25.	35.	65.	100.	400.	700.
1850O	412,000	13.	16.	25.	35.	65.	180.	550.	1,000.
1851	160,000	14.	18.	28.	50.	80.	100.	400.	700.
1851O	88,000	65.	100.	200.	300.	650.	1,100.	2,000.	
1852	177,060	15.	20.	30.	55.	90.	110.	375.	650.
1852O	96,000	80.	120.	175.	300.	550.	1,400.	3,000.	5,500.
1853, No arrows or rays	44,200	100.	120.	150.	250.	400.	700.	1,300.	1,800.

†Coinage for 1849O included with 1850O.

Arrows at Date, Rays Around Eagle 1853 Only

1853, 3 over 4

	Mintage	G-4	VG-8	F-12	VF-20	EF-40	AU-50	MS-60	MS-63
1853	} 15,210,020	$7.	$9.	$12.	$20.	$60.	$125.	$500.	$800.
1853, 3/4		20.	35.	75.	125.	150.	200.	900.	1,800.
1853O	1,332,000	6.	10.	16.	30.	90.	400.	1,100.	3,000.

Arrows at Date, No Rays 1854-1855

	Mintage	G-4	VG-8	F-12	VF-20	EF-40	AU-50	MS-60	MS-63
1854	12,380,000	$7.	$8.	$10.	$17.	$35.	$90.	$250.	$550.
1854O	1,484,000	7.	8.	10.	17.	35.	90.	300.	800.
1855	2,857,000	7.	8.	10.	17.	35.	90.	275.	550.
1855O	176,000	16.	25.	45.	100.	150.	340.	1,000.	3,000.
1855S	396,400	16.	25.	32.	60.	125.	300.	850.	2,000.

No Motto Above Eagle 1856-1865

	Mintage	G-4	VG-8	F-12	VF-20	EF-40	AU-50	MS-60	MS-63	PF-63
1856	7,264,000	$7.	$8.	$10.	$17.	$23.	$60.	$170.	$275.	$1,750.
1856O	968,000	7.	9.	13.	18.	40.	90.	500.	650.	
1856S	286,000	14.	20.	30.	80.	160.	275.	1,000.	3,500.	
1857	9,644,000	7.	8.	10.	17.	23.	60.	150.	250.	1,100.
1857O	1,180,000	7.	8.	10.	17.	27.	100.	400.	800.	
1857S	82,000	20.	35.	55.	150.	250.	400.	1,200.	2,500.	
1858 (*300+*)	7,368,000	7.	8.	10.	17.	23.	60.	150.	250.	850.
1858O	520,000	7.	8.	10.	20.	45.	150.	550.	1,000.	
1858S	121,000	18.	30.	45.	100.	200.	400.	2,000.		
1859 (800)	1,344,000	7.	8.	10.	17.	23.	60.	150.	400.	600.
1859O	260,000	8.	13.	18	26.	45.	150.	475.	1,000.	
1859S	80,000	30.	50.	90.	150.	400.	2,700.	—		
1860 (1,000)	805,400	7.	8.	10.	17.	23.	60	175.	275.	500.
1860O	388,000	7.	9.	12.	18.	32.	150.	450.	800.	
1860S	56,000	60.	100.	150.	325.	1,000.	1,750.			
1861 (1,000)	4,854,600	7.	8.	10.	17.	23.	60.	175.	275.	500.
1861S	96,000	18.	35.	75.	125.	300.	800.			
1862 (550)	932,550	7.	8.	10.	17.	23.	60.	175.	300.	500.
1862S	67,000	15.	22.	50.	90.	200.	400.	1,000.	2,500.	
1863 (460)	192,060	9.	13.	20.	30.	50.	120.	350.	400.	500.
1864 (470)	94,070	15.	25.	35.	55.	100.	175.	400.	500.	500.
1864S	20,000	100.	120.	250.	350.	800.	1,000.			
1865 (500)	59,300	16.	25.	40.	55.	110.	150.	350.	500.	500.
1865S	41,000	20.	35.	55.	120.	190.	400.	1,200.	1,500.	

Motto Above Eagle 1866-1873

1866 (725)	17,525	90.	175.	200.	300.	400.	500.	750.	1,000.	400.
1866S	28,000	70.	100.	200.	350.	450.	600.	1,400.	2,000.	
1867 (625)	20,625	70.	100.	150.	200.	250.	350.	475.	1,500.	400.
1867S	48,000	70.	100.	130.	175.	300.	400.	1,750.		
1868 (600)	30,000	35.	50.	75.	100.	125.	200.	400.	600.	400.
1868S	96,000	30.	40.	50.	90.	200.	350.	1,100.	1,500.	
1869 (600)	16,600	90.	110.	170.	200.	275.	400.	600.	1,000.	400.
1869S	76,000	21.	35.	70.	110.	180.	450.	1,000.	1,750.	
1870 (1,000)	87,400	18.	21.	35.	60.	90.	175.	400.	500.	400.

	Mintage	G-4	VG-8	F-12	VF-20	EF-40	AU-50	MS-60	MS-63	PF-63
1870CC	8,340	$900.	$1,400.	$2,600.	$4,750.	$8,000.	$10,000.			
1871 . . . . .(960)	119,160	10.	14.	20.	40.	60.	125.	225.	400.	375.
1871CC	10,890	600.	1,000.	1,600.	4,000.	8,000.	—			
1871S	30,900	90.	125.	175.	250.	400.	600.	1,300.	1,800.	
1872 . . . . .(950)	182,950	9.	13.	20.	30.	50.	90.	300.	700.	375.
1872CC	22,850	150.	250.	500.	900.	1,700.	2,500.	5,500.		
1872S	83,000	200.	300.	450.	600.	900.	1,250.	2,750.		
1873 . . . . .(600)	212,600	9.	13.	22.	35.	50.	90.	200.	400.	375.
1873CC	4,000				—			—		

Arrows at Date 1873-1874

	Mintage	G-4	VG-8	F-12	VF-20	EF-40	AU-50	MS-60	MS-63	PF-63
1873 . . . . .(540)	1,271,700	8.	10.	15.	35.	90.	175.	425.	600.	700.
1873CC	12,462	500.	900.	1,700.	3,000.	5,000.	8,000.	14,000.	25,000.	

	Mintage	G-4	VG-8	F-12	VF-20	EF-40	AU-50	MS-60	MS-63	PF-63
1873S	156,000	10.	13.	22.	45.	110.	200.	600.	1,000.	
1874 . . . . .(700)	471,900	8.	10.	15.	35.	90.	175.	450.	600.	700.
1874S	392,000	10.	12.	20.	45.	110.	175.	450.	600.	

No Arrows at Date 1875-1891

1877S, S over horizontal S

	Mintage	G-4	VG-8	F-12	VF-20	EF-40	AU-50	MS-60	MS-63	PF-63
1875 . . . . .(700)	4,293,500	7.	8.	10.	15.	20.	60.	125.	200.	300.
1875CC	140,000	20.	30.	60.	120.	200.	300.	700.	1,000.	
1875S	680,000	8.	14.	22.	35.	70.	125.	275.	500.	
1876 . . .(1,150)	17,817,150	7.	8.	10.	15.	20.	60.	175.	200.	300.
1876CC	4,944,000	7.	13.	16.	20.	35.	75.	200.	400.	
1876S	8,596,000	7.	8.	10.	15.	20.	60.	125.	200.	
1877 . . . . .(510)	10,911,710	7.	8.	10.	15.	20.	60.	125.	200.	300.
1877CC	4,192,000	7.	13.	16.	20.	35.	75.	200.	350.	
1877S	8,996,000	7.	8.	10.	15.	20.	60.	125.	200.	
1877S, Over Horizontal S . .		10.	15.	40.	50.	90.	125.	300.	500.	
1878 . . . . .(800)	2,260,800	7.	8.	10.	15.	20.	60.	125.	200.	300.
1878CC	996,000	7.	13.	17.	25.	50.	90.	225.	400.	
1878S	140,000	27.	50.	75.	100.	175.	250.	600.	900.	
1879 . . .(*1,100*)	14,700	40.	45.	75.	80.	100.	135.	200.	350.	300.
1880 . . .(1,355)	14,955	40.	45.	75.	80.	100.	135.	200.	350.	300.
1881 . . . . .(975)	12,975	50.	65.	85.	100.	120.	190.	225.	375.	300.
1882 . . .(1,100)	16,300	45.	50.	80.	100.	110.	150.	275.	375.	300.
1883 . . .(1,039)	15,439	45.	50.	80.	100.	110.	150.	275.	375.	300.
1884 . . . . .(875)	8,875	90.	100.	120.	125.	150.	200.	325.	400.	300.

	Mintage	G-4	VG-8	F-12	VF-20	EF-40	AU-50	MS-60	MS-63	PF-63
1885 .....(930)	14,530	$40.	$50.	$75.	$100.	$110.	$175.	$300.	$400.	$300.
1886 .....(886)	5,886	90.	110.	150.	175.	275.	375.	475.	500.	350.
1887 .....(710)	10,710	80.	90.	100.	125.	175.	200.	300.	400.	300.
1888 .....(832)	10,833	70.	80.	90.	135.	200.	225.	300.	375.	300.
1888S	1,216,000	7.	8.	10.	15.	22.	65.	150.	250.	
1889 .....(711)	12,711	50.	60.	90.	110.	120.	175.	300.	400.	400.
1890 .....(590)	80,590	20.	25.	35.	50.	80.	120.	250.	350.	325.
1891 .....(600)	3,920,600	7.	8.	10.	15.	22.	65.	150.	250.	325.
1891O	6,800	50.	65.	110.	325.	475.	500.	1,500.	2,000.	
1891S	2,216,000	7.	8.	10.	15.	23.	65.	150.	250.	

BARBER or LIBERTY HEAD TYPE 1892-1916

Like other silver coins of this type the quarter dollars minted from 1892 to 1916 were designed by Charles E. Barber. His initial B is found at the truncation of the neck of Liberty.

G-4 GOOD—*Date and legends readable. LIBERTY worn off headband.*
VG-8 VERY GOOD—*Minimum of 3 letters in LIBERTY readable.*
F-12 FINE—*LIBERTY completely readable but not sharp.*
VF-20 VERY FINE—*All letters in LIBERTY evenly plain.*
EF-40 EXTREMELY FINE—*LIBERTY bold, and its ribbon distinct.*
AU-50 ABOUT UNCIRCULATED—*Traces of light wear on only the high points of the design. Half of mint luster is present.*
MS-60 UNCIRCULATED—*No trace of wear. Light blemishes.*
MS-63 SELECT UNCIRCULATED—*Some distracting contact marks or blemishes in prime focal areas. Luster may be impaired.*
PF-63 PROOF— *Reflective surfaces with only a few blemishes in secondary focal places. No major flaws.*

Mint mark location is on the reverse below the eagle.

	Mintage	G-4	VG-8	F-12	VF-20	EF-40	AU-50	MS-60	MS-63	PF-63
1892 ....(1,245)	8,237,245	$2.00	$3.00	$8.00	$12.	$27.	$50.	$115.	$125.	$280.
1892O	2,460,000	3.00	5.00	10.00	18.	35.	60.	150.	200.	
1892S	964,079	8.00	15.00	20.00	30.	60.	125.	200.	400.	
1893 .....(792)	5,444,815	2.00	3.00	8.00	13.	30	50.	115.	150.	280.
1893O	3,396,000	3.00	4.00	9.00	14.	35.	60.	160.	200.	
1893S	1,454,535	3.00	8.00	15.00	30.	60.	125.	200.	500.	
1894 .....(972)	3,432,972	2.00	2.50	9.00	15.	30.	60.	110.	200.	280.
1894O	2,852,000	2.50	3.00	10.00	20.	35.	90.	160.	300.	
1894S	2,648,821	3.00	3.50	10.00	20.	35.	90.	160.	300.	
1895 .....(880)	4,440,880	2.00	2.50	9.00	14.	30.	60.	110.	200.	280.
1895O	2,816,000	2.50	3.50	12.00	25.	38.	90.	185.	400.	
1895S	1,764,681	3.00	6.00	15.00	30.	40.	100.	200.	400.	
1896 .....(762)	3,874,762	2.50	3.00	8.00	13.	32.	60.	125.	200.	280.
1896O	1,484,000	3.00	10.00	30.00	100.	150.	275.	450.	750.	
1896S	1,888,039	175.00	300.00	450.00	700.	1,000.	1,600.	2,100.	3,200.	
1897 .....(731)	8,140,731	2.00	3.00	8.00	12.	28.	50.	90.	125.	280.
1897O	1,414,800	3.00	10.00	30.00	90.	120.	275.	425.	750.	
1897S	542,229	8.00	18.00	60.00	100.	125.	275.	425.	750.	
1898 .....(735)	11,100,735	2.00	2.50	8.00	13.	30.	50.	90.	125.	280.
1898O	1,868,000	3.00	6.00	18.00	50.	100.	150.	300.	650.	
1898S	1,020,592	3.00	5.00	12.00	16.	30.	90.	200.	600.	
1899 .....(846)	12,624,846	2.00	2.50	8.00	12.	26.	50.	90.	125.	280.
1899O	2,644,000	3.00	5.00	9.00	16.	32.	100.	200.	400.	
1899S	708,000	4.00	8.00	16.00	30.	40.	125.	225.	550.	
1900 .....(912)	10,016,912	2.00	2.50	7.00	12.	25.	60.	90.	125.	280.
1900O	3,416,000	3.00	7.00	15.00	25.	45.	150.	250.	400.	
1900S	1,858,585	2.50	4.00	10.00	16.	30.	50.	175.	450.	

QUARTER DOLLARS

	Mintage	G-4	VG-8	F-12	VF-20	EF-40	AU-50	MS-60	MS-63	PF-63
1901 . . .(813)	8,892,813	$2.00	$3.00	$7.00	$12.	$30.	$60.	$100.	$120.	$280.
1901O	1,612,000	12.00	21.00	50.00	100.	175.	250.	400.	900.	
1901S	72,664	1,500.00	2,500.00	3,500.00	5,000.	6,000.	8,000.	9,000.	15,000.	
1902 . . .(777)	12,197,744	2.00	2.50	7.00	12.	30.	50.	90.	125.	280.
1902O	4,748,000	2.50	3.00	12.00	25.	50.	90.	200.	600.	
1902S	1,524,612	4.00	6.00	12.00	25.	50.	100.	220.	475.	
1903 . . .(755)	9,760,064	2.00	2.50	7.00	12.	30.	50.	90.	175.	280.
1903O	3,500,000	3.00	4.00	11.00	20.	32.	100.	150.	600.	
1903S	1,036,000	4.00	6.00	14.00	25.	45.	100.	210.	400.	
1904 . . .(670)	9,588,813	2.00	2.50	7.00	12.	25.	50.	90.	125.	280.
1904O	2,456,000	3.00	4.00	16.00	30.	90.	175.	350.	600.	
1905 . . .(727)	4,968,250	2.50	3.50	8.50	12.	30.	50.	90.	150.	280.
1905O	1,230,000	3.00	9.00	30.00	50.	90.	150.	200.	550.	
1905S	1,884,000	2.50	3.00	12.00	18.	40.	90.	175.	500.	
1906 . . .(675)	3,656,435	2.50	3.00	7.00	12.	25.	50.	90.	125.	280.
1906D	3,280,000	2.50	3.00	9.00	15.	26.	60.	110.	200.	
1906O	2,056,000	2.50	3.00	12.00	15.	30.	90.	135.	250.	
1907 . . .(575)	7,132,575	2.50	3.00	7.00	12.	25.	50.	90.	125.	280.
1907D	2,484,000	2.50	3.00	9.00	15.	26.	60.	125.	350.	
1907O	4,560,000	2.50	3.00	8.00	12.	25.	55.	100.	250.	
1907S	1,360,000	2.50	3.00	15.00	19.	45.	90.	200.	400.	
1908 . . .(545)	4,232,545	2.50	3.00	7.00	12.	25.	50.	90.	125.	280.
1908D	5,788,000	2.50	3.00	7.00	12.	25.	50.	110.	200.	
1908O	6,244,000	2.00	2.50	7.00	12.	25.	50.	100.	125.	
1908S	784,000	4.00	12.00	30.00	40.	100.	200.	350.	550.	
1909 . . .(650)	9,268,650	2.00	2.50	7.00	12.	25.	50.	90.	125.	280.
1909D	5,114,000	2.00	2.50	7.00	12.	25.	60.	110.	160.	
1909O	712,000	4.00	12.00	30.00	60.	120.	210.	375.	800.	
1909S	1,348,000	2.00	2.50	10.00	16.	30.	90.	150.	350.	
1910 . . .(551)	2,244,551	2.00	2.50	7.00	12.	25.	60.	90.	150.	280.
1910D	1,500,000	2.00	2.50	15.00	18.	35.	110.	175.	400.	
1911 . . .(543)	3,720,543	2.00	2.50	7.00	12.	25.	50.	90.	125.	280.
1911D	933,600	2.00	2.50	30.00	90.	125.	200.	300.	550.	
1911S	988,000	2.00	2.50	18.00	20.	50.	120.	175.	350.	
1912 . . .(700)	4,400,700	2.00	2.50	7.00	12.	25.	50.	90.	125.	280.
1912S	708,000	2.00	2.50	15.00	18.	35.	100.	175.	400.	
1913 . . .(613)	484,613	5.00	8.00	23.00	65.	185.	210.	550.	600.	325.
1913D	1,450,800	2.00	2.50	10.00	15.	32.	70.	140.	175.	
1913S	40,000	300.00	500.00	950.00	1,500.	2,000.	2,300.	2,700.	3,500.	
1914 . . .(380)	6,244,610	2.00	2.50	7.00	12.	25.	50.	90.	125.	325.
1914D	3,046,000	2.00	2.50	7.00	12.	25.	50.	90.	125.	
1914S	264,000	22.00	35.00	60.00	100.	175.	250.	420.	550.	
1915 . . .(450)	3,480,450	2.00	2.50	7.00	12.	25.	50.	90.	125.	325.
1915D	3,694,000	2.00	2.50	7.00	12.	25.	50.	90.	125.	
1915S	704,000	2.00	2.50	8.00	15.	32.	90.	125.	200.	
1916	1,788,000	2.00	2.50	7.00	12.	25.	50.	90.	125.	
1916D	6,540,800	2.00	2.50	7.00	12.	25.	50.	90.	125.	

QUARTER DOLLARS

STANDING LIBERTY TYPE 1916-1930

This design is by Hermon A. MacNeil, whose initial M is above and to the right of the date. Liberty bears a shield of protection in her left arm, while the right hand holds the olive branch of peace. There was a modification in 1917. The reverse has a new arrangement of stars and the eagle is higher. After 1924 the date was "recessed," thereby giving it greater protection from the effects of circulation.

G-4 GOOD—*Date and lettering readable. Top of date worn. Liberty's right leg and toes worn off. Left leg and drapery lines show much wear.*
VG-8 VERY GOOD—*Distinct date. Toes show faintly. Drapery lines visible above her left leg.*
F-12 FINE—*High curve of right leg flat from thigh to ankle. Left leg shows only slight wear. Drapery lines over right thigh seen only at sides of leg.*
VF-20 VERY FINE—*Garment line across right leg will be worn but show at sides.*
EF-40 EXTREMELY FINE—*Flattened only at high spots. Her toes are sharp. Drapery lines across right leg are evident.*
AU-50 ABOUT UNCIRCULATED—*Traces of light wear on only the high points of the design. Half of mint luster is present.*
MS-60 UNCIRCULATED—*No trace of wear. Light blemishes.*
MS-63 SELECT UNCIRCULATED—*Some distracting contact marks or blemishes in prime focal areas. Luster may be impaired.*

No stars below eagle 1916-1917

	Mintage	G-4	VG-8	F-12	VF-20	EF-40	AU-50	MS-60	MS-63
1916	52,000	$1,250.	$2,100.	$3,250.	$3,500.	$4,500.	$5,000.	$6,000.	$8,000.
1917, Variety 1	8,740,000	11.	17.	25.	30.	40.	90.	125.	150.
1917D, Variety 1	1,509,200	12.	17.	25.	32.	50.	90.	125.	175.
1917S, Variety 1	1,952,000	15.	20.	25.	35.	75.	100.	150.	200.

Stars below eagle 1917-1930

Mint mark position is on obverse at left of date.

1918S, 8 over 7

	Mintage	G-4	VG-8	F-12	VF-20	EF-40	AU-50	MS-60	MS-63
1917, Variety 2	13,880,000	10.	12.	15.	17.	25.	45.	70.	115.
1917D, Variety 2	6,224,400	15.	20.	30.	35.	50.	70.	100.	150.
1917S, Variety 2	5,552,000	15.	21.	35.	35.	45.	60.	100.	150.
1918	14,240,000	7.	8.	15.	17.	25.	45.	70.	115.
1918D	7,380,000	13.	15.	25.	30.	40.	70.	100.	175.
1918S	} 11,072,000	9.	11.	17.	20.	25.	45.	100.	150.
1918S, 8/7 ..		700.	900.	1,200.	1,500.	2,250.	4,500.	7,500.	15,000.
1919	11,324,000	17.	20.	25.	30.	35.	55.	70.	100.
1919D	1,944,000	35.	50.	80.	125.	200.	250.	350.	700.
1919S	1,836,000	35.	50.	80.	130.	250.	300.	375.	800.
1920	27,860,000	7.	10.	15.	17.	20.	35.	75.	115.
1920D	3,586,400	20.	25.	35.	40.	60.	90.	120.	375.
1920S	6,380,000	9.	12.	16.	20.	30.	50.	100.	375.
1921	1,916,000	75.	100.	150.	175.	225.	300.	400.	500.
1923	9,716,000	8.	10.	15.	17.	20.	35.	70.	110.
1923S	1,360,000	120.	150.	200.	300.	400.	450.	500.	600.
1924	10,920,000	8.	10.	12.	15.	20.	45.	65.	110.
1924D	3,112,000	20.	30.	40.	60.	80.	100.	125.	150.
1924S	2,860,000	12.	15.	20.	22.	80.	100.	135.	450.

QUARTER DOLLARS

Recessed Date 1925-1930

QUARTER DOLLARS

	Mintage	G-4	VG-8	F-12	VF-20	EF-40	AU-50	MS-60	MS-63
1925	12,280,000	$1.50	$2.50	$3.50	$7.	$16.	$35.	$60.	$100.
1926	11,316,000	1.50	2.50	3.50	7.	16.	35.	60.	100.
1926D	1,716,000	1.50	2.50	8.00	15.	25.	50.	70.	100.
1926S	2,700,000	1.50	2.50	6.00	11.	50.	100.	150.	350.
1927	11,912,000	1.50	2.50	3.50	7.	16.	35.	60.	100.
1927D	976,000	3.00	5.00	10.00	20.	50.	80.	120.	150.
1927S	396,000	10.00	12.00	30.00	100.	500.	1,400.	1,650.	3,000.
1928	6,336,000	1.50	2.50	3.50	7.	16.	35.	60.	100.
1928D	1,627,600	1.50	2.50	3.50	7.	16.	35.	60.	100.
1928S	2,644,000	1.50	2.50	3.50	7.	16.	35.	60.	
1929	11,140,000	1.50	2.50	3.50	7.	16.	35.	60.	
1929D	1,358,000	1.50	2.50	3.50	7.	16.	35.	60.	
1929S	1,764,000	1.50	2.50	3.50	7.	16.	35.	60.	
1930	5,632,000	1.50	2.50	3.50	7.	16.	35.	60.	
1930S	1,556,000	1.50	2.50	3.50	7.	16.	35.	60.	

WASHINGTON TYPE 1932 to Date

This type was intended to be a commemorative issue marking the two-hundredth anniversary of Washington's birth. John Flanagan, a New York sculptor, was the designer. The initals JF are found at the base of the neck. Mint mark is on reverse below wreath. 1932 to 1964. Starting in 1968 mint mark is on obverse at right of ribbon.

F-12 FINE—*Hairlines about ear are visible. Tiny feathers on eagle's breast are faintly visible.*
VF-20 VERY FINE—*Hair details worn but plain. Feathers at sides of eagle's breast are plain.*
EF-40 EXTREMELY FINE—*Hairlines sharp. Wear spots confined to top of eagle's legs and center of breast.*
AU-50 ABOUT UNCIRCULATED—*Traces of light wear on only the high points of the design. Half of mint luster is present.*
MS-60 UNCIRCULATED—*No trace of wear. Light blemishes.*
MS-63 SELECT UNCIRCULATED—*No trace of wear. Very few noticeable blemishes.*
MS-65—CHOICE UNCIRCULATED—*Only light scattered contact marks that are not distracting.Strong luster, good eye appeal.*
PF-65—*Choice Brilliant surfaces with no noticeable blemishes or flaws. May have a few scatered barely noticeable marks or hairlines.*

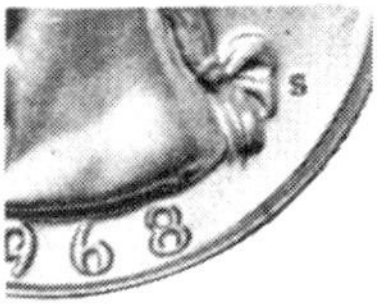

Starting in 1968 mint mark is on obverse at right of ribbon.

Silver Coinage—1932-1964

	Mintage	VG-8	F-12	VF-20	EF-40	MS-60	MS-63	MS-65	PF-65
1932	5,404,000	$2.00	$2.50	$3.00	$4.00	$12.00	$23.	$175.	
1932D	436,800	45.00	50.00	70.00	140.00	400.00	1,500.	10,000.	
1932S	4,080,00	45.00	50.00	60.00	70.00	200.00	450.	3,000.	
1934	31,912,052	.75	1.25	1.40	3.00	9.00	17.	40.	
1934D	3,527,200	1.00	1.25	1.40	5.00	70.00	150.	350.	
1935	32,484,000	.75	1.00	1.25	2.00	9.00	15.	40.	
1935D	5,780,000	1.00	1.25	2.00	5.00	80.00	120.	300.	
1935S	5,660,000	1.00	1.25	1.40	4.00	30.00	50.	120.	
1936 ..(3,837)	41,303,837		.75	.75	1.00	8.00	16.	40.	800.
1936D	5,374,000		1.00	5.00	18.00	170.00	300.	600.	
1936S	3,828,000		.75	1.50	4.00	40.00	60.	175.	
1937 ..(5,542)	19,701,542		.75	.75	.85	8.00	15.	40.	300.
1937D	7,189,600		.75	1.50	3.00	20.00	40.	60.	
1937S	1,652,000		.75	2.00	6.00	65.00	90.	120.	
1938 ..(8,045)	9,480,045		.75	2.00	5.00	35.00	50.	110.	175.
1938S	2,832,000		.75	1.50	4.00	35.00	50.	100.	
1939 ..(8,795)	33,548,795		.75	.75	.85	5.00	12.	25.	150.
1939D	7,092,000		.75	1.00	2.00	12.00	20.	40.	
1939S	2,628,000		.75	1.00	4.00	40.00	60.	125.	
1940 .(11,246)	35,715,246		.75	.75	.85	4.00	11.	25.	100.
1940D	2,797,600		.75	1.00	5.00	45.00	70.	125.	
1940S	8,244,000		.75	.75	1.00	7.00	13.	25.	
1941 .(15,287)	79,047,287		.75	.75	.85	2.00	6.	20.	100.
1941D	16,714,800		.75	.75	.85	12.00	22.	25.	

QUARTER DOLLARS

	Mintage	F-12	VF-20	EF-40	MS-60	MS-63	MS-65	PF-65
1941S	16,080,000	$.75	$.75	$.85	$7.50	$18.	$35.	
1942 . . . . .(21,123)	102,117,123	.75	.75	.85	2.00	4.	10.	$100.
1942D	17,487,200	.75	.75	1.00	6.00	12.	20.	
1942S	19,384,000	.75	.75	1.00	27.00	45.	90.	
1943	99,700,000	.75	.75	.85	2.00	4.	20.	
1943D	16,095,600	.75	.75	.85	8.00	16.	20.	
1943S	21,700,000	.75	.75	1.00	10.00	19.	25.	
1944	104,956,000	.75	.75	.85	2.00	4.	18.	
1944D	14,600,800	.75	.75	.85	4.00	10.	20.	
1944S	12,560,000	.75	.75	.85	5.00	12.	20.	
1945	74,372,000	.75	.75	.85	2.00	3.	20.	
1945D	12,341,600	.75	.75	.85	4.00	12.	20.	
1945S	17,004,001	.75	.75	.85	3.00	5.	15.	
1946	535,436,000	.75	.75	.85	2.00	3.	15.	
1946D	9,072,800	.75	.75	.85	2.00	3.	15.	
1946S	4,204,000	.75	.75	.85	2.00	3.	15.	
1947	22,556,000	.75	.75	.85	3.00	5.	15.	
1947D	15,338,400	.75	.75	.85	2.00	4.	15.	
1947S	5,532,000	.75	.75	.85	2.00	4.	15.	
1948	35,196,000	.75	.75	.85	2.00	3.	15.	
1948D	16,766,800	.75	.75	.85	2.00	4.	30.	
1948S	15,960,000	.75	.75	.85	2.00	3.	18.	
1949	9,312,000	.75	.75	.85	10.00	20.	30.	
1949D	10,068,400	.75	.75	.85	5.00	11.	22.	
1950 . . . . .(51,386)	24,971,512	.75	.75	.85	2.00	4.	13.	25.
1950D	} 21,075,600	.75	.75	.85	2.00	4.	13.	
1950D, D/S			25.00	75.00	125.00	200	700.	
1950S	} 10,284,004	.75	.75	.85	4.00	7.	30.	
1950S, S/D			25.00	80.00	140.00	200.	400.	
1951 . . . . .(57,500)	43,505,602	.75	.75	.85	1.25	3.	14.	25.
1951D	35,354,800	.75	.75	.85	1.25	3.	14.	
1951S	9,048,000	.75	.75	.85	4.00	12.	18.	
1952 . . . . .(81,980)	3,862,073	.75	.75	.85	1.25	3.	18.	20.
1952D	49,795,200	.75	.75	.85	1.25	3.	18.	
1952S	13,707,800	.75	.75	.85	4.00	10.	16.	
1953 . . . .(128,800)	18,664,920	.75	.75	.85	1.25	3.	16.	20.
1953D	56,112,400	.75	.75	.85	1.25	3.	14.	
1953S	14,016,000	.75	.75	.85	1.25	2.	12.	
1954 . . . .(233,300)	54,645,503	.75	.75	.85	1.25	4.	13.	10.
1954D	42,305,500	.75	.75	.85	1.25	3.	16.	
1954S	11,834,722	.75	.75	.85	1.25	2.	15.	
1955 . . . .(378,200)	18,558,381	.75	.75	.85	1.25	2.	10.	10.
1955D	3,182,400	.75	.75	.85	1.25	3.	20.	
1956 . . . .(669,384)	44,813,384	.75	.75	.75	1.00	3.	8.	4.
1956D	32,334,500	.75	.75	.75	1.00	2.	10.	
1957 . .(1,247,952)	4,779,952	.75	.75	.75	1.00	2.	10.	3.
1957D	77,924,160	.75	.75	.75	1.00	2.	10.	
1958 . . . .(875,652)	7,235,652	.75	.75	.75	1.00	2.	9.	4.
1958D	78,124,900	.75	.75	.75	1.00	2.	9.	
1959 . .(1,149,291)	25,533,291	.75	.75	.75	1.00	2.	9.	3.
1959D	62,054,232	.75	.75	.75	1.00	2.	9.	
1960 . .(1,691,602)	30,855,602	.75	.75	.75	1.00	2.	6.	2.
1960D	63,000,324	.75	.75	.75	1.00	2.	6.	
1961 . .(3,028,244)	40,064,244	.75	.75	.75	1.00	2.	6.	2.
1961D	83,656,928	.75	.75	.75	1.00	2.	6.	
1962 . .(3,218,019)	39,374,019	.75	.75	.75	1.00	2.	6.	2.
1962D	127,554,756	.75	.75	.75	1.00	2.	6.	
1963 . .(3,075,645)	77,391,645	.75	.75	.75	1.00	2.	6.	2.
1963D	135,288,184	.75	.75	.75	1.00	2.	6.	
1964 . .(3,950,762)	564,341,347	.75	.75	.75	1.00	2.	6.	2.
1964D	704,135,528	.75	.75	.75	1.00	2.	6.	

QUARTER DOLLARS

Clad Coinage—1965 to Date

	Mintage	MS-63	MS-65	PF-65
1965	1,819,717,540	$.30	$1.00	
1966	821,101,500	.30	1.00	
1967	1,524,031,848	.30	1.00	
1968	220,731,500	.50	1.50	
1968D	101,534,000	.30	1.00	
1968S, Pf	(3,041,506)			$.50
1969	176,212,000	.75	1.50	
1969D	114,372,000	.50	1.25	
1969S, Pf	(2,934,631)			.50
1970	136,420,000	.25	1.00	
1970D	417,341,364	.25	1.00	
1970S, Pf	(2,632,810)			.50
1971	109,284,000	$.30	$1.00	
1971D	258,634,428	.30	.50	
1971S, Pf	(3,220,733)			$.50
1972	215,048,000	.30	.75	
1972D	311,067,732	.30	1.00	
1972S, Pf	(3,260,996)			.50
1973	346,924,000	.30	1.00	
1973D	232,977,400	.30	1.00	
1973S, Pf	(2,760,339)			.50
1974	801,456,000	.30	1.00	
1974D	353,160,300	.30	2.00	
1974S, Pf	(2,612,568)			.50

BICENTENNIAL COINAGE DATED 1776-1976

	Mintage	MS-63	MS-65	PF-65
1776-1976, Copper-nickel clad	809,784,016	$.30	$1.00	
1776-1976D, Copper-nickel clad	860,118,839	.30	1.00	
1776-1976S, Copper-nickel clad	(7,059,099)			$.50
1776-1976S, Silver clad	*11,000,000*	1.00	2.00	
1776-1976S, Silver clad	(*4,000,000*)			2.00

*Approximate mintage.

Eagle Reverse Resumed (Dies slightly modified to lower relief)

	Mintage	MS-63	MS-65	PF-65
1977	468,556,000	$.27		$1.50
1977D	256,524,978	.27	$1.00	
1977S, Pf	(3,251,152)			.50
1978	521,452,000	.27	1.50	
1978D	287,373,152	.27	1.50	
1978S, Pf	(3,127,781)			.50
1979	515,708,000	.28	1.50	
1979D	489,789,780	.27	1.25	
1979S, Proof				
1979S, Pf, Filled S				.50
1979S, Pf, Clear S				1.00
1980P	635,832,000	.27	1.50	
1980D	518,327,487	.27	1.25	
1980S, Pf	(3,554,806)			.50
1981P	601,716,000	.27	1.50	
1981D	575,722,833	.27	1.00	
1981S, Pf	(4,063,083)			.75
1982P	500,931,000	2.00	5.00	
1982D	480,042,788	.70	4.00	
1982S, Pf	(3,857,479)			.75
1983P	673,535,000	4.00	18.00	
1983D	617,806,446	2.00	9.00	
1983S, Pf	(3,279,126)			1.00
1984P	676,545,000	.30	1.25	
1984D	546,483,064	.50	1.25	
1984S, Pf	(3,065,110)			1.00
1985P	775,818,962	.50	2.50	
1985D	519,962,888	.35	1.25	
1985S, Pf	(3,362,821)			$.75
1986P	551,199,333	$1.00	$1.25	
1986D	504,298,660	1.50		4.00
1986S, Pf	(3,010,497)			1.00
1987P	582,499,481	.27	1.50	
1987D	655,594,696	.27	1.00	
1987S, Pf	(4,227,728)			1.00
1988P	562,052,000	.50	1.75	
1988D	596,810,688	.27	1.50	
1988S, Pf	(3,262,948)			.75
1989P	512,868,000	.27	1.75	
1989D	896,535,597	.27	1.00	
1989S, Pf	(3,220,194)			.75
1990P	613,792,000	.27	1.50	
1990D	927,638,181	.28	1.00	
1990S, Pf	(3,299,559)			1.75
1991P	570,968,000	.30	1.75	
1991D	630,966,693	.30	1.50	
1991S, Pf	(2,867,787)			1.25
1992P	384,764,000	.27	4.00	
1992D	389,777,107	.35	1.50	
1992S, Pf	(2,858,981)			1.25
1992S, Silver Pf	(1,317,579)			1.50
1993P	639,276,000	.30	1.75	
1993D	645,476,128	.30	1.75	
1993S, Pf	(2,633,439)			1.25
1993S, Silver Pf	(761,353)			3.00

QUARTER DOLLARS

	Mintage	MS-63	MS-65	PF-65
1994P	825,600,000	$.30	$4.00	
1994D	880,034,110	.30	1.50	
1994S, Pf	(2,484,594)			$1.75
1994S, Silver Pf	(785,329)		5.00	
1995P	1,004,336,000	.30	1.75	
1995D	1,103,216,000	.30	1.75	
1995S, Pf	(2,117,496)			6.00
1995S, Silver Pf	(679,985)			6.00
1996P	925,040,000	.25	1.25	
1996D	906,868,000	.25	1.25	
1996S, Pf	(1,750,244)			$1.50
1996S, Silver Pf	(775,021)			4.00
1997P	595,740,000	$.25	1.25	
1997D	599,680,000	.25	1.25	
1997S Pf	(2,055,000)			3.00
1997S Silver Pf	(741,678)			8.00
1998P	896,268,000	.25	1.00	
1998D	821,000,000	.25	1.00	
1998S Pf	(2,086,507)			4.00
1998S Silver Pf	(878,792)			4.00

QUARTER DOLLARS

STATEHOOD QUARTER DOLLARS 1999-2008

The United States Mint 50 State Quarters® Program begun in 1999 will produce a series of 50 quarter dollar coins with special designs honoring each state. Five different designs will be issued each year during the period 1999-2008. States are being commemorated in the order of their entrance into statehood.

These are all legal tender coins of standard weight and composition. The obverse side depicting President George Washington has been modified slightly to include some of the wording previously used on the reverse. The modification was authorized by special legislation, and carried out by Mint Sculptor-Engraver William Cousins, whose initials have been added to the truncation of Washington's neck adjacent to those of the original designer, John Flanagan.

Each state theme is being proposed, and approved, by the governor of the state. Final designs will be created by mint personnel.

Circulation coins are made at the Philadelphia and Denver mints. Proof coins are made in San Francisco. Both copper-nickel and silver proof coins are made each year.

	Mintage	AU-50	MS-63	PF-65
1999P, Delaware	373,400,000	$.25	$.50	
1999D, Delaware	401,424,000	.25	.50	
1999S, Delaware Pf (3,713,359)				$1.50
1999S, Delaware Silver Pf (800,000)				2.50
1999P, Pennsylvania	349,000,000	.25	.50	
1999D, Pennsylvania	358,332,000	.25	.50	
1999S, Pennsylvania Pf (3,713,359)				1.50
1999S, Pennsylvania Silver Pf (800,000)				2.50
1999P, New Jersey	363,200,000	.25	.30	
1999D, New Jersey	299,028,000	.25	.35	
1999S, New Jersey Pf (3,713,359)				1.50
1999S, New Jersey Silver Pf (800,000)				2.50
1999P, Georgia	451,188,000	.25	.30	
1999D, Georgia	488,744,000	.25	.30	
1999S, Georgia Pf (3,713,359)				1.50
1999S, Georgia Silver Pf (800,000)				2.50
1999P, Connecticut	688,744,000	.25	.30	
1999D, Connecticut	657,880,000	.25	.30	
1999S, Connecticut Pf (3,713,359)				1.50
1999S, Connecticut Silver Pf (800,000)				2.50

Statehood Quarters

2000P, Massachusetts	628,600,000	.25	.30	
2000D, Massachusetts	535,184,000	.25	.30	
2000S, Massachusetts Pf . . . . .(4,020,083)				1.50
2000S, Massachusetts Silver Pf . .(856,400)				2.50
2000P, Maryland	678,200,000	.25	.30	
2000D, Maryland	556,532,000	.25	.30	
2000S, Maryland Pf . . . .(4,020,083)				1.50
2000S, Maryland Silver Pf . . . . .(856,400)				2.50
2000P, South Carolina	742,576,000	.25	.30	
2000D, South Carolina	566,208,000	.25	.30	
2000S, South Carolina Pf . . . . .(4,020,083)				1.50
2000S, South Carolina Silver Pf . .(856,400)				2.50
2000P, New Hampshire	673,040,000	.25	.30	
2000D, New Hampshire	495,976,000	.25	.30	
2000S, New Hampshire Pf . . . .(4,020,083)				1.50
2000S, New Hampshire Silver Pf .(856,400)				2.50
2000P, Virginia	943,000,000	.25	.30	
2000D, Virginia	651,616,000	.25	.30	
2000S, Virginia Pf . . . .(4,020,083)				1.50
2000S, Virginia Silver Pf . . . .(856,400)				2.50

2001P, New York	655,400,000	.25	.30	
2001D, New York	619,640,000	.25	.30	
2001S, New York Pf . . . .(3,093,274)				1.50
2001S, New York Silver Pf . . . . . .(889,697)				2.50
2001P, North Carolina	627,600,000	.25	.30	
2001D, North Carolina	427,876,000	.25	.30	
2001S, North Carolina Pf . . . . .(3,093,274)				1.50
2001S, North Carolina Silver Pf . .(889,697)				2.50
2001P, Rhode Island	423,000,000	.25	.30	
2001D, Rhode Island	447,100,000	.25	.30	
2001S, Rhode Island Pf . . . . . .(3,093,274)				1.50
2001S, Rhode Island Silver Pf . . .(889,697)				2.50
2001P, Vermont	423,400,000	.25	.30	
2001D, Vermont	459,404,000	.25	.30	
2001S, Vermont Pf . . . .(3,093,274)				1.50
2001S, Vermont Silver Pf . . . .(889,697)				2.50
2001P, Kentucky	353,000,000	.25	.30	
2001D, Kentucky	370,564,000	.25	.30	
2001S, Kentucky Pf . . . .(3,093,274)				1.50

Statehood Quarters

2001S, Kentucky Silver Pf . . . . . .(889,697)				2.50
2002P, Tennessee	361,600,000	.25	.30	
2002D, Tennessee	286,468,000	.25	.30	
2002S, Tennessee Pf . . . .(3,039,320)				1.50
2002S, Tennessee Silver Pf . . . . .(888,826)				2.50
2002P, Ohio	217,200,000	.25	.30	
2002D, Ohio	414,832,000	.25	.30	
2002S, Ohio Pf . . . .(761,600)	3,039,320			1.50
2002S, Ohio Silver Pf . . . .(888,826)				2.50
2002P, Louisiana	362,000,000	.25	.30	
2002D, Louisiana	402,204,000	.25	.30	
2002S, Louisiana Pf . . . .(3,039,320)				1.50
2002S, Louisiana Silver Pf . . . . . .(888,826)				2.50
2002P, Indiana	362,600,000	.25	.30	
2002D, Indiana	327,200,000	.25	.30	
2002S, Indiana Pf . . . .(3,039,320)				1.50
2002S, Indiana Silver Pf . . . .(888,826)				2.50
2002P, Mississippi	290,000,000	.25	.30	
2002D, Mississippi	289,600,000	.25	.30	
2002S, Mississippi Pf . . . .(3,039,320)				1.50
2002S, Mississippi Silver Pf . . . .(888,826)				2.50

2003P, Illinois	225,800,000	.25	.30	
2003D, Illinois	237,400,000	.25	.30	
2003S, Illinois Pf				1.50
2003S, Illinois Silver Pf				2.50
2003P, Alabama	225,000,000	.25	.30	
2003D, Alabama	232,400,000	.25	.30	
2003S, Alabama Pf				1.50
2003S, Alabama Silver Pf				2.50
2003P, Maine	217,400,000	.25	.30	
2003D, Maine	231,900,000	.25	.30	
2003S, Maine Pf				1.50
2003S, Maine Silver Pf				2.50
2003P, Missouri	225,000,000	.25	.30	
2003D, Missouri	228,200,000	.25	.30	
2003S, Missouri Pf				1.50
2003S, Missouri Silver Pf				2.50
2003P, Arkansas		.25	.30	
2003D, Arkansas		.25	.30	
2003S, Arkansas Pf				1.50
2003S, Arkansas Silver Pf				2.50

	Mintage	AU-50	MS-63	MS-65	PF-63	PF-65
2004P, Michigan	233,800,00					
2004D, Michigan	225,800,00					
2004S, Michigan						
2004S, Michigan Silver PF						
2004P, Florida	240,200,00					
2004D, Florida	241,600,00					
2004S, Florida						
2004S, Florida Silver PF						
2004P, Texas						
2004D, Texas						
2004S, Texas						
2004S, Texas Silver PF						
2004P, Iowa						
2004D, Iowa						
2004S, Iowa						
2004S, Iowa Silver PF						
2004P, Wisconsin						
2004D, Wisconsin						
2004S, Wisconsin						
2004S, Wisconsin Silver PF						
2005, California						
2005, Minnesota						
2005, Oregon						
2005, Kansas						
2005, West Virginia						
2006, Nevada						
2006, Nebraska						
2006, Colorado						
2006, North Dakota						
2006, South Dakota						
2007, Montana						
2007, Washington						
2007, Idaho						
2007, Wyoming						
2007, Utah						
2008, Oklahoma						
2008, New Mexico						
2008, Arizona						
2008, Alaska						
2008, Hawaii						

HALF DOLLARS — 1794 to Date

The half dollar, authorized by the Act of April 2, 1792, was not minted until December, 1794. The weight of the half dollar was 208 grains and its fineness .8924 when first issued. This standard was not changed until 1837 when the law of January 18, 1837 specified 206 1/4 grains, .900 fine. This fineness continued in use until 1965.

Arrows at the date in 1853 indicate the reduction of weight to 192 grains. During that year only, rays were added to the field on the reverse side. Arrows remained in 1854 and 1855. In 1873 the weight was raised to 192.9 grains and arrows were again placed at the date.

FLOWING HAIR TYPE 1794-1795

AG-3 ABOUT GOOD—*Clear enough to identify.*
G-4 GOOD—*Date and letters sufficient to be readable. Main devices outlined, but lack details.*
VG-8 VERY GOOD—*Major details discernible. Letters well formed but worn.*
F-12 FINE—*Hair ends distinguishable. Top hairlines show, but otherwise worn smooth.*
VF-20 VERY FINE—*Hair in center shows some detail. Other details more bold.*
EF-40 EXTREMELY FINE—*Hair above head and down neck detailed with slight wear.*
AU-50 ABOUT UNCIRCULATED—*Traces of light wear on only the high points of the design. Half of mint luster is present.*

2 Leaves under wings

3 Leaves under wings

	Mintage	AG-3	G-4	VG-8	F-12	VF-20	EF-40	AU-50
1794	23,404	$425.	$750.	$1,500.	$2,200.	$4,200.	$8,000.	$15,000.
1795	299,680	135.	275.	350.	500.	1,000.	2,750.	3,400
1795, Recut date . .		135.	275.	350.	500.	1,100.	2,900.	3,500.
1795,3 leaves under each wing		225.	450.	750.	1,500.	2,750.	5,500.	7,500.

DRAPED BUST TYPE, SMALL EAGLE REVERSE 1796-1797

Grading same as above for About Good to Fine.

VF-20 VERY FINE—*Right side of drapery slightly worn. Left side to curls is smooth.*
EF-40 EXTREMELY FINE—*All lines in drapery on bust will show distinctly around to hair curls.*
AU-50 ABOUT UNCIRCULATED—*Traces of light wear on only the high points of the design. Half of mint luster is present.*
MS-60 UNCIRCULATED—*No trace of wear. Light blemishes.*

1796, 15 Stars

1796, 16 Stars

DRAPED BUST TYPE, SMALL EAGLE REVERSE 1796-1797

	Mintage	AG-3	G-4	VG-8	F-12	VF-20	EF-40	AU-50
1796, 15 stars	3,918	$4,000.	$6,500.	$8,200.	$11,000.	$15,000.	$28,000.	$35,000.
1796, 16 stars		4,200.	6,800.	8,500.	12,000.	16,000.	29,000.	37,500.
1797, 15 stars		4,000.	6,500.	8,200.	11,000.	15,000.	28,000.	35,000.

DRAPED BUST TYPE, HERALDIC EAGLE REVERSE 1801-1807

	Mintage	G-4	VG-8	F-12	VF-20	EF-40	AU-50	MS-60
1801	30,289	$120.	$160.	$300.	$600.	$1,200.	$4,500.	$8,500.
1802	29,890	100.	130.	250.	400.	1,000.	4,300.	8,500.
1803		80.	100.	165.	275.	500.	2,200.	4,000.

1805, 5 over 4

1806, 6 over 5

	Mintage	G-4	VG-8	F-12	VF-20	EF-40	AU-50	MS-60
1805, 5/4	211,722	100.	150.	250.	350.	900.	2,000.	9,000.
1805		75.	100.	120.	210.	400.	1,000.	3,000.
1806 All kinds	839,576	75.	100.	120.	200.	400.	1,000.	2,700.
1806, 6/5		75.	100.	120.	200.	400.	1,000.	2,700.
1806, 6/inverted 6 .		80.	120.	200.	400.	800.	2,000.	4,500.
1807	301,076	75.	100.	120.	200.	400.	1,000.	2,700.

CAPPED BUST TYPE, Lettered Edge 1807-1836

John Reich designed this Capped Head concept of Liberty. The head of Liberty facing left was used on all U.S. coin denominations for the next thirty years.

G-4 GOOD—*Date and letters readable. Bust worn smooth with outline distinct.*
VG-8 VERY GOOD—*LIBERTY visible but faint. Legends distinguishable. Clasp at shoulder visible. Curl above it nearly smooth.*
F-12 FINE—*Clasp and adjacent curl clearly outlined with slight details.*
VF-20 VERY FINE—*Clasp at shoulder clear. Curl has wear only on highest point. Hair over brow distinguishable.*
EF-40 EXTREMELY FINE—*Clasp and adjacent curl fairly sharp. Brow and hair above distinct. Curls well defined.*
AU-50 ABOUT UNCIRCULATED—*Traces of light wear on only the high points of the design. Half of mint luster is present.*
MS-60 UNCIRCULATED—*No trace of wear. Light blemishes.*
MS-63 SELECT UNCIRCULATED—*Some distracting contact marks or blemishes in prime focal areas.*

First style 1807-1808

	Mintage	G-4	VG-8	F-12	VF-20	EF-40	AU-50	MS-60	MS-63
1807, All kinds	750,500	$25.	$30.	$45.	$90.	$200.	$500.	$1,200.	$2,000.
1808, 8/7	1,368,600 (both)	25.	30.	40.	70.	140.	300.	900.	1,250.
1808		22.	25.	35.	45.	100.	200.	700.	1,000.

Remodeled Portrait and Eagle 1809-1834

	Mintage	G-4	VG-8	F-12	VF-20	EF-40	AU-50	MS-60	MS-63
1809, All Kinds	1,405,810	$20.	$25.	$35.	$40.	$85.	$200.	$600.	$1,200.

	Mintage	G-4	VG-8	F-12	VF-20	EF-40	AU-50	MS-60	MS-63
1810	1,276,276	20.	25.	35.	40.	85.	200.	600.	1,200.
1811, All kinds	1,203,644	18.	22.	32.	38.	80.	150.	500.	900.

1812, 2 over 1

1813, 50 C. over UNI

1814, 4 over 3

	Mintage	G-4	VG-8	F-12	VF-20	EF-40	AU-50	MS-60	MS-63
1812, 2/1	1,628,059 (both)	20.	25.	38.	65.	140.	200.	900.	2,000.
1812		18.	22.	35.	55.	120.	180.	500.	800.
1813	1,241,903 (both)	18.	22.	35.	55.	120.	180.	500.	800.
1813, 50C/UNI		20.	26.	40.	70.	140.	240.	600.	2,000.
1814, 4/3	1,039,075 (both)	18.	25.	36.	60.	125.	180.	500.	600.
1814		18.	25.	35.	55.	120.	180.	500.	800.

1817, 7 over 3 **1817, 7 over 4** **1817 Punctuated Date**

	Mintage	G-4	VG-8	F-12	VF-20	EF-40	AU-50	MS-60	MS-63
1815, 5/2	47,150	$325.	$550.	$700.	$950.	$1,600.	$2,000.	$4,000.	$8,500.
1817, All kinds	1,215,567								
1817, 7/3		24.	40.	90.	175.	300.	500.	1,200.	3,200.
1817, 7/4				35,000.	50,000.	80,000.			
1817, Dated 181.7		18.	25.	32.	42.	85.	150.	475.	900.
1817		18.	22.	30.	40.	60.	140.	450.	850.

1818, 2nd 8 over 7 **1819, 9 over 8** **1820, 20 over 19**

	Mintage	G-4	VG-8	F-12	VF-20	EF-40	AU-50	MS-60	MS-63
1818, 8/7	} 1,960,322	18.	22.	30.	35.	60.	140.	500.	900.
1818		18.	22.	30.	35.	60.	140.	450.	825.
1819, 9/8	2,208,000	18.	22.	30.	35.	60.	140.	450.	825.
1819		18.	22.	30.	35.	60.	140.	450.	825.
1820, 20/19	751,122	18.	24.	32.	50.	120.	300.	600.	900.
1820		17.	22.	30.	35.	55.	130.	475.	850.
1821	1,305,797	17.	22.	30.	35.	55.	130.	450.	825.
1822	1,559,573	17.	22.	30.	35.	55.	130.	475.	850.
1823, All kinds	1,694,200	17.	22.	30.	35.	55.	130.	350.	725.

"Various Dates" 1828 Square Base 2 (probably 4 over 2 over 0) **1824, 4 over 1** **1828 Curl Base, Knob 2** **1828 Square Base 2**

	Mintage	G-4	VG-8	F-12	VF-20	EF-40	AU-50	MS-60	MS-63
1824, All kinds	3,504,954								
1824, over various dates		17.	22.	30.	35.	55.	130.	350.	725.
1824, 4/1		18.	24.	30.	35.	55.	130.	375.	725.
1824		12.	22.	30.	35.	55.	130.	400.	750.
1825	2,943,166	17.	22.	30.	35.	55.	130.	325.	700.
1826	4,004,180	17.	22.	30.	35.	55.	130.	325.	700.
1827, All kinds	5,493,400								
1827, 7/6		20.	28.	35.	40.	75.	140.	400.	750.
1827		17.	22.	30.	35.	55.	130.	325.	700.
1828, All kinds	3,075,200								
1828, Curl base no knob 2		17.	22.	30.	35.	55.	130.	325.	700.
1828, Curl base knob 2		22.	30.	40.	50.	75.	150.	485.	725.
1828, Square base		17.	22.	30.	35.	55.	130.	325.	700.

	Mintage	G-4	VG-8	F-12	VF-20	EF-40	AU-50	MS-60	MS-63
1829, 9/7	3,712,156	$18.	$24.	$32.	$38.	$60.	$140.	$325.	$800.
1829		17.	22.	30.	35.	55.	130.	300.	700.
1830	4,764,800	17.	22.	30.	35.	55.	130.	300.	700.
1831	5,873,660	17.	22.	30.	35.	55.	130.	300.	675.
1832	4,797,000	17.	22.	30.	35.	55.	130.	300.	675.
1833	5,206,000	17.	22.	30.	35.	55.	130.	300.	675.
1834, All kinds	6,412,004	17.	22.	30.	35.	55.	130.	300.	675.
1835	5,352,006	17.	22.	30.	35.	55.	130.	300.	675.
1836	6,545,000	17.	22.	30.	35.	55.	130.	300.	675.
1836, 50/00		20.	30.	40.	55.	90.	200.	600.	1,400.

Reeded Edge, Reverse "50 CENTS" 1836-1837

G-4 GOOD—*LIBERTY discernible on headband.*
VG-8 VERY GOOD—*Minimum of 3 letters in LIBERTY must be clear.*
F-12 FINE—*LIBERTY complete.*
VF-20 VERY FINE—*LIBERTY is sharp. Shoulder clasp is clear.*
EF-40 EXTREMELY FINE—*LIBERTY sharp and strong. Hair details show.*
AU-50 ABOUT UNCIRCULATED—*Traces of light wear on only the high points of the design. Half of mint luster is present.*
MS-60 UNCIRCULATED—*No trace of wear. Light blemishes.*
MS-63 SELECT UNCIRCULATED—*Some distracting contact marks or blemishes in prime focal areas. Luster may be impaired.*

	Mintage	G-4	VG-8	F-12	VF-20	EF-40	AU-50	MS-60	MS-63
1836	1,200	$385.	$450.	$600.	$750.	$1,000.	$2,800.	$5,200.	$6,500.
1837	3,629,820	20.	22.	27.	45.	75.	125.	425.	575.

Reeded Edge, Reverse "HALF DOL." 1838-1839

In 1838-39 the mint mark appears on the obverse; thereafter, it is on the reverse below the eagle.

	Mintage	G-4	VG-8	F-12	VF-20	EF-40	AU-50	MS-60	MS-63
1838	3,546,000	$18.	$22.	$30.	$45.	$75.	$125.	$425.	$650.
1838O	(20)						30,000.	50,000.	
1839	1,392,976	18.	22.	30.	45.	75.	125.	525.	700.
1839O	178,976	60.	85.	120.	175.	275.	400.	1,500.	2,300.

LIBERTY SEATED TYPE 1839-1891
No Motto Above Eagle 1839-1853

G-4 GOOD—*Scant rim. LIBERTY on shield worn off. Date and letters readable.*
VG-8 VERY GOOD—*Rim fairly defined. At least 3 letters in LIBERTY are evident.*
F-12 FINE—*LIBERTY complete, but weak.*
VF-20 VERY FINE—*LIBERTY mostly sharp.*
EF-40 EXTREMELY FINE—*LIBERTY entirely sharp. Scroll edges and clasp distinct.*
AU-50 ABOUT UNCIRCULATED—*Traces of light wear on only the high points of the design. Half of mint luster is present.*
MS-60 UNCIRCULATED—*No trace of wear. Light blemishes.*
MS-63 SELECT UNCIRCULATED—*Some distracting contact marks or blemishes in prime focal areas. Luster may be impaired.*

Drapery from Elbow starting 1839

1842 Small Date

	Mintage	G-4	VG-8	F-12	VF-20	EF-40	AU-50	MS-60	MS-63
1839, No Drapery from elbow		$18.	$28.	$50.	$140.	$325.	$450.	$2,600.	$8,500.
1839	1,972,400	10.	12.	18.	30.	50.	60.	275.	650.
1840	1,435,008	9.	13.	20.	35.	60.	70.	275.	650.
18400	855,100	9.	11.	17.	30.	48.	58.	300.	600.
1841	310,000	10.	13.	20.	65.	110.	140.	475.	750.
18410	401,000	9.	11.	17.	30.	50.	65.	375.	500.
1842, SmDt	2,012,764	9.	11.	17.	35.	55.	70.	350.	875.
1842, Med. Dt	2,012,764	9.	11.	17.	30.	50.	65.	300.	850.
18420, SmDt . . . . }	754,000	180.	350.	600.	1,100.	1,800.	2,500.	4,000.	—
18420, Med. Dt . . . . . . }		9.	10.	15.	28.	45.	60.	300.	600.
1843	3,844,000	9.	10.	15.	28.	45.	60.	300.	400.
18430	2,268,000	9.	10.	15.	28.	45.	60.	300.	450.
1844	1,766,000	9.	10.	15.	28.	45.	60.	300.	400.
18440	2,005,000	9.	10.	15.	28.	45.	60.	300.	450.
1845	589,000	9.	10.	17.	30.	50.	65.	380.	600.
18450	2,094,000	9.	10.	15.	28.	45.	60.	360.	400.
1846, All kinds	2,210,000	9.	10.	15.	23.	45.	60.	300.	500.
1846, / horizontal 6 (error)		40.	75.	120.	175.	300.	500.	1,000.	2,850.
18470	2,584,000	9.	10.	15.	23.	45.	60.	300.	575.
1848	580,000	14.	18.	28.	40.	75.	180.	420.	575.
18480	3,180,000	9.	10.	15.	23.	45.	60.	360.	575.
1849	1,252,000	9.	10.	15.	23.	45.	60.	340.	500.
18490	2,310,000	9.	10.	15.	23.	45.	60.	300.	650.
1850	227,000	50.	75.	140.	175.	275.	300.	700.	1,200.
18500	2,456,000	9.	10.	15.	23.	45.	60.	300.	425.
1851	200,750	60.	100.	175.	250.	260.	275.	700.	1,000.
18510	402,000	9.	10.	15.	23.	45.	60.	300.	400.
1852	77,130	125.	180.	280.	360.	400.	550.	800.	1,000.
18520	144,000	20.	30.	45.	70.	180.	225.	900.	2,500.
18530		30,000.	40,000.	50,000.	75,000.				

Arrows at Date, Rays Around Eagle 1853 Only

	Mintage	G-4	VG-8	F-12	VF-20	EF-40	AU-50	MS-60	MS-63
1853	3,532,708	$8.	$10.	$20.	$60.	$120.	$300.	$950.	$1,250.
1853O, All kinds	1,328,000	8.	11.	22.	65.	130.	340.	1,400.	1,800.
Arrows at Date, No Rays 1854-1855									
1854	2,982,000	8.	11.	18.	30.	55.	85.	360.	650.
1854O	5,240,000	8.	11.	18.	30.	55.	85.	360.	650.
1855/1854	} 759,500	15.	35.	70.	120.	220.	275.	675.	1,200.
1855	}	8.	11.	18.	30.	55.	85.	360.	650.
1855O	3,688,000	8.	11.	18.	30.	55.	85.	360.	650.
1855S	129,950	150.	185.	300.	600.	1,400.	2,500.	5,500.	
No Arrows at Date 1856-1866									
1856	938,000	7.50	11.	18.	22.	40.	80.	220.	400.
1856O	2,658,000	7.50	11.	20.	24.	40.	80.	220.	400.
1856S	211,000	12.00	18.	35.	80.	200.	350.	1,600.	
1857	1,988,000	7.50	11.	18.	22.	40.	80.	220.	400.
1857O	818,000	7.50	11.	20.	24.	40.	80.	240.	650.
1857S	158,000	18.00	30.	40.	80.	175.	400.	1,400.	

	Mintage	G-4	VG-8	F-12	VF-20	EF-40	AU-50	MS-60	MS-63	PF-63
1858 . .*(300+)*	4,226,000	$9.00	$10.	$17.	$22.	$40.	$80.	$220.	$400.	$1,300.
1858O	7,294,000	9.00	10.	17.	22.	40.	80.	220.	400.	
1858S	476,000	11.00	13.	20.	30.	55.	120.	525.	1,500.	
1859 . . .(800)	748,000	9.00	10.	17.	22.	45.	85.	225.	450.	900.
1859O	2,834,000	9.00	10.	17.	22.	45.	85.	225.	450.	
1859S	566,000	11.00	13.	20.	30.	80.	85.	250.	1,000.	
1860 . .(1,000)	303,700	11.00	13.	19.	28.	50.	85.	225.	450.	600.
1860O	1,290,000	9.00	10.	17.	22.	45.	80.	225.	450.	
1860S	472,000	11.00	13.	20.	25.	45.	80.	350.	1,000.	
1861 . .(1,000)	2,888,400	9.00	10.	17.	22.	45.	80.	225.	400.	600.
1861O	2,532,633	9.00	10.	17.	22.	45.	80.	225.	400.	
1861S	939,500	9.00	10.	17.	22.	45.	80.	275.	800.	
1862 . . .(550)	253,550	12.00	18.	25.	50.	75.	100.	450.	650.	600.
1862S	1,352,000	9.00	10.	17.	22.	45.	80.	275.	450.	
1863 . . .(460)	503,660	11.00	14.	20.	28.	55.	85.	300.	675.	600.
1863S	916,000	9.00	10.	17.	22.	45.	85.	275.	450.	
1864 . . .(470)	379,570	12.00	16.	21.	32.	55.	90.	300.	450.	600.
1864S	658,000	9.00	10.	17.	22.	45.	85.	275.	425.	
1865 . . .(500)	511,900	11.00	13.	20.	28.	50.	90.	300.	450.	600.
1865S	675,000	9.00	10.	17.	22.	45.	85.	275.	400.	
1866S, No motto	60,000	30.00	40.	85.	140.	300.	600.	2,200.	2,900.	

Motto "In God We Trust" Added Above Eagle 1866-1873

	Mintage	G-4	VG-8	F-12	VF-20	EF-40	AU-50	MS-60	MS-63	PF-63
1866 . . . . . .(725)	745,625	$7.	$8.	$15.	$20.	$40.	$80.	$220.	$450.	$400.
1866S	994,000	7.	8.	15.	20.	40.	90.	320.	550.	
1867 . . . . . .(625)	449,925	9.	12.	20.	25.	50.	95.	275.	475.	400.
1867S	1,196,000	7.	8.	15.	20.	40.	80.	300.	650.	
1868 . . . . . .(600)	418,200	9.	14.	22.	30.	70.	120.	325.	475.	400.
1868S	1,160,000	7.	8.	15.	20.	40.	90.	325.	600.	
1869 . . . . . .(600)	795,900	7.	8.	15.	20.	40.	90.	275.	450.	400.
1869S	656,000	7.	8.	15.	20.	42.	90.	350.	800.	
1870 . . . .(1,000)	634,900	7.	8.	15.	20.	40.	80.	300.	450.	400.
1870CC	54,617	250.	400.	650.	1,400.	4,500.	8,000.			
1870S	1,004,000	7.	8.	15.	20.	42.	90.	300.	600.	
1871 . . . . . .(960)	1,204,560	7.	8.	15.	20.	40.	90.	275.	450.	400.
1871CC	153,950	50.	90.	140.	240.	600.	1,200.	3,500.	12,500.	
1871S	2,178,000	7.	8.	15.	20.	42.	90.	300.	500.	
1872 . . . . . .(950)	881,550	7.	8.	15.	20.	40.	90.	275.	550.	400.
1872CC	257,000	22.	35.	80.	180.	375.	600.	1,800.	8,000.	
1872S	580,000	8.	9.	18.	20.	42.	120.	400.	800.	
1873 . . . . . .(600)	801,800	7.	8.	15.	20.	40.	95.	250.	450.	
1873CC	122,500	50.	80.	140.	240.	450.	850.	3,500.	12,500.	

Arrows at Date 1873-1874

1873 . . . . . .(550)	1,815,700	12.	18.	20.	48.	130.	160.	500.	850.	1,100.
1873CC	214,560	40.	70.	120.	275.	550.	850.	2,400.	5,500.	
1873S	228,000	15.	25.	40.	80.	150.	275.	750.	2,500.	
1874 . . . . . .(700)	2,360,300	12.	18.	20.	48.	130.	160.	500.	850.	1,100.
1874CC	59,000	100.	175.	260.	420.	700.	1,200.	3,500.	6,500.	
1874S	394,000	15.	25.	40.	80.	140.	220.	800.	1,250.	

No Arrows at Date 1875-1891

1875 . . . . . .(700)	6,027,500	7.	8.	15.	20.	35.	75.	220.	300.	350.
1875CC	1,008,000	7.	10.	20.	25.	45.	80.	250.	400.	

	Mintage	G-4	VG-8	F-12	VF-20	EF-40	AU-50	MS-60	MS-63	PF-63
1875S	3,200,000	$7.	$8.	$15.	$20.	$35.	$75.	$220.	$300.	
1876 ....(1,150)	8,419,150	7.	8.	15.	20.	35.	75.	220.	500.	$400.
1876CC	1,956,000	7.	8.	15.	20.	40.	80.	260.	300.	
1876S	4,528,000	7.	8.	15.	20.	35.	75.	220.	300.	
1877 ......(510)	8,304,510	7.	8.	15.	20.	35.	75.	220.	300.	400.
1877CC	1,420,000	7.	8.	15.	20.	40.	85.	260.	500.	
1877S	5,356,000	7.	8.	15.	20.	35.	75.	220.	300.	
1878 ......(800)	1,378,400	7.	8.	15.	20.	35.	75.	220.	300.	400.
1878CC	62,000	120.	170.	240.	400.	900.	1,200.	2,400.	8,500.	
1878S	12,000	3,000.	4,000.	5,500.	8,000.	9,000.	12,000.	15,000.	30,000.	
1879 ....(1,100)	5,900	80.	100.	120.	160.	200.	280.	425.	500.	400.
1880 ....(1,355)	9,755	80.	100.	120.	160.	180.	250.	375.	500.	400.
1881 ......(975)	10,975	80.	100.	120.	160.	180.	250.	375.	500.	400.
1882 ....(1,100)	5,500	90.	100.	120.	160.	200.	280.	425.	500.	400.
1883 ....(1,039)	9,039	80.	110.	120.	160.	180.	245.	375.	500.	400.
1884 ......(875)	5,275	90.	110.	120.	175.	200.	280.	450.	525.	400.
1885 ......(930)	6,130	80.	120.	130.	175.	180.	260.	475.	550.	400.
1886 ......(886)	5,886	90.	120.	130.	175.	180.	260.	475.	550.	400.
1887 ......(710)	5,710	90.	120.	130.	175.	180.	260.	475.	550.	400.
1888 ......(832)	12,833	85.	120.	125.	160.	180.	250.	425.	500.	400.
1889 ......(711)	12,711	85.	110.	125.	160.	180.	250.	425.	500.	400.
1890 ......(590)	12,590	85.	110.	125.	160.	180.	250.	425.	500.	400.
1891 ......(600)	200,600	15.	20.	25.	30.	65.	75.	300.	400.	400.

BARBER or LIBERTY HEAD TYPE 1892-1915

Like the dime and quarter dollar, this type was designed by Charles E. Barber, whose initial B is on the truncation of the neck.

G-4 GOOD—*Date and legends readable. LIBERTY worn off headband.*
VG-8 VERY GOOD—*Minimum of 3 letters readable in LIBERTY.*
F-12 FINE—*LIBERTY completely readable, but not sharp.*
VF-20 VERY FINE—*All letters in LIBERTY evenly plain.*
EF-40 EXTREMELY FINE—*LIBERTY bold, and its ribbon distinct.*
AU-50 ABOUT UNCIRCULATED—*Traces of light wear on only the high points of the design. Half of mint luster is present.*
MS-60 UNCIRCULATED—*No trace of wear. Light blemishes.*
MS-63 SELECT UNCIRCULATED—*Some distracting contact marks or blemishes in prime focal areas. Luster may be impaired.*
PF-63—*Reflective surfaces with only a few blemishes in secondary focal places. No major flaws.*

Mint mark location on reverse below eagle.

	Mintage	G-4	VG-8	F-12	VF-20	EF-40	AU-50	MS-60	MS-63	PF-63
1892 ....(1,245)	935,245	$10.	$12.	$22.	$35.	$140.	$160.	$220.	$350.	$400.
1892O	390,000	80.	100.	140.	180.	250.	275.	460.	750.	
1892S	1,029,028	75.	90.	120.	175.	240.	275.	460.	800.	
1893 ......(792)	1,826,792	8.	12.	22.	40.	100.	150.	300.	500.	400.
1893O	1,389,000	10.	20.	32.	65.	160.	200.	310.	600.	
1893S	740,000	40.	50.	100.	160.	240.	300.	620.	1,000.	
1894 ......(972)	1,148,972	10.	20.	32.	50.	120.	150.	260.	400.	400.
1894O	2,138,000	6.	10.	30.	50.	130.	160.	260.	450.	
1894S	4,048,690	7.	12.	25.	45.	120.	150.	255.	500.	
1895 ......(880)	1,835,218	6.	10.	24.	40.	110.	150.	260.	450.	400.
1895O	1,766,000	7.	12.	28.	50.	110.	165.	275.	650.	

	Mintage	G-4	VG-8	F-12	VF-20	EF-40	AU-50	MS-60	MS-63	PF-63
1895S	1,108,086	$10.	$14.	$35.	$60.	$125.	$175.	$275.	$600.	
1896 (762)	950,762	8.	10.	25.	45.	110.	150.	275.	425.	$400.
1896O	924,000	10.	15.	50.	80.	175.	300.	600.	1,500.	
1896S	1,140,948	30.	40.	65.	110.	180.	240.	600.	1,500.	
1897 (731)	2,480,731	4.	5.	15.	35.	65.	140.	220.	375.	400.
1897O	632,000	26.	50.	140.	300.	400.	500.	800.	1,400.	
1897S	933,900	50.	75.	125.	210.	340.	450.	675.	1,500.	
1898 (735)	2,956,735	4.	5.	12.	30.	75.	150.	200.	375.	400.
1898O	874,000	9.	15.	50.	100.	175.	240.	450.	1,300.	
1898S	2,358,550	5.	6.	18.	40.	100.	150.	375.	1,500.	
1899 (846)	5,538,846	4.	5.	14.	30.	65.	140.	200.	350.	400.
1899O	1,724,000	5.	6.	22.	40.	130.	160.	325.	550.	
1899S	1,686,411	5.	6.	22.	40.	100.	150.	300.	1,000.	
1900 (912)	4,762,912	4.	5.	14.	35.	65.	140.	200.	375.	400.
1900O	2,744,000	5.	7.	20.	40.	125.	160.	325.	1,400.	
1900S	2,560,322	5.	7.	18.	40.	100.	140.	275.	900.	
1901 (813)	4,268,813	4.	5.	14.	30.	60.	150.	200.	350.	400.
1901O	1,124,000	5.	7.	25.	55.	140.	200.	675.	2,000.	
1901S	847,044	9.	16.	50.	120.	275.	400.	800.	2,200.	
1902 (777)	4,922,777	4.	5.	14.	30.	60.	150.	200.	350.	400.
1902O	2,526,000	5.	7.	18.	35.	90.	150.	350.	950.	
1902S	1,460,670	5.	7.	20.	45.	110.	165.	300.	850.	
1903 (755)	2,278,755	4.	5.	14.	35.	70.	150.	210.	500.	375.
1903O	2,100,000	5.	7.	16.	40.	90.	160.	300.	650.	
1903S	1,920,772	5.	7.	16.	40.	95.	170.	300.	750.	
1904 (670)	2,992,670	4.	5.	14.	30.	65.	140.	200.	500.	375.
1904O	1,117,600	6.	9.	25.	60.	150.	210.	550.	1,250.	
1904S	553,038	8.	20.	75.	150.	310.	600.	1,200.	3,750.	
1905 (727)	662,727	4.	5.	20.	40.	90.	140.	230.	625.	375.
1905O	505,000	6.	10.	35.	65.	135.	170.	350.	750.	
1905S	2,494,000	5.	7.	16.	38.	90.	150.	300.	850.	
1906 (675)	2,638,675	4.	5.	14.	30.	65.	120.	200.	350.	375.
1906D	4,028,000	5.	5.	15.	36.	75.	120.	200.	350.	
1906O	2,446,000	4.	6.	16.	35.	80.	125.	275.	500.	
1906S	1,740,154	4.	5.	18.	40.	90.	140.	275.	500.	
1907 (575)	2,598,575	4.	5.	14.	26.	65.	120.	200.	350.	375.
1907D	3,856,000	4.	5.	14.	32.	70.	130.	200.	350.	
1907O	3,946,600	4.	5.	14.	32.	70.	140.	220.	375.	
1907S	1,250,000	4.	5.	22.	50.	115.	275.	400.	1,750.	
1908 (545)	1,354,545	4.	5.	14.	30.	65.	120.	200.	350.	375.
1908D	3,280,000	4.	5.	14.	30.	65.	120.	200.	350.	
1908O	5,360,000	4.	5.	14.	30.	70.	140.	210.	425.	
1908S	1,644,828	4.	5.	20.	42.	100.	150.	340.	1,100.	
1909 (650)	2,368,650	4.	5.	14.	30.	65.	120.	200.	350.	375.
1909O	925,400	7.	8.	18.	45.	120.	200.	340.	750.	
1909S	1,764,000	4.	5.	14.	32.	90.	140.	260.	500.	
1910 (551)	418,551	7.	9.	18.	50.	130.	145.	290.	500.	375.
1910S	1,948,000	4.	5.	14.	35.	85.	130.	250.	350.	
1911 (543)	1,406,543	4.	5.	14.	26.	65.	110.	180.	350.	375.
1911D	695,080	4.	5.	15.	30.	75.	125.	240.	400.	
1911S	1,272,000	4.	5.	14.	30.	75.	130.	250.	550.	
1912 (700)	1,550,700	4.	5.	14.	28.	70.	110.	200.	350.	375.
1912D	2,300,800	4.	5.	14.	28.	70.	110.	200.	350.	
1912S	1,370,000	4.	5.	14.	30.	75.	130.	240.	450.	

	Mintage	G-4	VG-8	F-12	VF-20	EF-40	AU-50	MS-60	MS-63	PF-63
1913 .....(627)	188,627	$10.	$15.	$50.	$90.	$160.	$300.	$450.	$750.	$500.
1913D	534,000	4.	5.	16.	35.	90.	120.	225.	400.	
1913S	604,000	4.	5.	18.	40.	90.	140.	275.	500.	
1914 .....(380)	124,610	15.	20.	80.	125.	210.	300.	450.	750.	700.
1914S	992,000	4.	5.	14.	30.	80.	140.	275.	450.	
1915 .....(450)	138,450	9.	15.	45.	90.	160.	300.	475.	1,100.	600.
1915D	1,170,400	4.	5.	11.	26.	60.	130.	200.	350.	
1915S	1,604,000	4.	5.	11.	26.	60.	130.	200.	350.	

LIBERTY WALKING TYPE 1916-1947

This type was designed by A. A. Weinman. The designer's monogram AAW appears under the tip of the wing feathers. On the 1916 coins and some of the 1917 coins the mint mark is located on the obverse below the motto.

G-4 GOOD—*Rims are defined. Motto IN GOD WE TRUST readable.*
VG-8 VERY GOOD—*Motto is distinct. About half of skirt lines at left are clear.*
F-12 FINE—*All skirt lines evident, but worn in spots. Details in sandal below motto are clear.*
VF-20 VERY FINE—*Skirt lines sharp including leg area. Little wear on breast and right arm.*
EF-40 EXTREMELY FINE—*All skirt lines bold.*
AU-50 ABOUT UNCIRCULATED—*Traces of light wear on only the high points of the design. Half of mint luster is present.*
MS-60 UNCIRCULATED—*No trace of wear. Light blemishes.*
MS-63 SELECT UNCIRCULATED—*No trace of wear. Slight blemishes. Attractive mint luster.*
PF-65—*Choice Brilliant surfaces with no noticeable blemishes or flaws. May have a few scatered barely noticeable marks or hairlines.*

1916-1917

1917-1947

Mint mark locations.

Choice uncirculated well-struck specimens are worth more than values listed.

	Mintage	G-4	VG-8	F-12	VF-20	EF-40	AU-50	MS-60	MS-63	PF-65
1916	608,000	$12.00	$15.00	$25.00	$50.	$70.	$100.	$135.	$180.	
1916D, (Obv.) ..	1,014,400	10.00	12.00	16.00	35.	65.	100.	140.	200.	
1916S (Obv.) ...	508,000	35.00	40.00	60.00	150.	250.	275.	450.	1,000.	
1917	12,292,000	2.00	2.50	3.50	8.	16.	25.	55.	75.	
1917D, (Obv.) ..	765,400	5.50	7.00	16.00	35.	70.	110.	215.	475.	
1917D, (Rev.) ...	1,940,000	3.00	3.50	10.00	30.	85.	200.	325.	700.	
1917S, (Obv.) ...	952,000	7.00	9.00	22.00	110.	275.	500.	1,000.	1,900.	
1917S, (Rev.) ...	5,554,000	2.50	3.00	5.00	12.	21.	60.	135.	750.	
1918	6,634,000	2.00	3.00	5.00	24.	60.	110.	210.	475.	
1918D	3,853,040	2.00	3.00	5.00	25.	75.	150.	475.	925.	
1918S	10,282,000	2.00	3.00	5.00	12.	25.	60.	185.	900.	
1919	962,000	7.00	9.00	14.00	65.	200.	250.	475.	1,250.	
1919D	1,165,000	5.00	7.00	15.00	75.	225.	475.	1,300.	5,000.	
1919S	1,552,000	5.00	7.00	10.00	60.	250.	600.	1,100.	2,500.	
1920	6,372,000	1.60	1.60	4.00	12.	25.	50.	110.	250.	
1920D	1,551,000	3.00	4.00	11.00	60.	135.	275.	500.	1,500.	
1920S	4,624,000	1.60	3.00	7.50	20.	65.	150.	285.	1,000.	
1921	246,000	50.00	70.00	110.00	300.	725.	1,100.	1,600.	2,250.	
1921D	208,000	70.00	90.00	150.00	325.	950.	1,250.	1,600.	2,500.	
1921S	548,000	12.00	16.00	50.00	300.	2,000.	3,000.	4,750.	10,000.	
1923S	2,178,000	3.50	4.00	8.00	25.	100.	550.	900.	1,500.	

	Mintage	G-4	VG-8	F-12	VF-20	EF-40	AU-50	MS-60	MS-63	PF-63	PF-65
1927S	2,392,000	$1.60	$1.75	$4.00	$13.00	$45.	$125.	$350.	$900.		
1928S	1,940,000	1.60	1.75	4.00	15.00	50.	125.	350.	$1,000.		
1929D	1,001,200	1.60	1.75	3.50	9.00	30.	100.	150.	300.		
1929S	1,902,000	1.60	1.75	3.50	8.50	35.	100.	150.	350.		
1933S	1,786,000	1.60	1.75	3.00	6.00	21.	100.	200.	475.		
1934	6,964,000	1.50	1.50	1.60	2.00	4.	12.	30.	45.		
1934D	2,361,000	1.50	1.50	1.60	3.00	12.	35.	60.	80.		
1934S	3,652,000	1.50	1.50	1.60	2.25	13.	40.	140.	350.		
1935	9,162,000	1.50	1.50	1.60	2.00	3.	8.	20.	25.		
1935D	3,003,800	1.50	1.50	1.60	2.25	12.	25.	60.	100.		
1935S	3,854,000	1.50	1.50	1.60	2.25	12.	40.	80.	175.		
1936 (3,901)	12,617,901	1.50	1.50	1.60	2.00	3.	8.	20.	25.	$675.	$2,000.
1936D	4,252,400	1.50	1.50	1.60	2.25	7.	15.	40.	50.		
1936S	3,884,000	1.50	1.50	1.60	2.25	7.	16.	65.	70.		
1937 (5,728)	9,527,728	1.50	1.50	1.60	2.00	3.	8.	18.	21.	250.	600.
1937D	1,676,000	1.50	1.50	2.00	3.00	12.	26.	80.	100.		
1937S	2,090,000	1.50	1.50	1.60	2.25	7.	16.	65.	90.		
1938 (8,152)	4,118,152	1.50	1.50	1.60	2.00	4.	15.	27.	50.	225.	500.
1938D	491,600	12.00	14.00	17.00	25.00	50.	90.	200.	250.		
1939 (8,808)	6,820,808	1.50	1.50	1.60	2.00	3.	8.	18.	21.	225.	475.
1939D	4,267,800	1.50	1.50	1.60	2.00	4.	8.	20.	30.		
1939S	2,552,000	1.50	1.50	1.60	2.00	6.	16.	45.	55.		

	Mintage	VG-8	F-12	VF-20	EF-40	AU-50	MS-60	MS-63	PF-63	PF-65
1940 (11,279)	9,167,279	$1.50	$1.50	$1.60	$2.	$4.	$13.	$20.	$175.	$450.
1940S	4,550,000	1.50	1.50	1.60	2.	5.	15.	30.		
1941 (15,412)	24,207,412	1.50	1.50	1.60	2.	4.	12.	20.	160.	400.
1941D	11,248,400	1.50	1.50	1.60	2.	4.	15.	25.		
1941S	8,098,000	1.50	1.50	1.60	2.	10.	30.	50.		
1942 (21,120)	47,839,120	1.50	1.50	1.60	2.	4.	12.	20.	175.	450.
1942D	10,973,800	1.50	1.50	1.60	2.	4.	14.	25.		
1942S	12,708,000	1.50	1.50	1.60	2.	4.	15.	23.		
1943	53,190,000	1.50	1.50	1.60	2.	4.	12.	15.		
1943D	11,346,000	1.50	1.50	1.60	2.	4.	16.	25.		
1943S	13,450,000	1.50	1.50	1.60	2.	4.	15.	20.		
1944	28,206,000	1.50	1.50	1.60	2.	4.	12.	15.		
1944D	9,769,000	1.50	1.50	1.60	2.	4.	14.	20.		
1944S	8,904,000	1.50	1.50	1.60	2.	4.	16.	23.		
1945	3,152,000	1.50	1.50	1.60	2.	4.	12.	15.		
1945D	9,966,800	1.50	1.50	1.60	2.	4.	12.	17.		
1945S	10,156,000	1.50	1.50	1.60	2.	4.	12.	18.		
1946	12,118,000	1.50	1.50	1.60	2.	4.	12.	15.		
1946D	2,151,000	1.50	1.50	1.60	2.	4.	12.	15.		
1946S	3,724,000	1.50	1.50	1.60	2.	4.	12.	15.		
1947	4,094,000	1.50	1.50	1.60	2.	4.	12.	15.		
1947D	3,900,600	1.50	1.50	1.60	2.	4.	12.	15.		

FRANKLIN-LIBERTY BELL TYPE 1948-1963

The Benjamin Franklin half dollar and the Roosevelt dime were both designed by John R. Sinnock. His initials appear below the shoulder.

VF-20 VERY FINE—*At least half of the lower and upper incused lines on the rim of the bell must show.*
EF-40 EXTREMELY FINE—*Wear spots appear at top of end curls and hair back of ears. On reverse, Liberty Bell will show wear at top and on lettering.*
MS-60 UNCIRCULATED—*No trace of wear. A few noticeable blemishes.*
MS-63 SELECT UNCIRCULATED—*No trace of wear. Light blemishes. Attractive mint luster.*
MS-65—CHOICE UNCIRCULATED—*Only light scattered contact marks that are not distracting. Strong luster, good eye appeal.*
PF-63—*Reflective surfaces with only a few blemishes in secondary focal places. No major flaws.*
PF-65—*Choice Brilliant surfaces with no noticeable blemishes or flaws. May have a few scatered barely noticeable marks or hairlines.*

Mint mark location

Choice, well -struck uncirculated halves command higher prices.

	Mintage	VF-20	EF-40	MS-60	MS-63	MS-65	PF-63	PF-65
1948	3,006,814	$1.75	$2.00	$5.00	$8.00	$35.00		
1948D	4,028,600	1.50	1.75	4.00	6.00	60.00		
1949	5,614,000	1.50	2.00	15.00	20.00	65.00		
1949D	4,120,600	1.50	3.00	15.00	22.00	375.00		
1949S	3,744,000	1.50	5.00	25.00	35.00	60.00		
1950 .....(51,386)	7,793,509	1.50	1.75	10.00	15.00	50.00	$115.00	$200.
1950D	8,031,600	1.50	1.75	9.00	15.00	200.00		
1951 .....(57,500)	16,859,602	1.50	1.75	4.00	7.00	30.00	65.00	150.
1951D	9,475,200	1.50	2.00	10.00	14.00	120.00		
1951S	13,696,000	1.50	1.75	9.00	13.00	50.00		
1952 .....(81,980)	21,274,073	1.50	1.75	3.00	7.00	27.00	35.00	100.
1952D	25,395,600	1.50	1.75	2.75	4.00	100.00		
1952S	5,526,000	1.50	2.00	15.00	20.00	50.00		
1953 ....(128,800)	2,796,920	1.75	2.00	6.00	10.00	100.00	26.00	55.
1953D	20,900,400	1.50	1.50	3.00	5.00	50.00		
1953S	4,148,000	1.50	2.00	7.00	10.00	27.00		
1954 ....(233,300)	13,421,502	1.50	1.50	2.00	4.00	27.00	18.00	45.
1954D	25,445,580	1.50	1.50	2.50	4.50	60.00		
1954S	4,993,400	1.50	1.50	3.00	4.50	25.00		
1955 ....(378,200)	2,876,381	3.50	4.00	5.00	7.00	25.00	14.00	40.
1956 ....(669,384)	4,701,384	1.50	1.50	2.00	5.00	20.00	5.00	20.
1957 ...(1,247,952)	6,361,952	1.50	1.50	2.00	4.50	20.00	5.00	12.
1957D	1,966,850	1.50	1.50	2.00	4.50	20.00		
1958 ....(875,652)	4,917,652	1.50	1.50	2.00	5.00	20.00	5.00	15.
1958D	23,962,412	1.50	1.50	2.00	4.50	20.00		
1959 ...(1,149,291)	7,349,291	1.50	1.50	2.00	4.50	50.00	3.00	12.
1959D	13,053,750	1.50	1.50	2.00	4.50	60.00		
1960 ...(1,691,602)	7,715,602	1.50	1.50	1.60	4.50	60.00	3.00	12.
1960D	18,215,812	1.50	1.50	2.00	6.00	20.00		
1961 ...(3,028,244)	11,318,244	1.50	1.50	2.00	4.00	65.00	2.50	17.
1961D	20,276,442	1.50	1.50	2.00	4.00	100.00		
1962 ...(3,218,019)	12,932,019	1.50	1.50	2.00	4.00	90.00	2.50	10.
1962D	35,473,281	1.50	1.50	2.00	4.00	120.00		
1963 ...(3,075,645)	25,239,645	1.50	1.50	2.00	4.00	28.00	2.50	12.
1963D	67,069,292	1.50	1.50	2.00	4.00	28.00		

KENNEDY TYPE 1964 to Date

Gilroy Roberts, former Chief Engraver of the Mint, designed the obverse of this coin. His stylized initials are on the truncation of the forceful bust of President John F. Kennedy. The reverse, which uses the presidential coat of arms for the motif, is the work of Chief Engraver Frank Gasparro.

1964 Mint mark location

1968 Mint mark location

Silver Coinage 1964

	Mintage	MS-63	PF-63	PF-65
1964 . . . .(3,950,762)	277,254,766	$1.50	$2.50	$4.00
1964D	156,205,446	1.50		

Silver-Clad Coinage 1965-1970

	Mintage	MS-63	PF-63	PF-65
1965	65,879,366	$.75		
1966	108,984,932	.75		
1967	295,046,978	.75		
1968D	246,951,930	.75		
1968S, Pf . . . .(3,041,506)			$1.00	$2.00
1969D	129,881,800	.75		
1969S, Pf . . . .(2,934,631)			1.00	2.00
1970D, (Issued only in mint sets)	2,150,000	7.00		
1970S, Pf . . . .(2,632,810)			4.00	6.00

Copper-Nickel Clad Coinage 1971-

	Mintage	MS-63	PF-63	PF-65
1971	155,164,000	$.55		
1971D	302,097,424	.55		
1971S, Pf	(3,220,733)		$.75	$1.25
1972	153,180,000	.60		
1972	141,890,000	.60		
1972S, Pf	(3,260,996)		.75	1.25
1973	64,964,000	$.55		
1973D	83,171,400	.55		
1973S, Pf	(2,760,339)		$.75	$1.00
1974	201,596,000	.55		
1974D	79,066,300	.55		
1974S, Pf	(2,612,568)		.75	1.00

BICENTENNIAL COINAGE DATED 1776—1976

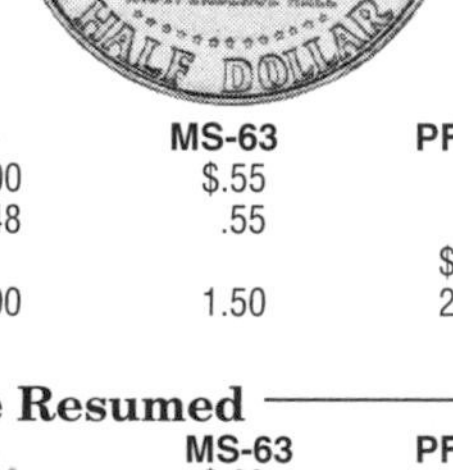

	Mintage	MS-63	PF-63	PF-65
1776-1976, Copper-nickel clad	234,308,000	$.55		
1776-1976D, Copper-nickel clad	287,565,248	.55		
1776-1976S, Copper-nickel clad (7,059,099)			$.75	$1.00
1776-1976S, Silver clad . . . . . .*(4,000,000)	*11,000,000	1.50	2.00	2.25

Eagle Reverse Resumed

	Mintage	MS-63	PF-63	PF-65
1977	43,598,000	$.60		
1977D	31,449,106	.60		

*Approximate mintage.

	Mintage	MS-63	PF-63	PF-65
1977S, Pf(3,251,152)			$1.00	$1.25
1978	14,350,000	$.60		
1978D	13,765,799	1.00		
1978S, Pf(3,127,781)			1.00	1.25
1979	68,312,000	.55		
1979D	15,815,422	.55		
1979S, Pf				
1979S, Pf, Filled S			1.00	1.25
1979S, Pf, Clear S			6.00	7.00
1980P	44,134,000	.55		
1980D	33,456,449	.55		
1980S, Pf(3,554,806)			1.00	1.50
1981P	29,544,000	.75		
1981D	27,839,533	.55		
1981S, Pf(4,063,083)			1.00	1.50
1982P	10,819,000	1.50		
1982D	13,140,102	1.50		
1982S, Pf(3,857,479)			1.00	1.50
1983P	34,139,000	1.75		
1983D	32,472,244	1.75		
1983S, Pf(3,279,126)			1.00	1.75
1984P	26,029,000	.75		
1984D	26,262,158	.75		
1984S, Pf(3,065,110)			1.00	2.00
1985P	18,706,962	1.00		
1985D	19,814,034	1.25		
1985S, Pf(3,362,821)			1.00	1.75
1986P	13,107,633	2.50		
1986D	15,336,145	2.00		
1986S, Pf(3,010,497)			4.00	4.50
1987P	*2,890,758	1.50		
1987D	*2,890,758	1.50		
1987S, Pf(4,227,728)			1.00	1.75
1988P	13,626,000	1.50		
1988D	1,200,096	1.00		
1988S, Pf(3,262,948)			2.00	2.50
1989P	24,542,000	1.00		
1989D	23,000,216	.90		
1989S, Pf(3,220,194)			1.50	2.00
1990P	22,278,000	1.00		
1990D	20,096,242	1.10		
1990S, Pf(3,299,559)			1.50	2.00
1991P	14,874,000	.75		
1991D	15,054,678	1.25		
1991S, Pf(2,867,787)			4.50	5.00
1992P	17,628,000	.50		
1992D	17,000,106	1.00		
1992S, Pf(2,858,981)			3.00	3.50
1992S, Silver Pf	(1,317,579)		4.00	5.00

	Mintage	MS-63	PF-63	PF-65
1993P	15,510,000	$.50		
1993D	15,000,006	.50		
1993S, Pf(2,633,439)			$5.00	$6.00
1993S, Silver Pf	(761,353)		9.00	10.00
1994P	23,718,000	.50		
1994D	23,828,110	.50		
1994S, Pf(2,484,594)			3.00	4.00
1994S, Silver Pf	(785,329)		15.00	18.00
1995P	26,496,000	.50		
1995D	26,288,000	.50		
1995S, Pf(2,117,496)			12.00	15.00
1995S, Silver Pf	(679,985)		40.00	50.00
1996P	24,442,000	.50		
1996D	24,744,000	.50		
1996S, Pf(1,750,244)			3.00	4.00
1996S, Silver Pf	(775,021)		20.00	25.00
1997P	20,882,000	.50		
1997D	19,876,000	.50		
1997S, Pf(2,055,000)			9.00	11.00
1997S, Silver Pf	(741,678)		40.00	50.00
1998P	15,646,000	.50		
1998D	15,064,000	.50		
1998S, Pf(2,086,507)			5.00	7.00
1998S, Silver Pf	878,792		9.00	14.00
1998S, Silver Matte Finish			125.00	150.00
1999P	8,900,000	.55		
1999D	10,682,000	.55		
1999S, Pf(2,543,401)			3.00	5.00
1999S, Silver Pf	(800,000)		7.00	12.00
2000P	22,600,000	.60		
2000D	19,466,000	.60		
2000S, Pf(3,082,483)			2.00	3.00
2000S, Silver Pf	(856,400)		4.00	5.00
2001P	21,200,000	4.00		
2001D	19,504,000	.55		
2001S, Pf(2,294,043)			4.00	5.00
2001S, Silver Pf	(889,697)		5.00	7.00
2002P	3,100,000	.65		
2002D	2,500,000	.65		
2002S, Pf(2,277,720)			2.00	3.00
2002S, Silver Pf	(761,600)		5.00	6.00
2003P		.65		
2003D		.65		
2003S, Pf			2.00	3.00
2003S, Silver Pf			5.00	6.00
2004P		.65		
2004D		.65		
2004S, Pf			2.00	3.00
2004S, Silver Pf			5.00	6.00

*Not issued for circulation; included with uncirculated and souvenir sets.

SILVER DOLLARS — 1794 to Date

The silver dollar was authorized by Congress April 2, 1792. Weight and fineness were specified at 416 grains and 892.4 fine. The first issues appeared in 1794 and until 1804 all silver dollars had the value stamped on the edge: HUNDRED CENTS, ONE DOLLAR OR UNIT. After a lapse in coinage of the silver dollar during the period 1804 to 1835, coins were made with either plain or reeded edges and the value was placed on the reverse side.

The weight was changed by the law of January 18, 1837 to 412½ grains, fineness .900. The coinage was discontinued by the Act of February 12, 1873 and reauthorized by the Act of February 28, 1878. The dollar was again discontinued after 1935, and since then only the copper-nickel pieces first authorized in 1971 have been coined for circulation.

FLOWING HAIR TYPE 1794-1795

AG-3 ABOUT GOOD—*Clear enough to identify.*
G-4 GOOD—*Date and letters readable. Main devices outlined, but lack details.*
VG-8 VERY GOOD—*Major details discernible. Letters well formed but worn.*
F-12 FINE—*Hair ends distinguishable. Top hairlines show, but otherwise worn smooth.*
VF-20 VERY FINE—*Hair in center shows some detail. Other details more bold.*
EF-40 EXTREMELY FINE—*Hair well defined but will show some wear.*
AU-50 ABOUT UNCIRCULATED—*Traces of light wear on only the high points of the design. Half of mint luster is present.*
MS-60 UNCIRCULATED—*No trace of wear. Light blemishes.*

	Mintage	AG-3	G-4	VG-8	F-12	VF-20	EF-40	AU-50	MS-60
1794	1,758	$6,000.	$12,000.	$18,000.	$22,000.	$40,000.	$70,000.	$100,000.	—
1795	*160,295*	350.	600.	800.	1,500.	2,300.	4,600.	8,000.	$18,000.

— DRAPED BUST TYPE, SMALL EAGLE REVERSE 1795-1798 —

AG-3 ABOUT GOOD—*Clear enough to identify.*
G-4 GOOD—*Bust outlined, no detail. Date readable, some leaves evident.*
VG-8 VERY GOOD—*Drapery worn except deepest folds. Hairlines smooth.*
F-12 FINE—*All drapery lines distinguishable. Hairlines near cheek and neck show some detail.*
VF-20 VERY FINE—*Left side of drapery worn smooth.*
EF-40 EXTREMELY FINE—*Drapery shows distinctly. Hair well outlined and detailed.*
AU-50 ABOUT UNCIRCULATED—*Traces of light wear on only the high points of the design. Half of mint luster is present.*
MS-60 UNCIRCULATED—*No trace of wear. Light blemishes.*

	Mintage	AG-3	G-4	VG-8	F-12	VF-20	EF-40	AU-50	MS-60
1795, BUST TYPE		$300.	$450.	$600.	$950.	$1,800.	$3,000.	$4,000.	$14,000
1796, All kinds	79,920	300.	450.	600.	950.	1,800.	3,000.	4,000.	14,000.
1797	57,776	300.	450.	600.	950.	1,800.	3,000.	4,000.	14,000.
1798, All kinds	*277,536*	300.	450.	600.	950.	1,800.	3,000.	4,000.	14,000.

SILVER DOLLARS
HERALDIC EAGLE REVERSE 1798-1804

G-4 GOOD—*Letters and date readable. E PLURIBUS UNUM obliterated.*
VG-8 VERY GOOD—*Motto partially readable. Only deepest drapery details visible. All other lines smooth.*
F-12 FINE—*All drapery lines distinguishable. Harlines near cheek and neck show some detail.*
VF-20 VERY FINE—*Left side of drapery worn smooth.*
EF-40 EXTREMELY FINE—*Drapery is distinct. Hair well detailed.*
AU-50 ABOUT UNCIRCULATED—*Traces of light wear on only the high points of the design. Half of mint luster is present.*
MS-60 UNCIRCULATED—*No trace of wear. Light blemishes.*

	Mintage	G-4	VG-8	F-12	VF-20	EF-40	AU-50	MS-60
1798, Heraldic Eagle		$300.	$350.	$500.	$900.	$1,500.	$2,500.	$7,500.
1799, All kinds	423,515	300.	350.	500.	900.	1,500.	2,500.	7,500.
1800, All kinds	220,920	300.	350.	500.	900.	1,500.	2,500.	7,500.
1801	54,454	300.	350.	500.	900.	1,500.	2,500.	7,500.
1802, All kinds	41,650	300.	350.	500.	900.	1,500.	2,500.	7,500.
1803	85,634	300.	350.	500.	900.	1,500.	2,500.	8,000.
1804, Variety 1, O Above Cloud							Proof	1,000,000.
1804, Variety 2, O Above Space BTW. Cloud							Proof	800,000.

GOBRECHT SILVER DOLLARS

Silver dollars of 1836, 1838, and 1839 were mostly made as trial pieces, but some were made in quantities for general circulation. There was no regular issue of dollars 1805 to 1835 inclusive.

	VF-20	EF-40	AU-50	PF-60
1836, c. GOBRECHT F. on base. Rev. Eagle flying upward amid stars. Plain edge. Although scarce, this is the most common variety and was issued for circulation as regular coinage	$3,000.	$5,000.	$7,000.	$8,000.
1838, Similar obv., designer's name omitted, stars added around border. Rev. Eagle flying left in plain field. Reeded edge	6,000.	8,000.	10,000.	12,000.
1839, Obv. as above. Rev. Eagle in plain field. Reeded edge. Issued for circulation as regular coinage	6,000.	8,000.	9,000.	11,000.

SILVER DOLLARS

LIBERTY SEATED TYPE — REGULAR ISSUES 1840-1873

In 1840 silver dollars were again issued for general circulation, and the seated figure of Liberty device was adopted for the obverse, and a heraldic eagle on the reverse.

VG-8 VERY GOOD—*Any 3 letters of LIBERTY at least two-thirds complete.*
F-12 FINE—*All 7 letters of LIBERTY visible though weak.*
VF-20 VERY FINE—*LIBERTY is strong but its ribbon shows slight wear.*
EF-40 EXTREMELY FINE—*Horizontal lines of shield complete. Eagle's eye plain.*
AU-50 ABOUT UNCIRCULATED—*Traces of light wear on only the high points of the design. Half of mint luster is present.*
MS-60 UNCIRCULATED—*No trace of wear. Light marks or blemishes.*
PF-60—*Surface may have several contact marks, hairlines or light rubs. Luster may be dull and eye appeal lacking.*
PF-63—*Reflective surfaces with only a few blemishes in secondary focal places. No major flaws.*

Mint mark location is on the reverse below eagle.

	Mintage	VG-8	F-12	VF-20	EF-40	AU-50	MS-60	PF-60	PF-63
1840	61,005	$75.	$100.	$150.	$225.	$300.	$800.	$5,000.	$12,000.
1841	173,000	60.	90.	125.	200.	250.	750.	5,000.	12,000.
1842	184,618	60.	90.	125.	200.	250.	650.	5,000.	12,000.
1843	165,100	60.	90.	125.	200.	250.	700.	5,000.	12,000.
1844	20,000	70.	100.	150.	225.	300.	1,000.	5,000.	13,000.
1845	24,500	70.	100.	150.	225.	300.	2,000.	5,000.	12,000.
1846	110,600	60.	90.	125.	200.	250.	650.	5,000.	12,000.
1846O	59,000	75.	100.	150.	250.	350.	1,500.		
1847	140,750	60.	90.	125.	200.	250.	650.	5,000.	12,000.
1848	15,000	125.	200.	275.	375.	500.	1,200.	5,000.	12,000.
1849	62,600	60.	90.	125.	200.	250.	700.	5,000.	14,000.
1850	7,500	150.	250.	300.	500.	700.	2,300.	5,000.	12,000.
1850O	40,000	100.	125.	225.	500.	1,200.	3,000.		
1851	1,300	1,500.	2,500.	4,000.	5,000.	7,000.	9,000.	9,000.	15,000.
1852	1,100	1,000.	2,100.	3,500.	4,500.	6,000.	9,000.	10,000.	17,000.
1853	46,110	80.	125.	150.	250.	400.	900.	6,000.	12,000.
1854	33,140	400.	550.	800.	1,400.	1,800.	2,500.	5,000.	8,000.
1855	26,000	300.	500.	700.	1,000.	1,200.	2,500.	5,000.	8,000.
1856	63,500	125.	175.	225.	400.	600.	1,600.	2,500.	5,000.
1857	94,000	125.	175.	225.	400.	600.	1,100.	2,200.	4,000.
1858 . . . .(*300+*)		1,200.	1,500.	2,000.	2,500.	3,000.		3,000.	4,500.
1859 . . . . .(800)	256,500	100.	135.	185.	250.	300.	800.	1,000.	1,500.
1859O	360,000	60.	90.	125.	200.	250.	650.		
1859S	20,000	100.	150.	250.	500.	1,000.	4,000.		
1860 . . . .(1,330)	218,930	80.	110.	160.	225.	275.	600.	1,000.	1,500.
1860O	515,000	60.	90.	125.	250.	650.			
1861 . . . .(1,000)	78,500	200.	250.	350.	450.	600.	1,000.	1,000.	1,500.
1862 . . . . .(550)	12,090	150.	250.	350.	450.	600.	1,000.	1,000.	1,500.
1863 . . . . .(460)	27,660	125.	150.	200.	275.	400.	1,000.	900.	1,500.
1864 . . . . .(470)	31,170	90.	125.	175.	250.	375.	900.	1,500.	1,500.
1865 . . . . .(500)	47,000	90.	125.	150.	250.	375.	900.	900.	1,500.

Motto "In God We Trust" Added to Reverse

	Mintage	VG-8	F-12	VF-20	EF-40	AU-50	MS-60	PF-60	PF-63
1866 . . . .(725)	49,625	$75.	$120.	$150.	$200.	$300.	$700.	$800.	$1,400.
1867 . . . .(625)	47,525	75.	120.	150.	200.	300.	700.	800.	1,400.
1868 . . . .(600)	162,700	65.	100.	150.	200.	300.	700.	800.	1,400.
1869 . . . .(600)	424,300	65.	100.	150.	200.	300.	700.	800.	1,400.
1870 . . . .(1,000)	416,000	65.	100.	150.	200.	250.	500.	800.	1,400.
1870CC	11,758	150.	225.	350.	650.	1,000.	3,500.		
1870S			30,000.	50,000.	100,000.	200,000.	300,000.		
1871 . . . .(960)	1,074,760	65.	100.	150.	200.	250.	500.	800.	1,400.
1871CC	1,376	1,000.	2,000.	3,000.	4,000.	6,000.	20,000.		
1872 . . . .(950)	1,106,450	65.	100.	150.	200.	250.	500.	800.	1,400.
1872CC	3,150	500.	800.	1,400.	2,000.	3,000.	8,500.		
1872S	9,000	100.	150.	275.	400.	900.	3,300.		
1873 . . . .(600)	293,600	65.	100.	150.	200	250.	500.	800.	1,400.
1873CC	2,300	2,000.	3,000.	5,000.	7,000.	10,000.	30,000.		

TRADE DOLLARS 1873-1885

This coin was issued for circulation in the Orient to compete with dollar-size coins of other countries. It weighed 420 grains compared to 412 1/2 grains, the weight of the regular silver dollar.

VG-8 VERY GOOD—*About half of mottoes IN GOD WE TRUST and E PLURIBUS UNUM will show. Rim on both sides well defined.*
F-12 FINE—*Mottoes and LIBERTY readable but worn.*
EF-40 EXTREMELY FINE—*Mottoes and LIBERTY are sharp. Only slight wear on rims.*
AU-50 ABOUT UNCIRCULATED—*Traces of light wear on only the high points of the design. Half of mint luster is present.*
MS-60 UNCIRCULATED—*No trace of wear. Light blemishes.*
MS-63 SELECT UNCIRCULATED—*Some distracting contact marks or blemishes in prime focal areas. Luster may be impaired.*
PF-63—*Reflective surfaces with only a few blemishes in secondary focal places. No major flaws.*

1875S
S over CC

TRADE DOLLARS 1873-1885

	Mintage	VG-8	F-12	EF-40	AU-50	MS-60	MS-63	PF-63
1873 . . . .(865)	397,500	$35.	$45.	$75.	$100.	$250.	$600.	$1,000.
1873CC	124,500	50.	75.	200.	500.	1,000.	5,000.	
1873S	703,000	35.	45.	75.	100.	250.	600.	
1874 . . . .(700)	987,800	35.	45.	75.	100.	250.	600.	1,000.
1874CC	1,373,200	50.	75.	100.	150.	450.	2,000.	
1874S	2,549,000	35.	45.	75.	100.	250.	600.	
1875 . . . .(700)	218,900	60.	110.	200.	300.	650.	1,000.	1,000.
1875CC	1,573,700	50.	75.	100.	150.	325.	900.	
1875S	} 4,487,000	35.	45.	75.	100.	250.	600.	
1875S, S/CC		80.	120.	300.	500.	1,000.	4,000.	
1876 . . . .(1,150)	456,150	35.	45.	75.	100.	250.	600.	1,000.
1876CC	509,000	50.	75.	125.	200.	900.	5,000.	
1876S	5,227,000	35.	45.	75.	100.	250.	600.	
1877 . . . .(510)	3,039,710	35.	45.	75.	100.	275.	600.	1,000.
1877CC	534,000	50.	75.	150.	200.	450.	2,500.	
1877S	9,519,000	35.	45.	75.	100.	250.	600.	
1878 . . . .(900)								1,000.
1878CC	97,000	125.	250.	800.	1,200.	4,000.	8,000.	
1878S	4,162,000	35.	45.	75.	100.	250.	600.	
1879 . . . .(1,541)								1,000.
1880 . . . .(1,987)								1,000.
1881 . . . .(960)								1,100.
1882 . . . .(1,097)								1,100.
1883 . . . .(979)								1,100.
1884 . . . .(10)								100,000.
1885 . . . .(5)								250,000.

LIBERTY HEAD OR MORGAN TYPE 1878-1921

George T. Morgan, formerly a pupil of Wyon at the Royal Mint in London, designed the new dollar. His initial M is found at the truncation of the neck, at the last tress. It also appears on the reverse on the left-hand loop of the ribbon.

Sharply struck "Proof-like" coins have a highly reflective surface and usually command substantial premiums.

VF-20 VERY FINE—*Two-thirds of hairlines from top of forehead to ear must show. Ear well defined. Feathers on eagle's breast worn.*
EF-40 EXTREMELY FINE—*All hairlines strong and ear bold. Eagle's feathers all plain but slight wear on breast and wing tips.*
AU-50 ABOUT UNCIRCULATED—*Slight trace of wear. Most of mint luster is present although marred by bag marks.*
MS-60 UNCIRCULATED—*No trace of wear. Has full mint luster, but may be noticeably marred by scuff marks or bag abrasions.*
MS-63 SELECT UNCIRCULATED—*No trace of wear, full mint luster, few noticeable surface marks.*
MS-65—CHOICE UNCIRCULATED—*Only light scattered contact marks that are not distracting. Strong luster, good eye appeal.*

Most uncirculated silver dollars have scratches or nicks because of handling of mint bags. Choice sharply struck coins with full brilliance and without blemishes are worth more than listed values.

8 Tail Feathers, 1878 Philadelphia Only
Mint mark location on the reverse below wreath

	Mintage	VF-20	EF-40	AU-50	MS-60	MS-63	MS-65
1878, 8 Feathers . .(500)	750,000	$9.	$13.	$16.	$40.	$50.	$500.
1878, 7 Feathers . .(250)	9,759,550	7.	10.	12.	25.	35.	500.
1878, Clear double Feathers		12.	14.	22.	45.	100.	1,200.
1878CC	2,212,000	40.	50.	60.	85.	140.	750.
1878S	9,774,000	7.	8.	10.	20.	30.	100.
1879 . . . .(1,100)	14,807,100	7.	8.	10.	15.	25.	400.
1879CC, CC / CC	756,000	50.	150.	300.	900.	2,000.	1,000.
1879O	2,887,000	7.	8.	10.	25.	65.	1,200.
1879S,	9,110,000	7.	8.	10.	15.	20.	60.
1880 . . . .(1,355)	12,601,355	7.	8.	10.	15.	20.	300.
1880CC, All Kinds	591,000	60.	75.	100.	200.	250.	500.
1880O	5,305,000	7.	8.	10.	25.	150.	5,000.
1880S	8,900,000	7.	8.	10.	15.	20.	60.
1881 . . . .(984)	9,163,984	7.	8.	10.	15.	20.	300.
1881CC	296,000	100.	125.	150.	175.	200.	300.
1881O	5,708,000	7.	8.	10.	15.	20.	500.
1881S	12,760,000	7.	8.	10.	15.	20.	60.
1882 . . . .(1,100)	11,101,100	7.	8.	10.	15.	22.	140.
1882CC	1,133,000	40.	45.	50.	75.	90.	150.
1882O	6,090,000	7.	8.	10.	15.	20.	250.
1882S	9,250,000	7.	8.	10.	15.	20.	60.
1883 . . . .(1,039)	12,291,039	7.	8.	10.	15.	20.	70.
1883CC	1,204,000	40.	45.	50.	75.	90.	150.
1883O	8,725,000	7.	8.	10.	15.	20.	60.
1883S	6,250,000	8.	11.	50.	225.	850.	5,000.
1884 . . . .(875)	14,070,875	7.	8.	10.	15.	20.	100.
1884CC	1,136,000	40.	45.	50.	75.	90.	150.
1884O	9,730,000	7.	8.	10.	15.	20.	60.
1884S	3,200,000	8.	15.	100.	1,800.	10,000.	75,000.
1885 . . . .(930)	17,787,930	7.	8.	10.	15.	20.	60.
1885CC	228,000	100.	125.	150.	200.	250.	500.
1885O	9,185,000	7.	8.	10.	15.	20.	60.
1885S	1,497,000	7.	15.	40.	60.	90.	500.
1886 . . . .(886)	19,963,886	7.	8.	10.	15.	20.	60.
1886O	10,710,000	7.	9.	30.	200.	1,500.	75,000.
1886S	750,000	15.	25.	35.	100.	150.	1,000.
1887 . . . .(710)	20,290,710	7.	8.	10.	15.	20.	60.
1887O	11,550,000	7.	8.	10.	18.	45.	1,200.
1887S	1,771,000	7.	8.	15.	40.	100.	1,200.
1888 . . . .(832)	19,183,932	7.	8.	10.	15.	20.	70.
1888O	12,150,000	7.	8.	10.	18.	20.	150.
1888S	657,000	25.	35.	45.	100.	150.	1,000.
1889 . . . .(811)	21,726,811	7.	8.	10.	15.	20.	100.
1889CC	350,000	500.	1,000.	2,000.	6,000.	12,000.	100,000.
1889O	11,875,000	7.	8.	16.	50.	150.	1,500.

Proof Morgan Dollars where indicated in mintage records (quantity shown in parentheses) are valued approximately as follows:

Proof-60 $400.00 **Proof-63** $850.00 **Proof-65** $2,700

	Mintage	VF-20	EF-40	AU-50	MS-60	MS-63	MS-65
1890S	8,230,373	$7.	$8.	$11.	$20.	$40.	$250.
1891 ...(650)	8,694,206	7.	8.	13.	20.	65.	2,000.
1891CC	1,618,000	40.	50.	75.	150.	300.	1,500.
1891O	7,954,529	8.	11.	20.	50.	125.	2,500.
1891S	5,296,000	7.	8.	11.	25.	50.	350.
1892 ..(1,245)	1,037,245	8.	11.	30.	65.	150.	1,200.
1892CC	1,352,000	50.	125.	175.	300.	700.	2,500.
1892O	2,744,000	9.	11.	27.	60.	125.	1,500.
1892S	1,200,000	22.	75.	850.	10,000.	24,000.	65,000.
1893 ...(792)	378,792	45.	65.	100.	200.	400.	2,500.
1893CC	677,000	125.	500.	750.	1,000.	2,000.	18,000.
1893O	300,000	65.	125.	300.	800.	2,800.	80,000.
1893S	100,000	2,500.	3,500.	9,000.	30,000.	50,000.	150,000.
1894 ...(972)	110,972	400.	500.	800.	1,000.	2,000.	8,000.
1894O	1,723,000	20.	30.	90.	275.	1,500.	16,000.
1894S	1,260,000	25.	50.	150.	220.	400.	2,000.
1895 ...(880)	12,880		†12,000.	†15,000.	†18,000.	†25,000.	†30,000.
1895O	450,000	90.	125.	500.	6,000.	16,000.	75,000.
1895S	400,000	110.	225.	500.	800.	2,000.	7,000.
1896 ...(762)	9,976,762	7.	8.	10.	15.	20.	75.
1896O	4,900,000	7.	8.	60.	400.	3,500.	60,000.
1896S	5,000,000	20.	70.	200.	500.	900.	5,000.
1897 ...(731)	2,822,731	7.	8.	10.	15.	20.	75.
1897O	4,004,000	7.	8.	45.	275.	2,000.	18,000.
1897S	5,825,000	7.	8.	11.	25.	40.	200.
1898 ...(735)	5,884,735	7.	8.	10.	15.	20.	90.
1898O	4,440,000	7.	8.	10.	15.	20.	60.
1898S	4,102,000	7.	12.	35.	90.	150.	500.
1899 ...(846)	330,846	20.	25.	35.	45.	80.	250.
1899O	12,290,000	7.	8.	10.	15.	20.	60.
1899S	2,562,000	10.	15.	40.	125.	175.	500.
1900 ...(912)	8,830,912	7.	8.	10.	15.	20.	70.
1900O	12,590,000	7.	8.	10.	15.	20.	60.
1900S	3,540,000	8.	15.	30.	100.	150.	400.
1901 ...(813)	6,962,813	15.	25.	150.	825.	6,000.	75,000.
1901O	13,320,000	7.	8.	10.	15.	20.	75.
1901S	2,284,000	12.	20.	60.	140.	250.	1,200.
1902 ...(777)	7,994,777	7.	8.	10.	18.	40.	150.
1902O	8,636,000	7.	8.	10.	15.	20.	60.
1902S	1,530,000	35.	45.	100.	125.	225.	1,000.
1903 ...(755)	4,652,755	15.	20.	25.	30.	35.	100.
1903O	4,450,000	90.	100.	125.	150.	170.	250.
1903S	1,241,000	35.	125.	600.	1,400.	2,300.	2,600.
1904 ...(650)	2,788,650	7.	8.	15.	30.	100.	1,500.
1904O	3,720,000	7.	8.	10.	15.	20.	60.
1904S	2,304,000	22.	80.	275.	500.	900.	2,500.
1921	44,690,000	6.	7.	8.	8.	12.	50.
1921D	20,345,000	6.	7.	8.	14.	25.	100.
1921S	21,695,000	6.	7.	8.	11.	25.	500.

†Values are for proofs.

Proof Morgan Dollars where indicated in mintage records (quantity shown in parenthesis) are valued approximately as follows:

Proof-60 $400.00 **Proof-63** $850.00 **Proof-65** $2,700

SILVER DOLLARS
PEACE TYPE 1921-1935

Anthony De Francisci, a medalist, designed this dollar. His monogram is located in the field of the coin under the neck of Liberty.

VF-20 VERY FINE—*Hair over eye well worn. Some strands over ear well defined. Some eagle feathers on top and outside edge of right wing will show.*

EF-40 EXTREMELY FINE—*Hairlines over brow and ear are strong though slightly worn. Outside wing feathers at right and those at top are visible but faint.*

AU-50 ABOUT UNCIRCULATED—*Slight trace of wear. Most of mint luster is present although marred by contact marks.*

MS-60 UNCIRCULATED—*No trace of wear. Has full mint luster but may be noticeably marred by stains, surface marks or bag abrasions.*

MS-63 SELECT UNCIRCULATED—*No trace of wear, full mint luster, few noticeable surface marks.*

MS-63 SELECT UNCIRCULATED—*No trace of wear, full mint luster, few noticeable surface marks.*

MS-65—CHOICE UNCIRCULATED—*Only light scattered contact marks that are not distracting. Strong luster, good eye appeal.*

PF-65 CHOICE PROOF—*Brilliant surfaces with no noticable blemishes or flaws. Few scattered barely noticeable marks or hairlines.*

Most uncirculated silver dollars have scratches or nicks because of handling of mint bags. Choice sharply struck coins with full brilliance and without blemishes are worth more than listed values.

Mint mark location is on reverse below one.

	Mintage	VF-20	EF-40	AU-50	MS-60	MS-63	MS-65	PF-65
1921	1,006,473	$30.00	$35.00	$45.	$80.	$140.	$700.	$15,000.
1922	51,737,000	6.00	6.50	7.	8.	12.	60.	15,000.
1922D	15,063,000	6.00	6.50	7.	10.	18.	125.	
1922S	17,475,000	6.00	6.50	7.	10.	25.	500.	
1923	30,800,000	6.00	6.50	7.	8.	12.	60.	
1923D	6,811,000	6.00	6.50	7.	18.	45.	250.	
1923S	19,020,000	6.00	6.50	7.	10.	25.	1,500.	
1924	11,811,000	6.00	6.50	7.	8.	13.	62.	
1924S	1,728,000	7.00	9.00	25.	70.	185.	2,000.	
1925	10,198,000	6.00	6.50	7.	8.	13.	62.	
1925S	1,610,000	6.00	7.00	12.	25.	60.	5,000.	
1926	1,939,000	6.00	6.50	8.	12.	25.	100.	
1926D	2,348,700	6.00	6.50	11.	25.	60.	150.	
1926S	6,980,000	6.00	6.50	8.	15.	30.	200.	
1927	848,000	7.00	10.00	18.	28.	55.	500.	
1927D	1,268,900	7.00	9.00	35.	70.	120.	1,250.	
1927S	866,000	7.00	9.00	25.	65.	125.	2,500.	
1928	360,649	125.00	150.00	175.	200.	250.	1,250.	
1928S	1,632,000	10.00	12.00	20.	55.	200.	5,000.	
1934	954,057	7.00	9.00	15.	40.	75.	250.	
1934D	1,569,500	7.00	8.00	15.	40.	125.	400.	
1934S	1,011,000	22.00	50.00	25.	700.	1,400.	2,500.	
1935	1,576,000	7.00	8.00	12.	25.	40.	150.	
1935S	1,964,000	7.00	9.00	35.	90.	150.	300.	

EISENHOWER DOLLARS 1971-1978

Honoring both President Dwight D. Eisenhower and the first landing of man on the moon, this design is the work of Chief Engraver Frank Gasparro, whose initials are on the truncation and below the eagle. The reverse is an adaptation of the official *Apollo 11* insignia.

Mint mark location is above the date.

	Mintage	EF-40	MS-63	PF-63	PF-65
1971, Copper-nickel clad	47,799,000	$1.05	$1.40		
1971D, Copper-nickel clad	68,587,424	1.05	1.25		
1971S, Silver clad (4,265,234)	6,868,530		2.50	$2.50	$3.50
1972, Copper-nickel clad	75,890,000	1.05	1.25		
1972D, Copper-nickel clad	92,548,511	1.05	1.25		
1972S, Silver clad (1,811,631)	2,193,056		2.50	3.50	
1973, Copper-nickel clad	*2,000,056	1.50	6.00		
1973D, Copper-nickel clad	*2,000,000	1.50	6.00		
1973S, Copper-nickel clad (2,760,339)				3.00	5.00
1973S, Silver clad (1,013,646)	1,883,140	3.50		10.00	15.00
1974, Copper-nickel clad	27,366,000	1.05	1.30		
1974D, Copper-nickel clad	45,517,000	1.05	1.30		
1974S, Copper-nickel clad (2,612,568)				2.50	3.50
1974S, Silver clad (1,306,579)	1,900,156		2.50	2.50	3.50

*1,769,258 of each sold only in sets and not released for circulation. Unissued coins destroyed at mint.

BICENTENNIAL COINAGE DATED 1776-1976

Obverse and Reverse Variety 2 **Reverse Var. 1**

Variety 1: Design in low relief, bold lettering on reverse.
Variety 2: Sharp design, delicate lettering on reverse.

BICENTENNIAL DOLLARS

	Mintage	EF-40	MS-63	PF-63	PF-65
1776-1976, Copper-nickel clad, variety 1	4,019,000	$1.10	$1.50		
1776-1976, Copper-nickel clad, variety 2	113,318,000	1.10	1.20		
1776-1976D,Copper-nickel clad, variety 1	21,048,710	1.10	1.40		
1776-1976D,Copper-nickel clad, variety 2	82,179,564	1.10	1.20		
1776-1976S,Copper-nickel clad, variety 1	(2,845,450)			$0.50	$5.00
1776-1976S,Copper-nickel clad, variety 2	(4,149,730)			2.50	3.50
1776-1976S,Silver clad variety 1	*11,000,000	1.50	4.00		
1776-1976S,Silver clad variety 1	*(4,000,000)			5.00	9.00

*Approximate mintage.

EAGLE REVERSE RESUMED

	Mintage	EF-40	MS-63	PF-63	PF-65
1977, Copper-nickel clad	12,596,000	$1.05	$1.50		
1977D, Copper-nickel clad	32,983,006	1.05	1.25		
1977S, Copper-nickel clad	(3,251,152)			$2.50	$3.50
1978, Copper-nickel clad	25,702,000	1.05	1.25		
1978D, Copper-nickel clad	33,012,890	1.05	1.25		
1978S, Copper-nickel clad	(3,127,781)			2.50	4.50

SUSAN B. ANTHONY DOLLARS 1979-1999

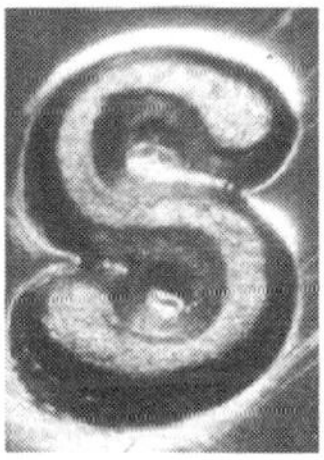

Clear S

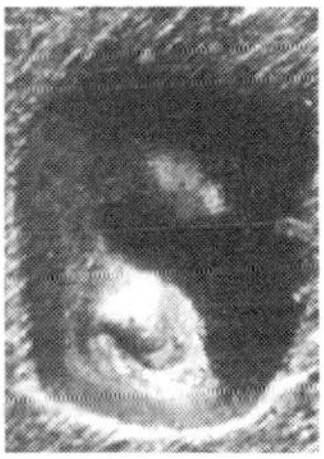

Filled S

	Mintage	MS-63	PF-63	PF-65
1979P, Narrow rim		$1.00		
1979P, Wide rim		2.50		
1979D	288,015,744	1.00		
1979S	109,576,000	1.00		
1979S, Proof, Filled S			$2.50	$5.00
1979S, Proof, Clear S			35.00	50.00
1980P	27,610,000	1.00		
1980D	41,628,708	1.00		
1980S	20,422,000	1.00		

	Mintage	MS-63	PF-63	PF-65
1980S, Proof	(3,554,806)		$2.50	$5.00
1981P	3,000,000	2.00		
1981D	3,250,000	2.00		
1981S	3,492,000	2.00		
1981S, Proof	(4,063,083)		2.50	4.00
1981S, Proof, Clear S			80.00	110.00
1999P	29,592,000	1.05		
1999P Proof			4.00	5.00
1999D	11,776,000	1.15		

The design of this coin was selected in national competition from among 120 submissions that were considered by a panel appointed by Treasury Secretary Robert Rubin. The adopted motif depicts Sacagawea, a young Native American Shoshone as conceived by artist Glenna Goodacre. On her back she carries Jean Baptiste, her infant son. The reverse shows an eagle in flight designed by mint engraver Thomas D. Rogers, Sr.

The composition exemplifies the spirit of Liberty, Peace, and Freedom shown by Sacagawea in her conduct as interpreter and guide to explorers Meriwether Louis and William Clark during their famed journey westward from the great northern plains to the Pacific.

These coins have a distinctive golden color and a plain edge to distinguish them from other denominations or coins of a similar size. The change in composition and appearance was mandated under the United States Dollar Coin Act of 1997.

Several distinctive finishes can be identified on the Sacagawea dollars as a result of the mint attempting to adjust the dies, blanks, strikes or finishing to produce coins with minimum spotting and a better surface color. One group of 5,000 pieces, dated 2000, with a special finish were presented to sculptor Glenna Goodacre in payment for the obverse design. Unexplained error coins made from mismatched dies (a 50-state quarter obverse combined with a Sacagawea dollar reverse) are extremely rare.

Designers: Obv. Glenna Goodacre; Rev. Thomas D. Rogers, Sr.; weight 8.1 grams; composition: pure copper core with outer layers of manganese brass. The alloy contains .770 copper, .120 zinc, .070 manganese, and .040 nickel; diameter 26.5 mm; plain edge; mints: Philadelphia, Denver, San Francisco; 22-karat gold numismatic specimens dated 2000W were struck at West Point in 1999.

	Mintage	MS-63	PF-63	PF-65
2000P	767,140,000	$1.00		
2000D	518,916,000	1.00		
2000S, Proof (3,082,483)			$3.00	$5.00
2001P	62,468,000	1.00		
2001D	70,939,500	1.00		
2001S, Proof (2,294,043)			6.00	15.00
2002P	3,865,610	1.10		
2002D	3,732,000	1.10		
2002S, Proof (2,319,766)			3.00	10.00
2003P		1.10		
2003D		1.10		
2003S, Proof			3.00	9.00
2004P		1.10		
2004D		1.10		
2004S, Proof			3.00	9.00

GOLD DOLLARS 1849-1889

Coinage of the gold dollar was authorized by the Act of March 3, 1849. The weight was 25.8 grains, fineness .900. The first type, struck until 1854, is known as the Liberty Head or small-sized type.

In 1854 the piece was made larger in diameter and thinner. The design was changed to a feather headdress on a female, generally referred to as the Indian Head or large-sized type. In 1856 the type was changed slightly by enlarging the size of the head.

LIBERTY HEAD TYPE 1849-1854

VF-20 VERY FINE—*LIBERTY on headband complete and readable. Knobs on coronet are defined.*
EF-40 EXTREMELY FINE—*Slight wear on Liberty's hair. Knobs on coronet sharp.*
AU-50 ABOUT UNCIRCULATED—*Trace of wear over eye and on coronet.*
AU-55-CHOICE ABOUT UNCIRCULATED—*Evidence of friction on design high points. Most of mint luster remains.*
MS-60 UNCIRCULATED—*No trace of wear. Light marks and blemishes.*
MS-63 SELECT UNCIRCULATED—*Some distracting contact marks or blemishes in prime focal areas. Luster may be impaired.*

Mint mark is below wreath.

	Mintage	VF-20	EF-40	AU-50	AU-55	MS-60	MS-63
1849	} 688,567	$100.	$140.	$170.	$190.	$280.	$1,200.
1849, Small Head, no L		100.	140.	150.	160.	250.	1,100.
1849C	11,634	650.	950.	1,400.	2,500.	6,000.	14,000.
1849D	21,588	850.	1,150.	1,450.	2,250.	3,750.	8,500.
1849O	215,00	110.	175.	230.	375.	500.	2,250.
1850	481,953	100.	140.	150.	165.	260.	800.
1850C	6,966	700.	975.	1,750.	3,250.	5,750.	17,000.
1850D	8,382	850.	1,200.	2,000.	3,500.	6,500.	19,000.
1850O	14,000	185.	270.	550.	1,050.	2,100.	4,250.
1851	3,317,671	100.	140.	150.	165.	190.	800.
1851C	41,267	750.	975.	1,200.	1,400.	1,900.	4,000.
1851D	9,882	900.	1,200.	1,550.	2,250.	4,000.	11,000.
1851O	290,000	120.	155.	175.	225.	550.	1,750.
1852	2,045,351	100.	145.	155.	165.	200.	800.
1852C	9,434	725.	950.	1,200.	1,600.	2,750.	7,500.
1852D	6,360	875.	1,200.	1,600.	3,000.	6,500.	18,000.
1852O	140,000	105.	175.	240.	450.	825.	4,500.
1853	4,076,051	100.	145.	155.	165.	200.	800.
1853C	11,515	750.	1,000.	1,500.	2,100.	3,800.	9,500.
1853D	6,583	900.	1,200.	1,800.	3,250.	6,750.	21,000.
1853O	290,000	115.	155.	170.	225.	450.	825.
1854	855,502	100.	145.	155.	165.	200.	1,250.
1854D	2,935	900.	1,550.	4,250.	5,250.	8,500.	25,000.
1854S	14,632	225.	310.	500.	850.	1,550.	1,900.

INDIAN HEAD TYPE, Small Head 1854-1856

VF-20 VERY FINE—*Feather curl tips outlined but details worn.*
EF-40 EXTREMELY FINE—*Slight wear on tips of feather curls on headdress.*
AU-50 ABOUT UNCIRCULATED—*Trace of wear on headdress.*
AU-55-CHOICE ABOUT UNCIRCULATED—*Evidence of friction on design high points. Most of mint luster remains.*
MS-60 UNCIRCULATED—*No trace of wear. Light marks and blemishes.*
MS-63 SELECT UNCIRCULATED—*Some distracting contact marks or blemishes in prime focal areas. Luster may be impaired.*
PF-63—*Reflective surfaces with only a few blemishes in secondary focal places. No major flaws.*

	Mintage	VF-20	EF-40	AU-50	AU-55	MS-60	MS-63	PF-63
1854	783,943	$210.	$325.	$400.	$900.	$2,600.	$11,000.	$60,000.
1855	758,269	210.	325.	400.	900.	2,600.	11,000.	55,000.
1855C	9,803	850.	2,500.	7,000.	11,000.	23,000.		
1855D	1,811	3,250.	6,500.	17,000.	22,500.	37,500.	70,000.	
1855O	55,000	300.	400.	975.	2,000.	5,250.	17,500.	
1856S	24,600	550.	950.	1,700.	2,750.	6,000.	24,000.	

GOLD DOLLARS

INDIAN HEAD TYPE, Large Head 1856-1889

VF-20 VERY FINE—*Curled feathers have slight detail. Details worn smooth at eyebrow, hair below headdress and behind ear and bottom curl.*
EF-40 EXTREMELY FINE—*Slight wear above and to right of eye and on top of curled feathers.*
AU-50 ABOUT UNCIRCULATED—*Trace of wear on headdress.*
AU-55-CHOICE ABOUT UNCIRCULATED—*Evidence of friction on design high points. Most of mint luster remains.*
MS-60 UNCIRCULATED—*No trace of wear. Light marks and blemishes.*
MS-63 SELECT UNCIRCULATED—*Some distracting contact marks or blemishes in prime focal areas. Luster may be impaired.*
PF-63 PROOF — *Reflective surfaces with only a few blemishes in secondary focal places. No major flaws.*

	Mintage	VF-20	EF-40	AU-50	AU-55	MS-60	MS-63	PF-63
1856	1,762,936	$105.	$150.	$160.	$185.	$200.	$750.	$15,000.
1856D	1,460	2,650.	4,250.	5,250.	8,000.	20,000.		
1857	774,789	100.	145.	160.	185.	200.	750.	8,000.
1857C	13,280	750.	1,050.	2,100.	3,500.	8,250.	22,500.	
1857D	3,533	900.	1,375.	2,800.	3,500.	8,000.	25,000.	
1857S	10,000	375.	450.	825.	1,250.	4,350.	15,000.	
1858	117,995	100.	145.	165.	175.	200.	750.	4,750.
1858D	3,477	900.	1,200.	2,350.	4,750.	7,250.	24,500.	
1858S	10,000	275.	375.	950.	1,200.	4,000.	11,750.	
1859 (80)	168,324	100.	145.	165.	175.	200.	750.	3,500.
1859C	5,235	750.	1,000.	2,400.	3,750.	7,500.	24,000.	
1859D	4,952	900.	1,200.	2,250.	3,250.	8,000.	15,500.	
1859S	15,000	175.	375.	775.	1,250.	3,850.	11,000.	
1860 (154)	36,668	100.	145.	165.	175.	260.	850.	3,350.
1860D	1,566	1,800.	2,850.	4,750.	6,000.	11,500.	40,000.	
1860S	13,000	245.	360.	525.	700.	1,750.	3,750.	
1861 (349)	527,499	100.	145.	165.	175.	210.	725.	3,900.
1861D		5,000.	7,250.	13,000.	15,000.	22,500.	42,500.	
1862 (35)	1,361,390	100.	145.	165.	175.	200.	725.	4,100.
1863 (50)	6,250	325.	625.	1,200.	1,450.	2,850.	5,000.	4,000.
1864 (50)	5,950	270.	350.	575.	625.	725.	2,000.	5,500.
1865	3,725	270.	350.	550.	625.	1,050.	2,350.	3,900.
1866 (30)	7,130	270.	350.	500.	550.	725.	1,500.	4,000.
1867 (50)	5,250	310.	375.	475.	575.	850.	1,450.	4,000.
1868 (25)	10,525	210.	300.	360.	425.	725.	1,500.	4,500.
1869 (25)	5,925	260.	375.	475.	525.	800.	1,400.	4,750.
1870 (35)	6,335	210.	300.	360.	400.	625.	1,400.	4,850.
1870S	3,000	350.	550.	850.	1,100.	1,700.	5,000.	
1871 (30)	3,930	210.	275.	350.	400.	550.	1,200.	3,600.
1872 (30)	3,530	215.	260.	325.	375.	650.	1,600.	5,250.
1873, Cl 3 (25)	1,825	300.	575.	675.	725.	1,150.	2,750.	11,500.
1873, Open 3	123,300	100.	145.	160.	170.	200.	725.	
1874 (20)	198,820	100.	145.	160.	170.	200.	725.	5,750.
1875 (20)	420	1,400.	2,800.	3,700.	3,900.	4,600.	6,750.	11,000.
1876 (45)	3,245	210.	260.	340.	360.	475.	775.	3,800.
1877 (20)	3,920	125.	250.	340.	360.	475.	775.	4,600.
1878 (20)	3,020	150.	260.	340.	360.	475.	775.	3,800.
1879 (30)	3,030	135.	200.	235.	250.	375.	775.	4,000.
1880 (36)	1,636	115.	150.	170.	190.	300.	700.	3,650.
1881 (87)	7,707	115.	150.	170.	190.	300.	700.	3,600.
1882 (125)	5,125	125.	150.	170.	190.	300.	750.	3,250.
1883 (207)	11,007	120.	150.	170.	190.	300.	750.	3,250.
1884 (1,006)	6,236	120.	150.	170.	190.	300.	750.	3,250.
1885 (1,105)	12,261	120.	150.	170.	190.	300.	750.	3,250.
1886 (1,016)	6,016	120.	150.	170.	190.	300.	750.	3,250.
1887 (1,043)	8,543	120.	150.	170.	190.	300.	750.	3,250.
1888 (1,079)	16,580	120.	150.	170.	190.	300.	750.	3,250.
1889 (1,779)	30,729	120.	150.	170.	190.	275.	750.	3,250.

QUARTER EAGLES—1796-1929
($2.50 GOLD PIECES)

Although authorized by the Act of April 2, 1792, coinage of quarter eagles was not begun until 1796.

CAPPED BUST TO RIGHT 1796-1807

No Stars on Obverse 1796 Only

F-12 FINE—*Hair worn smooth on high spots. E PLURIBUS UNUM weak but readable.*
VF-20 VERY FINE—*Some wear on high spots.*
EF-40 EXTREMELY FINE—*Only slight wear on hair and cheek.*
AU-50 ABOUT UNCIRCULATED—*Traces of light wear on only the high points of the design. Half of mint luster is present.*
AU-55-CHOICE ABOUT UNCIRCULATED—*Evidence of friction on design high points. Most of mint luster remains.*
MS-60 UNCIRCULATED—*No trace of wear. Light blemishes.*

Stars on Obverse 1796-1807 →

	Mintage	F-12	VF-20	EF-40	AU-50	AU-55	MS-60
1796, No stars on obverse	963	$17,500.	$25,000.	$47,500.	$57,500.	$65,000.	$115,000.
1796, Stars on obverse	432	15,000.	25,000.	40,000.	55,000.	60,000.	105,000.
1797	427	10,000.	12,500.	20,000.	35,000.	40,000.	75,000.
1798	1,094	3,250.	5,250.	7,000.	14,000.	20,000.	35,000.
1802, 2/1	3,035	3,250.	5,250.	6,000.	8,000.	10,000.	15,000.
1804, 13-Star reverse	} 3,327	17,500.	22,500.	50,000.	85,000.	100,000.	150,000.
1804, 14-Star reverse		3,250.	5,000.	6,500.	8,000.	10,000.	15,000.
1805	1,781	3,250.	5,000.	6,500.	8,000.	10,500.	16,000.
1806, 6/4, stars 8L, 5R	1,136	3,500.	5,250.	6,750.	8,500.	12,000.	17,500.
1806, 6/5, stars 7L, 6R	480	4,500.	6,500.	9,000.	15,000.	22,000.	45,000.
1807	6,812	3,250.	4,800.	5,750.	8,500.	10,000.	14,000.

CAPPED BUST TO LEFT, Large Size 1808

F-12 FINE—*E PLURIBUS UNUM and LIBERTY on headband readable but weak.*
VF-20 VERY FINE—*Motto and LIBERTY clear.*
EF-40 EXTREMELY FINE—*All details of hair are plain.*
AU-50 ABOUT UNCIRCULATED—*Traces of light wear on only the high points of the design. Half of mint luster is present.*
AU-55-CHOICE ABOUT UNCIRCULATED—*Evidence of friction on design high points. Most of mint luster remains.*
MS-60 UNCIRCULATED—*No trace of wear. Light blemishes.*

	Mintage	F-12	VF-20	EF-40	AU-50	AU-55	MS-60
1808	2,710.	$15,000.	$20,000.	$27,500.	$50,000.	$55,000.	$70,000.

CAPPED HEAD TO LEFT 1821-1834

Those dated 1829-1834 are smaller in diameter than the 1821-1827 pieces.

	Mintage	F-12	VF-20	EF-40	AU-50	AU-55	MS-60
1821	6,448	$3,500.	$4,750.	$6,000.	$7,500.	$8,250.	$15,000.
1824, 4/1	2,600	3,500.	4,750.	6,000.	7,500.	8,250.	14,000.
1825	4,434	3,500.	4,750.	6,000.	7,500.	8,250.	12,000.
1826, 6/5	760	4,000.	5,000.	6,250.	7,750.	8,750.	22,500.
1827	2,800	4,200.	5,250.	7,000.	8,000.	9,000.	14,000.
1829	3,403	3,500.	4,250.	5,000.	6,500.	7,500.	9,500.
1830	4,540	3,500.	4,250.	5,000.	6,500.	7,500.	9,500.

QUARTER EAGLES

	Mintage	F-12	VF-20	EF-40	AU-50	AU-55	MS-60
1831	4,520	$3,500.	$4,250.	$5,000.	$6,500.	$7,500.	$9,500.
1832	4,400	3,500.	4,250.	5,000.	6,500.	7,500.	9,750.
1833	4,160	3,500.	4,250.	5,250.	6,750.	7,750.	10,000.
1834, Motto	4,000	5,000.	7,500.	12,000.	15,000.	17,500.	25,000.

CLASSIC HEAD TYPE, No Motto on Reverse 1834-1839

In 1834 the quarter eagle was redesigned. A ribbon binding the hair, bearing the word liberty, replaces the Liberty cap. The motto was omitted from the reverse.

F-12 FINE—*LIBERTY readable and complete. Curl under ear oulined but no detail.*
VF-20 VERY FINE—*LIBERTY plain. Hair curl has detail.*
EF-40 EXTREMELY FINE—*Small amount of wear on top of hair and below L in LIBERTY. Wear evident on wing.*
AU-50 ABOUT UNCIRCULATED—*Trace of wear on coronet and hair above ear.*
AU-55-CHOICE ABOUT UNCIRCULATED—*Evidence of friction on design high points. Most of mint luster remains.*
MS-60 UNCIRCULATED—*No trace of wear. Light blemishes.*
MS-63 SELECT UNCIRCULATED—*Some distracting contact marks or blemishes in prime focal areas. Luster may be impaired.*
PF-63—*Reflective surfaces with only a few blemishes in secondary focal places. No major flaws.*

Mint mark location.

	Mintage	F-12	VF-20	EF-40	AU-50	AU-55	MS-60	MS-63
1834, No motto	112,234	$185.	$240.	$350.	$500.	$650.	$1,500.	$4,250.
1835	131,402	185.	240.	350.	500.	650.	1,600.	5,000.
1836	547,986	185.	240.	350.	500.	675.	1,500.	4,500.
1837	45,080	225.	285.	450.	850.	1,100.	2,400.	7,500.
1838	47,030	200.	240.	350.	675.	900.	1,500.	5,000.
1838C	7,880	650.	900.	1,500.	4,500.	6,000.	17,500.	27,500.
1839	27,021	200.	275.	500.	1,000.	1,250.	3,250.	12,500.
1839C	18,140	650.	850.	1,500.	2,500.	4,000.	14,000.	32,000.
1839D	13,674	650.	875.	2,000.	4,000.	5,250.	13,500.	32,500.
1839O	17,781	250.	385.	675.	1,100.	1,500.	4,000.	14,500.

CORONET TYPE 1840-1907

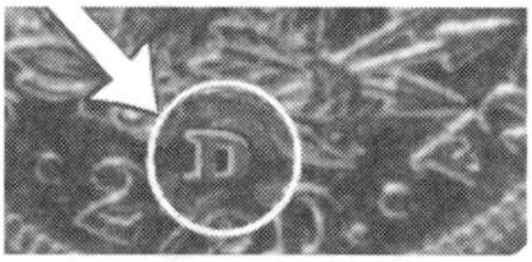

Mint mark location.

4 Plain 4

4 Crosslet 4

	Mintage	VF-20	EF-40	AU-50	AU-55	MS-60	MS-63	PF-63
1840	18,859	$135.	$650.	$2,000.	$2,350.	$4,750.	$9,000.	
1840C	12,822	850.	1,200.	3,100.	4,250.	8,750.	25,000.	
1840D	3,532	2,100.	6,250.	10,000.	15,000.	27,500.		
1840O	33,580	185.	600.	1,400.	2,500.	8,000.	19,500.	
1841,		35,000.	70,000.	75,000.	80,000.			$110,000.
1841C	10,281	850.	1,200.	2,500.	5,500.	13,000.	32,500.	
1841D	4,164	1,250.	3,100.	7,750.	10,000.	20,000.	42,500.	
1842	2,823	700.	1,850.	4,750.	7,000.	15,000.	37,500.	42,500.
1842C	6,729	1,000.	2,300.	5,250.	7,500.	20,000.	32,500.	
1842D	4,643	1,250.	2,750.	8,250.	12,500.	25,000.	23,500.	
1842O	19,800	260.	800.	1,650.	3,250.	8,250.	22,500.	
1843	100,546	125.	175.	275.	500.	900.	2,350.	42,500.
1843C	26,064	850.	1,200.	2,100.	3,250.	6,250.	15,000.	
1843D	36,209	1,000.	1,450.	2,100.	5,500.	7,250.	21,500.	
1843O	364,002	135.	180.	265.	550.	1,250.	6,000.	
1844	6,784	275.	650.	1,450.	3,250.	5,500.	16,500.	42,500.
1844C	11,622	900.	1,550.	5,000.	7,250.	13,500.	34,000.	
1844D	17,332	1,000.	1,400.	2,000.	3,500.	5,000.	19,500.	

	Mintage	VF-20	EF-40	AU-50	AU-55	MS-60	MS-63	PF-63
1845	91,051	$190.	$230.	$275.	$375.	$875.	$3,500.	$42,500.
1845D	19,460	1,000.	1,400.	2,600.	5,000.	10,000.	26,000.	
1845O	4,000	725.	1,650.	4,500.	5,250.	11,500.	37,500.	
1846	21,598	200.	375.	650.	1,500.	4,000.	17,500.	42,500.
1846C	4,808	975.	1,850.	6,500.	8,500.	13,000.	27,000.	
1846D	19,303	1,000.	1,400.	2,000.	3,500.	8,000.	20,000.	
1846O	62,000	220.	300.	800.	1,500.	4,750.	14,500.	
1847	29,814	170.	275.	625.	850.	2,650.	6,500.	
1847C	23,226	850.	1,200.	1,800.	2,500.	4,800.	11,000.	
1847D	15,784	975.	1,425.	2,000.	3,500.	7,500.	18,500.	
1847O	124,000	165.	275.	750.	1,250.	2,750.	13,500.	
1848	6,500	375.	650.	1,350.	2,250.	4,500.	11,750.	42,500.

CAL. Above Eagle on Reverse

California Gold Quarter Eagle

In 1848 about two hundred and thirty ounces of gold were sent to Secretary of War Marcy by Col. R. B. Mason, Military Governor of California. The gold was turned over to the mint and made into quarter eagles. The distinguishing mark "CAL." was punched above the eagle on the reverse side, while the coins were in the die.

	Mintage	VF-20	EF-40	AU-50	AU-55	MS-60	MS-63	PF-63
1848, CAL. above eagle	1,389	$7,500.	$16,000.	$22,000.	$24,000.	$31,000.	$42,500.	
1848C	16,788	850.	1,250.	2,350.	4,000.	10,500.	27,500.	
1848D	13,771	1,000.	1,450.	2,250.	3,800.	8,000.	24,500.	
1849	23,294	215.	360.	650.	975.	1,900.	5,500.	
1849C	10,220	850.	1,300.	3,750.	6,000.	17,500.	40,000.	
1849D	10,945	1,000.	1,400.	2,750.	4,250.	12,000.	20,000.	
1850	252,923	130.	165.	275.	375.	800.	2,900.	
1850C	9,148	850.	1,200.	2,650.	5,000.	13,500.	30,000.	
1850D	12,148	975.	1,200.	2,450.	4,750.	11,000.	30,000.	
1850O	84,000	160.	350.	900.	1,350.	3,750.	11,750.	
1851	1,372,748	130.	155.	175.	190.	240.	925.	
1851C	14,923	850.	1,200.	3,500.	4,500.	9,250.	27,500.	
1851D	11,264	1,000.	1,500.	3,000.	4,750.	9,000.	23,500.	
1851O	148,000	140.	160.	650.	1,250.	3,500.	11,000.	
1852	1,159,681	130.	155.	175.	190.	250.	925.	
1852C	9,772	850.	1,300.	3,350.	5,000.	13,500.	26,000.	
1852D	4,078	1,000.	1,950.	5,500.	6,250.	12,500.	37,500.	
1852O	140,000	140.	230.	700.	1,200.	3,750.	9,250.	
1853	1,404,668	130.	155.	175.	195.	275.	900.	
1853D	3,178	1,300.	2,450.	3,800.	5,500.	12,500.	37,500.	
1854	596,258	130.	155.	175.	195.	275.	1,175.	
1854C	7,295	850.	1,550.	3,900.	5,250.	11,000.	31,000.	
1854D	1,760	2,100.	4,000.	8,500.	12,500.	20,000.	60,000.	
1854O	153,000	130.	165.	325.	550.	1,200.	2,750.	
1854S	246	32,500.	60,000.	140,000.	—	—		
1855	235,480	130.	155.	175.	195.	280.	1,250.	
1855C	3,677	1,050.	2,350.	4,650.	6,500.	19,500.	35,000.	
1855D	1,123	2,500.	5,750.	13,500.	20,000.	38,000.	62,500.	
1856	384,240	130.	155.	175.	200.	300.	1,175.	$32,500.
1856C	7,913	900.	1,750.	3,000.	5,000.	11,500.	24,500.	
1856D	874	5,000.	7,500.	18,500.	22,500.	45,000.	92,500.	
1856O	21,100	155.	525.	925.	2,400.	4,000.	23,500.	
1856S	72,120	150.	275.	675.	1,200.	3,350.	9,750.	
1857	214,130	130.	155.	175.	210.	300.	1,200.	30,000.
1857D	2,364	1,000.	1,950.	2,950.	4,750.	9,750.	24,500.	
1857O	34,000	150.	275.	750.	1,250.	3,250.	9,500.	
1857S	69,200	150.	260.	650.	2,000.	4,250.	10,750.	

	Mintage	VF-20	EF-40	AU-50	AU-55	MS-60	MS-63	PF-63
1858	47,377	$130.	$185.	$265.	$350.	$950.	$2,500.	$21,000.
1858C	9,056	850.	1,200.	2,250.	2,600.	7,520.	26,000.	
1859 (80)	39,444	130.	190.	300.	400.	925.	2,400.	14,000.
1859D	2,244	1,250.	2,250.	3,600.	5,000.	14,500.	50,000.	
1859S	15,200	235.	700.	1,900.	2,600.	5,000.	13,000.	
1860 (112)	22,675	130.	190.	350.	400.	850.	2,000.	13,500.
1860C	7,469	850.	1,400.	2,800.	5,750.	16,500.	29,000.	
1860S	35,600	165.	500.	850.	1,200.	3,000.	7,500.	
1861 (90)	1,283,878	135.	155.	180.	195.	250.	775.	14,500.
1861S	24,000	260.	675.	2,250.	3,100.	5,750.	13,500.	
1862, 2/1	} 98,543	650.	1,300.	2,600.	3,200.	6,250.		
1862 (35)		150.	235.	375.	450.	925.	2,850.	12,500.
1862S	8,000	650.	1,600.	3,300.	4,750.	13,500.	28,500.	
1863, Pfs only (30)	30							33,500.
1863S	10,800	360.	1,100.	2,400.	4,000.	10,500.	20,000.	
1864 (50)	2,874	4,250.	8,500.	17,500.	20,000.	29,500.		8,000.
1865 (25)	1,545	3,600.	5,500.	14,500.	16,000.	29,500.		11,500.
1865S	23,376	160.	475.	1,100.	1,500.	3,350.	7,500.	
1866 (30)	3,110	950.	2,650.	4,250.	5,500.	9,000.	20,000.	8,000.
1866S	38,960	210.	475.	1,100.	1,650.	4,750.	15,500.	
1867 (50)	3,250	275.	600.	875.	1,250.	3,750.	7,000.	8,000.
1867S	28,000	180.	475.	1,250.	1,500.	3,100.	9,000.	
1868 (25)	3,625	170.	300.	500.	650.	1,175.	5,500.	9,000.
1868S	34,000	140.	225.	825.	1,200.	3,000.	11,000.	
1869 (25)	4,345	180.	250.	550.	900.	2,400.	3,750.	6,500.
1869S	29,500	165.	360.	625.	1,250.	3,400.	6,750.	
1870 (35)	4,555	175.	325.	575.	950.	2,850.	6,000.	6,750.
1870S	16,000	140.	325.	600.	1,250.	3,500.	12,000.	
1871 (30)	5,350	180.	250.	450.	625.	1,750.	3,000.	6,750.
1871S	22,000	140.	210.	415.	575.	1,725.	3,600.	
1872 (30)	3,030	280.	600.	825.	1,750.	3,600.	10,500.	5,750.
1872S	18,000	140.	280.	700.	1,200.	3,450.	9,000.	
1873 (25)	178,025	125.	155.	185.	200.	220.	625.	5,500.
1873S	27,000	160.	280.	675.	800.	2,100.	6,250.	
1874 (20)	3,940	185.	280.	550.	725.	1,650.	4,500.	7,250.
1875 (20)	420	2,650.	3,850.	6,500.	7,750.	10,500.	17,500.	8,750.
1875S	11,600	125.	225.	600.	900.	3,350.	6,750.	
1876 (45)	4,221	215.	500.	700.	1,250.	2,600.	4,600.	5,500.
1876S	5,000	175.	400.	725.	1,500.	2,600.	7,250.	
1877 (20)	1,652	280.	600.	825.	1,150.	2,350.	7,500.	6,000.
1877S	35,400	125.	150.	180.	210.	475.	1,750.	
1878 (20)	286,260	125.	150.	180.	200.	300.	650.	8,750.
1878S	178,000	125.	150.	180.	200.	260.	1,500.	
1879 (30)	88,990	125.	150.	175.	190.	260.	675.	6,250.
1879S	43,500	150.	210.	375.	725.	1,650.	4,000.	
1880 (36)	2,996	135.	260.	475.	625.	1,000.	2,800.	6,250.
1881 (51)	691	1,400.	2,200.	3,350.	4,000.	6,750.	12,500.	5,000.
1882 (67)	4,067	150.	225.	310.	390.	525.	1,800.	4,500.
1883 (82)	2,002	150.	300.	750.	975.	1,800.	4,750.	4,500.
1884 (73)	2,023	150.	300.	450.	600.	1,175.	2,250.	4,500.
1885 (87)	887	475.	1,300.	1,800.	2,000.	3,500.	6,000.	4,750.
1886 (88)	4,088	140.	200.	325.	375.	850.	2,100.	4,750.
1887 (122)	6,282	135.	190.	260.	300.	525.	1,750.	4,350.
1888 (97)	16,098	125.	170.	210.	220.	240.	650.	4,350.
1889 (48)	17,648	125.	160.	200.	210.	250.	650.	5,250.
1890 (93)	8,813	135.	175.	220.	240.	375.	850.	4,500.
1891 (80)	11,040	125.	155.	180.	200.	310.	675.	4,250.
1892 (105)	2,545	130.	180.	250.	290.	575.	1,950.	4,250.
1893 (106)	30,106	125.	150.	170.	190.	225.	600.	4,250.
1894 (122)	4,122	130.	170.	240.	260.	600.	1,250.	4,250.
1895 (119)	6,119	125.	160.	210.	225.	300.	675.	4,250.

QUARTER EAGLES

	Mintage	VF-20	EF-40	AU-50	AU-55	MS-60	MS-63	PF-63
1896 ....(132)	19,202	$125.	$150.	$175.	$190.	$220.	$600.	$4,250.
1897 ....(136)	29,904	125.	150.	175.	190.	220.	600.	4,100.
1898 ....(165)	24,165	125.	150.	175.	190.	220.	600.	4,250.
1899 ....(150)	27,350	125.	150.	175.	190.	220.	600.	4,100.
1900 ....(205)	67,205	125.	160.	200.	210.	220.	600.	4,100.
1901 ....(223)	91,323	125.	150.	175.	190.	220.	600.	4,100.
1902 ....(193)	133,733	125.	150.	175.	190.	220.	600.	4,100.
1903 ....(197)	201,257	125.	150.	175.	190.	220.	600.	4,100.
1904 ....(170)	160,960	125.	150.	175.	190.	220.	600.	4,100.
1905 ....(144)	217,944	125.	150.	175.	190.	220.	600.	4,100.
1906 ....(160)	176,490	125.	150.	175.	190.	220.	600.	4,100.
1907 ....(154)	336,448	125.	150.	175.	190.	220.	600.	4,100.

INDIAN HEAD TYPE 1908-1929

Bela Lyon Pratt was the designer of this and the similar half eagle piece. The coin has no raised milling and the main devices and legends are incuse.

Mint mark location is on reverse left of fasces.

VF-20 VERY FINE—*Hair cord knot distinct. Feathers at top of head clear. Cheekbone worn.*
EF-40 EXTREMELY FINE—*Cheekbone, war bonnet and headband feathers slightly worn.*
AU-50 ABOUT UNCIRCULATED—*Trace of wear on cheekbone and headdress.*
MS-60 UNCIRCULATED—*No trace of wear. Light blemishes.*
MS-63 SELECT UNCIRCULATED—*Some distracting contact marks or blemishes in prime focal areas. Luster may be impaired.*
MS-64 UNCIRCULATED—*Shows a few scattered contact marks. Good eye appeal and attractive luster.*
PF-63 PROOF — *Reflective surfaces with only a few blemishes in secondary focal places. No major flaws.*

	Mintage	VF-20	EF-40	AU-50	MS-60	MS-63	MS-64	Matte PF-63
1908 ....(236)	565,057	$125.	$135.	$140.	$210.	$1,000.	$1,400.	$5,250.
1909 ....(139)	441,899	125.	135.	140.	200.	1,600.	2,000.	5,250.
1910 ....(682)	492,682	125.	135.	140.	200	1,500.	2,400.	5,250.
1911 ....(191)	704,191	125.	135.	140.	200.	1,000.	1,700.	5,250.
1911D	55,680	900.	1,250.	1,750.	4,500.	18,500.	24,000.	
1912 ....(197)	616,197	125.	135.	140.	210.	1,800.	2,500.	5,250.
1913 ....(165)	722,165	125.	135.	140.	210.	1,000.	1,800.	5,250.
1914 ....(117)	240,117	135.	150.	160.	300.	4,350.	7,250.	5,250.
1914D	448,000	125.	135.	140.	210.	1,600.	3,900.	5,250.
1915 ....(100)	606,100	125.	135.	140.	190.	1,000.	1,650.	5,400.
1925D	578,000	125.	130.	140.	185.	875.	1,100.	
1926	446,000	125.	130.	140.	185.	875.	1,100.	
1927	388,000	125.	130.	140.	185.	875.	1,100.	
1928	416,000	125.	130.	140.	185.	875.	1,100.	
1929	532,000	125.	130.	140.	185.	875.	1,100.	

THREE DOLLAR GOLD PIECES—1854-1889

The three dollar gold piece was authorized by the Act of February 21, 1853. The coin was first struck in 1854. It was never popular and saw very little circulation.

Mint mark location is on reverse below wreath

VF-20 VERY FINE—*Eyebrow, hair about forehead and ear and bottom curl are worn smooth. Curled feather ends have faint details showing.*
EF-40 EXTREMELY FINE—*Light wear above and to right of eye and on top of curled feathers.*
AU-50 ABOUT UNCIRCULATED—*Trace of wear on top of curled feathers and in hair above and to right of eye.*
AU-55-CHOICE ABOUT UNCIRCULATED—*Evidence of friction on design high points. Most of mint luster remains.*
MS-60 UNCIRCULATED—*No trace of wear. Light blemishes.*
MS-63 SELECT UNCIRCULATED—*Some distracting contact marks or blemishes in prime focal areas. Luster may be impaired.*
PF-63 PROOF — *Reflective surfaces with only a few blemishes in secondary focal places. No major flaws.*

	Mintage	VF-20	EF-40	AU-50	AU-55	MS-60	MS-63	PF-63
1854	138,618	$525.	$700.	$1,050.	$1,250.	$1,950.	$4,650.	$45,000.
1854D	1,120	6,250.	11,000.	21,000.	30,000.	50,000.		
1854O	24,000	725.	1,400.	2,400.	5,500.	13,000.	21,000.	
1855	50,555	525.	700.	1,050.	1,250.	2,000.	5,250.	27,500.
1855S	6,600	775.	1,650.	4,250.	6,000.	18,500.	62,500.	

THREE DOLLAR GOLD PIECES

	Mintage	VF-20	EF-40	AU-50	AU-55	MS-60	MS-63	PF-63
1856	26,010	$525.	$775.	$1,100.	$1,250.	$2,000.	$5,250.	$14,500.
1856S	34,500	550.	950.	1,700.	3,500.	7,000.	16,000.	
1857	20,891	525.	750.	1,100.	1,350.	2,250.	7,000.	12,500.
1857S	14,000	600.	1,500.	3,750.	5,000.	12,000.		
1858	2,133	650.	1,150.	1,700.	2,800.	5,500.	12,500.	14,500.
1859 (80)	15,638	550.	650.	1,100.	1,350.	2,000.	5,000.	10,500.
1860 (119)	7,155	575.	700.	1,100.	1,500.	2,200.	5,250.	7,500.
1860S	7,000	650.	1,350.	4,000.	6,250.	11,000.	29,000.	
1861 (113)	6,072	600.	850.	1,300.	1,500.	2,600.	6,000.	10,000.
1862 (35)	5,785	600.	850.	1,300.	1,500.	2,600.	6,000.	8,000.
1863 (39)	5,039	625.	900.	1,300.	1,500.	2,750.	5,750.	8,750.
1864 (50)	2,680	650.	825.	1,300.	1,500.	2,700.	6,000.	9,500.
1865 (25)	1,165	850.	1,800.	3,750.	4,250.	5,750.	10,500.	12,500.
1866 (30)	4,030	650.	800.	1,250.	1,500.	2,600.	6,850.	9,500.
1867 (50)	2,650	650.	825.	1,100.	1,600.	2,600.	6,750.	9,500.
1868 (25)	4,875	550.	775.	1,200.	1,450.	2,250.	5,500.	10,000.
1869 (25)	2,525	625.	775.	1,300.	1,500.	2,850.	7,500.	10,000.
1870 (35)	3,535	575.	800.	1,300.	1,600.	3,000.	7,750.	8,000.
1870S, (*Unique*)								
1871 (30)	1,330	650.	875.	1,200.	1,450.	2,900.	6,500.	8,750.
1872 (30)	2,030	600.	825.	1,200.	1,400.	2,600.	7,000.	10,500.
1873, Open 3 (Orig) (25)	25	2,350.	3,500.	6,500.	9,500.			16,000.
1873, Closed 3		2,200.	3,500.	6,600.	10,000.	19,000.	27,500.	
1874 (20)	41,820	500.	750.	1,000.	1,250.	1,850.	4,650.	12,500.
1875, PfS only (20)	20	15,500.	22,000.	36,000.	40,000.			63,500.
1876, PfS only (45)	45	4,250.	7,500.	10,500.	13,000.			19,500.
1877 (20)	1,488	925.	2,150.	4,100.	5,500.	8,900.	25,000.	12,500.
1878 (20)	82,324	500.	750.	1,000.	1,250.	1,900.	4,500.	12,500.
1879 (30)	3,030	525.	775.	1,000.	1,400.	2,000.	4,750.	10,500.
1880 (36)	1,036	575.	1,300.	1,700.	1,825.	2,350.	5,000.	10,000.
1881 (54)	554	950.	1,800.	3,400.	3,750.	4,500.	8,250.	8,000.
1882 (76)	1,576	650.	800.	1,300.	1,500.	2,300.	5,000.	8,000.
1883 (89)	989	625.	1,000.	1,675.	1,900.	2,450.	5,000.	8,000.
1884 (106)	1,106	625.	1,200.	1,750.	1,900.	2,450.	5,250.	8,000.
1885 (109)	910	625.	1,200.	1,700.	2,100.	2,600.	5,400.	8,000.
1886 (142)	1,142	600.	950.	1,750.	2,000.	2,900.	5,900.	8,000.
1887 (160)	6,160	550.	600.	1,300.	1,450.	2,300.	4,700.	8,000.
1888 (291)	5,291	550.	600.	1,100.	1,400.	2,000.	4,650.	8,000.
1889 (129)	2,429	550.	650.	950.	1,300.	2,100.	4,650.	8,000.

FOUR DOLLAR GOLD OR "STELLA"

These pattern coins were first suggested by the Hon. John A. Kasson, then U.S. Minister to Austria; and it was through the efforts of Dr. W. W. Hubbell, who patented the goloid metal used in making the goloid metric dollars, that we have these beautiful and interesting pieces. Only those struck in gold are listed.

	Mintage	EF-40	AU-50	PF-60	PF-63	PF-65
1879, Flowing hair	(425)	$32,500.	$37,500.	$50,000.	$80,000.	$110,000.
1879, Coiled hair (*12 Known*)		70,000.	87,500.	92,500.	135,000.	275,000.
1880, Flowing hair (*17 Known*)		57,500.	62,500.	72,500.	110,000.	200,000.
1880, Coiled hair (*8 Known*)		110,000.	145,000.	170,000.	285,000.	390,000.

HALF EAGLES — 1795-1929
($5.00 GOLD PIECES)

The half eagle was the first gold coin struck for the United States. The $5.00 piece was authorized to be coined by the Act of April 2, 1792, and the first type weighed 135 grains, 916 2/3 fine. The weight was changed by the Act of June 28, 1834 to 129 grains, 899.225 fine. Fineness became .900 by the Act of January 18, 1837.

CAPPED BUST TO RIGHT, SMALL EAGLE 1795-1798

F-12 FINE—*Hair worn smooth but with distinct outline. For heraldic type, E PLURIBUS UNUM is faint but readable.*
VF-20 VERY FINE—*Slight to noticeable wear on high spots such as hair, turban, eagle's head and wings.*
EF-40 EXTREMELY FINE—*Slight wear on hair and highest part of cheek.*
AU-50 ABOUT UNCIRCULATED—*Traces of light wear on only the high points of the design. Half of mint luster is present.*
AU-55-CHOICE ABOUT UNCIRCULATED—*Evidence of friction on design high points. Most of mint luster remains.*
MS-60 UNCIRCULATED—*No trace of wear. Light blemishes.*
MS-63 SELECT UNCIRCULATED—*Some distracting contact marks or blemishes in prime focal areas. Luster may be impaired.*

	Mintage	F-12	VF-20	EF-40	AU-50	AU-55	MS-60	MS-63
1795, Small eagle	8,707	$7,500.	$10,000.	$13,500.	$18,000.	$21,000.	$27,500.	$95,000.

1796, 6 over 5

1797, 15 Stars

1797, 16 Stars

	Mintage	F-12	VF-20	EF-40	AU-50	AU-55	MS-60	MS-63
1796, 6/5	6,196	$8,000.	$10,500.	$15,000	$20,000.	$22,500.	$40,000.	$105,000.
1797, 15 stars	3,609	9,000.	12,500.	22,500.	40,000.	55,000.	85,000.	
1797, 16 stars	3,609	9,000.	12,500.	20,000.	35,000.	45,000.	80,000.	
1798, Small eagle, (*7 Known*)			65,000.	100,000.	175,000.	250,000.		

CAPPED BUST TO RIGHT, HERALDIC EAGLE 1795-1807

	Mintage	F-12	VF-20	EF-40	AU-50	AU-55	MS-60	MS-63
1795, Heraldic eagle		$6,000.	$9,000.	$15,000.	$25,000.	$35,000.	$55,000.	$115,000.
1797, 7/5		6,000.	9,000.	16,500.	30,000.	42,500.	100,000.	
1798, Lg. 8, 13 star rev	24,867	1,500.	2,200.	3,000.	6,000.	7,500.	12,500.	
1798, Lg. 8, 14 star rev		1,800.	2,500.	4,500.	10,000.	12,000.	20,000.	
1799	7,451	1,600.	2,200.	3,000.	5,000.	5,750.	11,000.	32,500.
1800	37,628	1,500.	2,000.	2,500.	4,500.	5,000.	6,500.	13,000.
1802, 2/1	53,176	1,500.	2,000.	2,500.	4,000.	4,500.	6,250.	12,000.
1803, 3/2	33,506	1,500.	2,000.	2,500.	4,000.	4,500.	6,250.	12,000.

HALF EAGLES

	Mintage	F-12	VF-20	EF-40	AU-50	AU-55	MS-60	MS-63
1804	30,475	$1,500.	$2,000.	$2,500.	$4,000.	$4,500.	$6,250.	$12,000.
1805	33,183	1,500.	2,000.	2,500.	4,000.	4,500.	6,250.	12,000.
1806	64,093	1,500.	2,000.	2,500.	4,000.	4,500.	6,250.	12,000.
1807	32,488	1,500.	2,000.	2,500.	4,000.	4,500.	6,250.	12,000.

CAPPED DRAPED BUST TO LEFT 1807-1812

F-12 FINE—*LIBERTY readable but partly weak.*
VF-20 VERY FINE—*Headband edges slightly worn. LIBERTY is bold.*
EF-40 EXTREMELY FINE—*Slight wear on highest portions of hair. 80% of major curls are plain.*
AU-50 ABOUT UNCIRCULATED—*Traces of lightwear on only the high points of the design. Half of mint luster is present.*
AU-55-CHOICE ABOUT UNCIRCULATED—*Evidence of friction on design high points. Most of mint luster remains.*
MS-60 UNCIRCULATED—*No trace of wear. Light blemishes.*
MS-63 SELECT UNCIRCULATED—*Some distracting contact marks or blemishes in prime focal areas. Luster may be impaired.*

	Mintage	F-12	VF-20	EF-40	AU-50	AU-55	MS-60	MS-63
1807	51,605	$1,300.	$1,600.	$2,200.	$3,250.	$4,000.	$5,000.	$9,500.
1808, 8/7	55,578	1,500.	2,200.	2,500.	4,000.	5,250.	7,500.	17,500.
1808		1,300.	1,600.	2,200.	3,250.	4,000.	5,000.	10,000.
1809, 9/8	33,875	1,300.	1,600.	2,200.	3,250.	4,000.	5,000.	10,000.
1810, All kinds	100,287	1,300.	1,600.	2,200.	3,250.	4,000.	5,000.	9,500.
1811	99, 581	1,300.	1,600.	2,200.	3,250.	4,000.	5,000.	9,500.
1812	58,087	1,300.	1,600.	2,200.	3,250.	4,000.	5,000.	9,500.

CAPPED HEAD TO LEFT 1813-1829

	Mintage	F-12	VF-20	EF-40	AU-50	AU-55	MS-60	MS-63
1813	95,428	$1,500.	$1,850.	$2,500.	$3,500.	$4,000.	$5,500.	$9,500.
1814, 4/3	15,454	1,750.	2,000.	2,750.	4,000.	4,750.	6,500.	15,000.
1815	635	25,000.	35,000.	50,000.	75,000.	85,000.	110,000.	150,000.
1818, All kinds	48,588	1,750.	2,000.	2,500.	4,000.	4,750.	6,500.	13,500.
1819	51,723	7,500.	12,500.	17,500.	25,000.	30,000.	40,000.	65,000.
1820, All kinds	263,806	1,750.	2,000.	2,500.	4,000.	4,750.	7,500.	15,000.
1821	34,641	4,000.	8,500.	13,500.	20,000.	25,000.	45,000.	100,000.
1822, (*3 known*)	17,796			1,000,000.				
1823	14,485	1,750.	2,500.	3,500.	5,000.	6,500.	10,500.	22,500.
1824	17,340	3,500.	7,500.	10,500.	15,000.	17,500.	25,000.	42,500.
1825, 5/1	29,060	3,500.	5,500.	8,000.	12,500.	15,000.	25,000.	45,000.
1825, 5/4 (*2 known*)				200,000.				
1826	18,069	2,500.	5,000.	6,500.	10,000.	12,500.	17,500.	35,000.
1827	24,913	4,000.	6,500.	8,500.	12,500.	15,000.	25,000.	45,000.
1828, 8/7	28,029	10,000.	15,000.	27,500.	40,000.	45,000.	80,000.	125,000.
1828		4,000.	8,000.	12,500.	20,000.	25,000.	45,000.	65,000.
1829, Large Date	57,442	10,000.	18,000.	25,000.	40,000.	45,000.	75,000.	125,000.

CAPPED HEAD TO LEFT (reduced diameter) 1829-1834

	Mintage	F-12	VF-20	EF-40	AU-50	AU-55	MS-60	MS-63
1829, Small Date		$25,000.	$35,000.	$50,000.	$70,000.	$75,000.	$85,000.	$125,000.
1830		9,000.	12,500.	13,500.	15,500.	17,500.	25,000.	45,000.
1831		9,000.	12,500.	13,500.	15,500.	17,500.	25,000.	45,000.
1832, Curved-base 2, 12 stars (6 known)	157,487	25,000.	35,000.	50,000.	75,000.			
1832, Sq-base 2, 13 stars		9,000.	12,500.	13,500.	15,500.	17,500.	25,000.	45,000.
1833		9,000.	12,500.	13,500.	15,500.	17,500.	25,000.	45,000.
1834		9,000.	12,500.	13,500.	15,500.	17,500.	27,500.	47,500.

HALF EAGLES

CLASSIC HEAD TYPE 1834-1838

	Mintage	F-12	VF-20	EF-40	AU-50	AU-55	MS-60	MS-63
1834	.657, 460	$185.	$250.	$350.	$600.	$850.	$2,000.	$4,500.
1835	371,534	185.	250.	350.	600.	850.	2,000.	4,500.
1836	553,147	185.	250.	350.	600.	850.	2,000.	4,500.
1837	207,121	200.	275.	400.	600.	1,000.	2,250.	8,000.
1838	286,588	200.	275.	400.	625.	1,000.	2,250.	8,000.
1838C	17,179	750.	1,200.	2,500.	6,000.	8,500.	13,000.	40,000.
1838D	20,583	700.	1,000.	2,500.	5,000.	7,500.	15,000.	22,500.

CORONET TYPE, No Motto Above Eagle 1839-1866

VF-20 VERY FINE—*LIBERTY bold. Major lines show in neck hair.*

EF-40 EXTREMELY FINE—*Neck hair details clear. Slight wear on top and lower part of coronet, and hair.*

AU-50 ABOUT UNCIRCULATED—*Trace of wear on coronet and hair above eye.*

MS-60 UNCIRCULATED—*No trace of wear. Light blemishes.*

MS-63 SELECT UNCIRCULATED—*Some distracting contact marks or blemishes in prime focal areas. Luster may be impaired.*

PF-63—*Reflective surfaces with only a few blemishes in secondary focal places. No major flaws.*

Mint mark above date 1839 only, below eagle 1840-1908.

	Mintage	VF-20	EF-40	AU-50	AU-55	MS-60	MS-63	PF-63
1839	118,143	$185.	$325.	$800.	$1,250.	$2,750.	$16,000.	
1839C	17,205	1,000.	1,875.	4,000.	5,750.	14,000.	42,000.	
1839D	18,939	1,000.	1,500.	3,650.	5,500.	13,000.		
1840	137,382	160.	250.	875.	1,375.	2,600.	7,500.	
1840C	18,992	1,000.	1,750.	4,750.	8,000.	17,500.	47,500.	
1840D	22,896	1,000.	1,450.	4,750.	5,250.	10,500.	33,500.	
1840O	40,120	220.	575.	1,275.	2,250.	7,000.	17,500.	
1841	15,833	260.	625.	1,250.	1,550.	3,550.	7,750.	$47,500.
1841C	21,467	950.	1,300.	2,150.	4,000.	11,500.	32,500.	
1841D	29,392	1,000.	1,300.	2,250.	4,000.	10,000.	19,000.	

1842 Large Date

Large Letters

Small Letters

	Mintage	VF-20	EF-40	AU-50	AU-55	MS-60	MS-63	PF-63
1842, Small Letter	27,578 (both)	$230.	$750.	$2,200.	$3,750.	$9,500.	$16,750.	$57,500.
1842, Large Letter		475.	1,400.	2,000.	3,250.	7,750.	17,500.	
1842C, Small Date	27,432 (both)	7,250.	16,500.	30,000.	40,000.	77,500.		
1842C, Large Date		950.	1,400.	2,350.	4,750.	12,000.	27,500.	
1842D, Small Date	59,608 (both)	1,000.	1,350.	2,200.	3,750.	10,500.	25,000.	
1842D, Large Date		1,675.	4,250.	10,000.	14,000.	33,500.		
1842O	16,400	700.	2,100.	6,750.	8,000.	15,500.	30,000.	
1843	611,205	150.	180.	250.	375.	1,200.	7,250.	
1843C	44,277	950.	1,300.	2,650.	3,750.	8,000.	24,000.	

	Mintage	VF-20	EF-40	AU-50	AU-55	MS-60	MS-63
1843D	98,452	$1,000.	$1,300.	$2,250.	$3,750.	$8,000.	$17,500.
1843O, Small Letter	19,075	375.	1,000.	1,650.	3,250.	13,500.	28,000.
1843O, Large Letter	82,000	175.	775.	1,375.	3,000.	8,500.	19,500.
1844	340,330	150.	165.	260.	350.	1,400.	6,500.
1844C	23,631	950.	2,100.	4,500.	6,000.	15,500.	30,000.
1844D	88,982	1,000.	1,550.	2,450.	3,500.	7,500.	18,000.
1844O	364,600	180.	265.	410.	1,000.	3,000.	10,000.
1845	417,099	150.	165.	250.	425.	1,450.	6,500.
1845D	90,629	1,000.	1,300.	2,250.	3,250.	8,250.	19,000.
1845O	41,000	275.	475.	1,900.	3,000.	7,000.	19,500.
1846	395, 942	150.	165.	250.	425.	1,750.	9,500.
1846C	12,995	1,000.	2,000.	4,500.	5,500.	16,000.	50,000.
1846D	80,294	1,000.	1,450.	2,500.	3,250.	9,000.	16,500.
1846O	58,000	265.	675.	2,200.	3,250.	8,250.	20,000.
1847	915,981	150.	170.	230.	325.	1,000.	5,250.
1847C	84,151	950.	1,350.	2,400.	3,000.	9,250.	19,500.
1847D	64,405	1,000.	1,350.	2,200.	3,250.	7,250.	13,500.
1847O	12,000	1,300.	5,000.	6,750.	9,000.	18,000.	26,500.
1848	260,775	155.	190.	290.	400.	1,050.	8,500.
1848C	64,472	950.	1,350.	2,500.	4,750.	14,000.	36,000.
1848D	47,465	1,000.	1,350.	2,200.	3,750.	10,000.	21,000.
1849	133,070	150.	185.	500.	800.	1,900.	9,500.
1849C	64,823	950.	1,350.	2,100.	4,000.	9,500.	20,000.
1849D	39,036	1,000.	1,350.	2,300.	3,500.	9,500.	22,000.
1850	64,491	190.	425.	750.	850.	2,600.	13,000.
1850C	63,591	950.	1,350.	2,100.	2,500.	8,000.	17,000.
1850D	43,984	1,000.	1,300.	2,800.	5,500.	19,500.	
1851	377,505	150.	165.	250.	500.	2,000.	7,250.
1851C	49,176	950.	1,300.	2,250.	4,750.	11,000.	37,500.
1851D	62,710	1,000.	1,300.	2,200.	4,250.	10,000.	19,500.
1851O	41,000	400.	1,000.	2,750.	4,250.	8,500.	14,000.
1852	573,901	150.	170.	230.	375.	850.	5,000.
1852C	72,574	950.	1,350.	2,100.	2,400.	4,800.	15,500.
1852D	91,584	1,000.	1,350.	2,200.	3,750.	9,000.	21,500.
1853	305,770	150.	170.	250.	375.	1,000.	6,500.
1853C	65,571	950.	1,350.	2,200.	3,100.	6,000.	20,000.
1853D	89,678	1,000.	1,350.	2,200.	3,200.	7,250.	18,000.
1854	160,675	150.	170.	360.	800.	1,450.	6,000.
1854C	39,283	950.	1,350.	2,700.	3,500.	10,000.	33,000.
1854D	56,413	1,000.	1,350.	2,200.	3,500.	7,500.	22,500.
1854O	46,000	210.	370.	975.	1,650.	5,750.	14,500.
1854S	268	—	—	250,000.	—		
1855	117,098	150.	165.	250.	400.	1,250.	6,000.
1855C	39,788	950.	1,400.	2,300.	3,500.	10,500.	28,000.
1855D	22,432	1,000.	1,350.	2,250.	3,500.	11,500.	31,000.
1855O	11,100	425.	1,500.	3,250.	4,500.	14,500.	
1855S	61,000	275.	650.	1,550.	3,750.	11,000.	
1856	197,990	150.	170.	230.	400.	1,600.	8,000.
1856C	28,457	950.	1,300.	2,300.	4,100.	14,500.	
1856D	19,786	1,000.	1,300.	2,600.	3,750.	7,750.	28,500.
1856O	10,000	450.	850.	3,250.	4,500.	8,750.	
1856S	105,100	215.	425.	875.	1,750.	4,750.	21,500.
1857	98,188	150.	170.	275.	400.	1,100.	5,250.
1857C	31,360	950.	1,300.	2,250.	3,500.	6,250.	24,000.
1857D	17,046	1,000.	1,300.	2,500.	3,500.	9,250.	30,000.
1857O	13,000	450.	975.	3,250.	4,250.	10,000.	39,000.
1857S	87,000	215.	375.	800.	2,000.	6,750.	13,500.
1858	15,136	170.	375.	500.	950.	2,750.	6,500.

	Mintage	VF-20	EF-40	AU-50	AU-55	MS-60	MS-63	PF-63
1858C	38,856	$950.	$1,350.	$2,200.	$3,250.	$7,250.	$27,500.	
1858D	15,362	1,000.	1,350.	2,200.	3,750.	8,750.		
1858S	18,600	475.	1,600.	3,850.	8,000.	21,500.		
1859 (80)	16,814	225.	425.	575.	1,200.	5,000.		$25,000.
1859C	31,847	950.	1,350.	2,650.	3,750.	10,500.	35,000.	
1859D	10,366	1,000.	1,350.	2,250.	4,250.	10,000.	29,000.	
1859S	13,220	875.	2,500.	3,750.	5,750.	20,000.		
1860 (62)	19,825	190.	400.	775.	950.	2,800.	11,500.	20,000.
1860C	14,813	950.	1,500.	2,300.	4,000.	9,250.		
1860D	14,635	1,000.	1,450.	2,500.	5,000.	12,000.	36,000.	
1860S	21,200	750.	1,500.	4,000.	7,250.	18,000.		
1861 (66)	688,150	150.	175.	255.	375.	850.	2,150.	20,000.
1861C	6,879	1,200.	2,500.	4,750.	6,000.	16,000.	50,000.	
1861D	1,597	3,000.	4,750.	10,000.	12,000.	35,000.	85,000.	
1861S	18,000	600.	3,000.	4,000.	5,500.	22,500.		
1862 (35)	4,465	350.	1,000.	2,000.	2,750.	10,000.	25,000.	17,500.
1862S	9,500	2,000.	4,000.	7,000.	8,250.	30,000.		
1863 (30)	2,472	750.	2,500.	4,000.	5,500.	15,000.		17,500.
1863S	17,000	850.	2,500.	6,500.	8,000.	18,000.		
1864 (50)	4,220	400.	1,250.	2,750.	3,500.	8,000.		17,500.
1864S	3,888	3,000.	7,500.	15,000.	17,500.	30,000.		
1865 (25)	1,295	750.	1,500.	5,500.	6,750.	10,000.		17,500.
1865S	27,612	650.	1,500.	2,500.	3,500.	10,000.	15,000.	
1866S	9,000	1,000.	2,200.	6,500.	9,000.	22,500.		

Motto Above Eagle 1866-1908

VF-20 VERY FINE—*Half of hairlines above coronet missing. Hair curls under ear evident, but worn. Motto and its ribbon sharp.*
EF-40 EXTREMELY FINE—*Small amount of wear on top of hair and below L in LIBERTY. Wear evident on wing tips and neck of eagle.*
AU-50 ABOUT UNCIRCULATED—*Trace of wear on tip of coronet and hair above eye.*
AU-55 CHOICE ABOUT UNCIRCULATED—*Evidence of friction on design high points. Most of mint luster remains.*
MS-60 UNCIRCULATED—*No trace of wear. Light blemishes.*
MS-63 SELECT UNCIRCULATED—*Some distracting contact marks or blemishes in prime focal areas. Luster may be impaired.*
PF-63 PROOF—*Reflective surfaces with only a few blemishes in secondary focal places. No major flaws.*

	Mintage	VF-20	EF-40	AU-50	AU-55	MS-60	MS-63	PF-63
1866 (30)	6,730	$400.	$900.	$2,000.	$2,500.	$8,000.		$13,000.
1866S	34,920	500.	1,500.	4,500.	5,500.	14,000.		
1867 (50)	6,920	250.	900.	2,000.	2,500.	6,500.		12,500.
1867S	29,000	750.	1,550.	4,500.	6,000.	15,000.		
1868 (25)	5,725	400.	650.	1,500.	2,000.	6,000.		13,000.
1868S	52,000	250.	1,000.	1,900.	2,500.	10,000.		
1869 (25)	1,785	500.	1,250.	1,700.	2,200.	8,500.		13,000.
1869S	31,000	300.	1,000.	1,700.	2,200.	13,500.		
1870 (35)	4,035	400.	1,200.	1,200.	1,800.	8,500.		13,000.
1870CC	7,675	3,000.	9,000.	17,500.	22,000.			
1870S	17,000	450.	1,250.	4,500.	5,500.	15,000.		
1871 (30)	3,230	500.	850.	1,850.	2,250.	7,500.		12,000.
1871CC	20,770	750.	2,250.	7,500.	9,000.	35,000.		
1871S	25,000	250.	500.	1,500.	2,000.	7,500.		
1872 (30)	1,690	450.	1,000.	1,500.	2,000.	7,500.	$10,000.	12,000.
1872CC	16,980	750.	2,500.	10,000.	15,000.	35,000.		
1872S	36,400	250.	350.	1,500.	1,850.	7,500.		
1873 (25)	112,505	115.	150.	200.	225.	450.	2,200.	12,000.
1873CC	7,416	1,250.	6,000.	15,000.	18,500.	35,000.		
1873S	31,000	250.	750.	1,850.	2,150.	10,000.		
1874 (20)	3,508	300.	850.	1,250.	1,500.	6,500.	12,500.	12,000.

	Mintage	VF-20	EF-40	AU-50	AU-55	MS-60	MS-63	PF-63
1874CC	21,198	$500.	$1,200.	$6,000.	$7,500.	$25,000.		
1874S	16,000	300.	1,200.	2,500.	3,000.	11,000.		
1875 (20)	220	20,000.	27,500.	40,000.	45,000.			$40,000.
1875CC	11,828	900.	2,500.	7,500.	8,500.	35,000.		
1875S	9,000	300.	1,100.	2,500.	3,000.	8,000.		
1876 (45)	1,477	675.	1,300.	2,000.	2,250.	6,000.	13,000.	10,000.
1876CC	6,887	800.	3,500.	8,500.	10,500.	27,500.		
1876S	4,000	850.	1,800.	5,000.	6,000.	12,500.		
1877 (20)	1,152	500.	1,500.	2,000.	2,750.	7,000.	15,000.	13,000.
1877CC	8,680	600.	2,000.	6,500.	8,500.	28,500.		
1877S	26,700	200.	250.	700.	800.	4,000.	10,000.	
1878 (20)	131,740	100.	115.	150.	160.	225.	1,000.	15,000.
1878CC	9,054	1,500.	4,500.	12,500.	15,000.	32,500.		
1878S	144,700	100.	120.	155.	165.	250.	2,000.	
1879 (30)	301,950	100.	115.	145.	160.	225.	1,000.	12,000.
1879CC	17,281	300.	950.	2,250.	3,000.	14,000.		
1879S	426,200	100.	115.	145.	160.	400.	1,500.	
1880 (36)	3,166,436	100.	115.	125.	135.	150.	500.	10,000.
1880CC	51,017	300.	500.	1,000.	1,400.	6,000.		
1880S	1,348,900	100.	120.	125.	130.	145.	500.	
1881 (42)	5,708,802	100.	120.	125.	130.	145.	500.	9,500.
1881 CC	13,886	350.	850.	4,000.	5,500.	14,000.	35,000.	
1881S	969,000	100.	120.	125.	130.	145.	500.	
1882 (48)	2,514,568	100.	120.	125.	130.	145.	500.	9,500.
1882 CC	82,817	250.	400.	500.	650.	5,000.	25,000.	
1882S	969,000	100.	120.	125.	130.	145.	500.	
1883 (61)	233,461	100.	120.	125.	130.	145.	750.	9,500.
1883 CC	12,598	300.	750.	2,000.	2,500.	10,000.		
1883S	83,200	100.	120.	175.	200.	450.	1,250.	
1884 (48)	191,078	100.	120.	125.	160.	400.	1,480.	9,500.
1884 CC	16,402	350.	600.	1,800.	2,400.	10,600.		
1884S	177,000	100.	120.	125.	135.	180.	1,260.	
1885 (66)	601,506	100.	120.	125.	130.	145.	500.	9,500.
1885S	1,211,500	100.	120.	125.	130.	145.	485.	
1886 (72)	388,432	100.	120.	125.	130.	145.	650.	9,200.
1886S	3,268,000	100.	120.	125.	130.	145.	485.	
1887, PfS only (87)	87							30,000.
1887S	1,912,000	100.	120.	125.	130.	145.	500.	
1888 (95)	18,296	100.	120.	125.	130.	145.	700.	7,500.
1888S	293,900	100.	130.	185.	225.	750.	2,000.	
1889 (45)	7,565	160.	220.	285.	320.	625.	1,250.	8,500.
1890 (88)	4,328	240.	265.	340.	500.	1,250.	3,400.	8,400.
1890CC	53,800	180.	210.	320.	350.	650.	2,800.	
1891 (53)	61,413	95.	130.	150.	185.	280.	980.	7,000.
1891CC	208,000	175.	210.	325.	340.	425.	1,800.	
1892 (92)	753,572	85.	100.	110.	120.	135.	460.	8,500.
1892CC	82,968	175.	210.	360.	420.	980.	3,300.	
1892O	10,000	280.	580.	800.	1,000.	2,000.		
1892S	298,400	85.	115.	150.	175.	285.	1,820.	
1893 (77)	1,528,197	85.	100.	110.	120.	135.	430.	8,050.
1893CC	60,000	160.	250.	400.	485.	850.	3,750.	
1893O	110,000	135.	180.	285.	350.	585.	3,800.	
1893S	224,000	95.	115.	120.	130.	145.	450.	
1894 (75)	957,955	85.	100.	110.	120.	135.	430.	8,050.
1894O	16,600	120.	200.	310.	375.	820.	3,250.	
1894S	55,900	150.	215.	315.	380.	1,800.	6,400.	
1895 (81)	1,345,936	85.	100.	110.	120.	135.	430.	7,150.
1895S	112,000	120.	150.	235.	310.	2,000.	3,750.	
1896 (103)	59,063	85.	100.	110.	120.	145.	535.	6,850.

HALF EAGLES

	Mintage	VF-20	EF-40	AU-50	AU-55	MS-60	MS-63	PF-63
1896S	155,400	$120.	$145.	$175.	$240.	$685.	$3,600.	
1897 (83)	867,883	85.	100.	110.	115.	135.	450.	$7,150.
1897S	354,000	100.	125.	145.	180.	525.	3,200.	
1898 (75)	633,495	85.	100.	110.	115.	140.	475.	7,450.
1898S	1,397,400	95.	115.	125.	130.	145.	550.	
1899 (99)	1,710,729	85.	100.	110.	120.	135.	450.	6,750.
1899S	1,545,000	90.	105.	115.	125.	145.	560.	
1900 (230)	1,405,730	85.	100.	110.	120.	135.	450.	6,650.
1900S	329,000	90.	110.	120.	130.	145.	525.	
1901 (140)	616,040	85.	100.	110.	120.	135.	450.	6,650.
1901S, 1/0	} 3,648,000	100.	125.	140.	160.	200.	500.	
1901S		85.	100.	110.	120.	135.	450.	
1902 (162)	172,562	85.	100.	110.	120.	135.	450.	6,650.
1902S	939,000	85.	100.	110.	120.	135.	450.	
1903 (154)	227,024	85.	100.	110.	120.	135.	450.	6,650.
1903S	1,855,000	85.	100.	110.	120.	135.	450.	
1904 (136)	392,136	85.	100.	110.	120.	135.	450.	6,725.
1904S	97,000	95.	130.	160.	195.	550.	2,400.	
1905 (108)	302,308	85.	100.	110.	120.	135.	450.	6,975.
1905S	880,700	95.	120.	135.	165.	325.	875.	
1906 (85)	348,820	85.	100.	110.	120.	135.	450.	6,650.
1906D	320,000	85.	100.	110.	120.	135.	450.	
1906S	598,000	90.	105.	115.	125.	140.	585.	
1907 (92)	626,192	85.	100.	110.	120.	135.	450.	6,725.
1907D	888,000	85.	100.	110.	120.	135.	450.	
1908	421,874	85.	100.	110.	120.	135.	450.	

INDIAN HEAD TYPE 1908-1929

This type conforms to the quarter eagle of the same date. The incuse designs and lettering make this a unique series, along with the quarter eagle, in United States coinage.

VF-20 VERY FINE—*Noticeable wear on large middle feathers and tip of eagle's wing.*
EF-40 EXTREMELY FINE—*Cheekbone, war bonnet and headband feathers slightly worn. Feathers on eagle's upper wing show considerable wear.*
AU-50 ABOUT UNCIRCULATED—*Trace of wear on cheekbone and headdress.*
AU-55-CHOICE ABOUT UNCIRCULATED—*Evidence of friction on design high points. Most of mint luster remains.*
MS-60 UNCIRCULATED—*No trace of wear. Light blemishes.*
MS-63 SELECT UNCIRCULATED—*Some distracting contact marks or blemishes in prime focal areas. Luster may be impaired.*
PF-63—*Reflective surfaces with only a few blemishes in secondary focal places. No major flaws.*

Scarcer coins with well struck mint marks command higher prices.

Mint mark location

	Mintage	VF-20	EF-40	AU-50	AU-55	MS-60	MS-63	Matte PF-63
1908 (167)	578,012	$125.	$135.	$150.	$160.	$235.	$1,100.	$7,000.
1908D	148,000	125.	135.	150.	160.	235.	1,100.	
1908S	82,000	200.	240.	260.	285.	750.	1,700.	
1909 (78)	627,138	125.	135.	150.	160.	235.	1,100.	7,000.
1909D	3,423,560	125.	135.	150.	160.	235.	1,100.	
1909O	34,200	975.	1,150.	1,800.	1,950.	6,400.	31,500.	
1909S	297,200	150.	160.	185.	220.	800.	6,800.	
1910 (250)	604,250	125.	135.	150.	160.	235.	1,100.	7,000.
1910D	193,600	135.	145.	165.	175.	250.	1,340.	

HALF EAGLES

	Mintage	VF-20	EF-40	AU-50	AU-55	MS-60	MS-63	Matte PF-63
1910S	770,200	$165.	$180.	$195.	$220.	$590.	$3,400.	
1911 ....(139)	915,139	125.	135.	150.	160.	235.	1,100.	$7,000.
1911D	72,500	260.	285.	350.	480.	2,200.	23,000.	
1911S	1,416,000	160.	170.	185.	200.	375.	1,750.	
1912 ....(144)	790,144	125.	135.	150.	160.	235.	1,100.	7,900.
1912S	392,000	185.	200.	220.	275.	1,100.	9,400.	
1913 ....(99)	916,000	125.	135.	150.	160.	235.	1,100.	7,700.
1913S	408,000	165.	180.	250.	280.	850.	9,000.	
1914 ....(125)	247,125	125.	135.	150.	160.	235.	1,100.	7,200.
1914D	247,000	130.	140.	160.	170.	245.	1,850.	
1914S	263,000	185.	200.	220.	250.	725.	8,500.	
1915 ....(75)	588,075	125.	135.	150.	160.	235.	1,100.	9,300.
1915S	164,000	175.	220.	245.	360.	1,275.	11,500.	
1916S	240,000	180.	195.	210.	225.	380.	1,740.	
1929	662,000	3,500.	4,000.	4,400.	4,500.	5,000.	6,600.	

EAGLES ($10.00 Gold Pieces) — 1795-1933

Coinage authority including specified weights and fineness of the eagle conforms to that of the half eagle. The small eagle reverse was used until 1797 when the large, heraldic eagle replaced it.

CAPPED BUST TO RIGHT, SMALL EAGLE 1795-1797

F-12 FINE—*Details on turban and head obliterated.*
VF-20 VERY FINE—*Neck hairlines and details under turban and over forehead are worn but distinguishable.*
EF-40 EXTREMELY FINE—*Definite wear on hair to left of eye and strand of hair across and around turban, also on eagle's wing tips.*
AU-50 ABOUT UNCIRCULATED—*Traces of light wear on only the high points of the design. Half of mint luster is present.*
AU-55 CHOICE ABOUT
MS-60 UNCIRCULATED—*No trace of wear. Light blemishes.*
MS-63 SELECT UNCIRCULATED—*Some distracting contact marks or blemishes in prime focal areas. Luster may be impaired.*

	Mintage	F-12	VF-20	EF-40	AU-50	AU-55	MS-60	MS-63
1795	5,583	$8,750.	$11,200.	$16,000.	$22,000.	$26,000.	$38,000.	$63,000.
1796	4,146	9,650.	12,300.	18,000.	24,000.	28,500.	42,500.	74,000.
1797, Small eagle	3,615	12,600.	15,400.	20,000.	44,000.	58,000.	115,000.	

CAPPED BUST TO RIGHT, HERALDIC EAGLE 1797-1804

	Mintage	F-12	VF-20	EF-40	AU-50	AU-55	MS-60	MS-63
1797, Large eagle	10,940	$4,200.	$5,600.	$7,200.	$12,000.	$14,000.	$20,000.	$42,000.
1798, 8 over 7, 9 stars left., 4 right. ..	900	5,000.	8,000.	15,600.	23,000.	28,000.	58,000.	160,000.
1798, 8 over 7, 7 stars left., 6 right. ..	842	9,000.	15,000.	36,000.	80,000.	98,000.	140,000.	

EAGLES

	Mintage	F-12	VF-20	EF-40	AU-50	AU-55	MS-60	MS-63
1799	37,449	$3,800.	$4,800.	$6,400.	$8,600.	$10,200.	$13,000.	$21,000.
1800	5,999	3,800.	4,800.	6,400.	9,000.	11,000.	17,000.	40,000.

	Mintage	F-12	VF-20	EF-40	AU-50	AU-55	MS-60	MS-63
1801	44,344	3,800.	4,800.	6,400.	8,600.	10,200.	13,000.	21,000.
1803	15,017	3,800.	4,860.	6,500.	9,000.	10,200.	13,000.	30,000.
1804	3,757	3,860.	5,000.	6,800.	11,400.	14,200.	22,000.	70,000.

CORONET TYPE, No Motto Above Eagle 1838-1866

In 1838 the weight and diameter of the eagle were reduced and the obverse and reverse were redesigned. Liberty now faces left and the word liberty is placed on the coronet.

VF-20 VERY FINE—*Hairlines above coronet partly worn. Curls under ear worn but defined.*
EF-40 EXTREMELY FINE—*Small amount of wear on top of hair and below L in LIBERTY. Wear evident on wing tips and neck of eagle.*
AU-50 ABOUT UNCIRCULATED—*Trace of wear on tip of coronet and hair above eye.*
AU-55 CHOICE ABOUT UNCIRCULATED—*Evidence of friction on design high points. Most of mint luster remains.*
MS-60 UNCIRCULATED—*No trace of wear. Light blemishes.*
MS-63 SELECT UNCIRCULATED—*Some distracting contact marks or blemishes in prime focal areas. Luster may be impaired.*
PF-63—*Choice Brilliant surfaces with no noticeable blemishes or flaws. May have a few scatered barely noticeable marks or hairlines.*

Mint mark location on reverse below eagle.

	Mintage	VF-20	EF-40	AU-50	AU-55	MS-60	MS-63	PF-63
1838	7,200	$560.	$1,575.	$3,400.	$4,800.	$22,000.	$60,000.	
1839, Large Letter	25,801	560.	1,075.	3,000.	4,000.	20,000.	36,000.	
1839, Small Letter	12,447	775.	1,950.	4,000.	5,200.	22,000.	64,000.	
1840	47,338	210.	350.	800.	1,000.	6,800.		
1841	63,131	200.	340.	640.	800.	5,000.	18,000.	
1841O	2,500	1,120.	2,700.	7,200.	9,600.	22,000.		
1842	81,507	200.	290.	700.	1,000.	6,800.	18,000.	
1842O	27,400	200.	340.	1,400.	2,000.	11,700.		
1843	75,462	200.	340.	800.	1,200.	7,500.		
1843O	175,162	200.	320.	620.	800.	7,200.		
1844	6,361	580.	1,640.	3,200.	4,000.	10,800.		
1844O	118,700	200.	340.	1,040.	1,240.	9,800.		
1845	26,153	360.	440.	1,260.	1,500.	10,000.		
1845O	47,500	240.	425.	1,120.	1,400.	9,400.	30,000.	
1846	20,095	385.	560.	3,200.	4,200.	15,800.		
1846O	81,780	280.	400.	2,000.	2,520.	10,800.	27,000.	
1847	862,258	200.	270.	320.	400.	2,100.	16,500.	
1847O	571,500	200.	270.	340.	420.	3,750.	14,000.	
1848	145,484	200.	280.	480.	580.	3,420.	18,000.	$135,000.
1848O	35,850	340.	680.	2,000.	2,480.	9,400.	20,000.	
1849	653,618	200.	270.	340.	400.	2,400.	9,200.	

	Mintage	VF-20	EF-40	AU-50	AU-55	MS-60	MS-63	PF-63
1849O	23,900	$230.	$1,360.	$3,200.	$3,980.	$15,800.		
1850	291,451	200.	270.	340.	425.	2,650.	$12,600.	
1850O	57,500	240.	450.	1,960.	2,420.	11,300.		
1851	176,328	200.	285.	350.	460.	3,160.	21,200.	
1851O	263,000	205.	280.	560.	680.	4,160.	15,600.	
1852	263,106	200.	270.	335.	460.	3,160.	18,000.	
1852O	18,000	330.	620.	2,280.	4,000.	17,000.		
1853, 3/2	} 201,253	300.	460.	1,100.	1,380.	10,400.		
1853		200.	270.	340.	420.	2,600.	13,100.	
1853O	51,000	205.	285.	600.	985.	9,100.		
1854	54,250	205.	310.	440.	560.	4,360.		
1854O	52,500	200.	425.	960.	1,160.	6,260.	25,000.	
1854S	123,826	200.	270.	495.	680.	7,160.	28,000.	
1855	121,701	200.	275.	340.	425.	2,660.	12,300.	
1855O	18,000	350.	740.	3,400.	4,020.	15,600.		
1855S	9,000	750.	1,360.	4,460.	5,340.	22,400.		
1856	60,490	200.	270.	350.	425.	2,650.	9,100.	
1856O	14,500	410.	700.	2,300.	2,800.	11,200.		
1856S	68,000	200.	350.	640.	785.	6,680.		
1857	16,606	235.	520.	1,160.	1,385.	9,280.		
1857O	5,500	490.	1,140.	1,975.	2,380.	13,800.		
1857S	26,000	235.	500.	1,260.	1,340.	7,725.	10,800.	
1858	2,521	2,800.	4,120.	6,450.	7,820.	25,000.		
1858O	20,000	200.	460.	1,020.	1,235.	6,185.		
1858S	11,800	825.	1,875.	3,320.	4,020.	19,800.		
1859 (80)	16,093	220.	390.	625.	780.	5,880.		$39,000.
1859O	2,300	2,360.	4,400.	8,780.	9,860.	32,000.		
1859S	7,000	1,100.	2,960.	7,485.	8,680.	28,000.		
1860 (50)	15,105	235.	410.	720.	845.	5,200.	11,300.	28,000.
1860O	11,100	320.	700.	1,380.	1,680.	8,800.		
1860S	5,000	1,360.	2,975.	9,200.	10,800.	28,000.		
1861 (69)	113,233	200.	270.	310.	360.	1,920.		26,000.
1861S	15,500	825.	1,875.	3,480.	4,200.	22,000.		
1862 (35)	10,995	300.	590.	1,325.	1,485.	7,600.		26,000.
1862S	12,500	950.	1,910.	3,080.	3,720.	24,000.		
1863 (30)	1,248	2,275.	4,720.	9,600.	10,800.	32,000.	59,000.	25,000.
1863S	10,000	780.	2,060.	4,985.	5,260.	15,600.		
1864 (50)	3,580	975.	2,200.	4,420.	5,280.	9,200.		26,000.
1864S	2,500	2,700.	6,590.	15,800.	17,800.	36,000.		
1865 (25)	4,005	1,025.	1,440.	4,020.	4,825.	22,000.		26,000.
1865S	16,700	1,890.	5,125.	9,600.	11,400.	31,000.		
1866S	8,500	950.	2,060.	7,220.	8,800.	30,000.		

Motto Above Eagle 1866-1907

Mint mark location on the reverse below eagle.

VF-20 VERY FINE—*Half of hairlines over coronet visible. Curls under ear worn but defined. IN GOD WE TRUST and its ribbon are sharp.*

EF-40 EXTREMELY FINE—*Small amount of wear on top of hair and below L in LIBERTY. Wear evident on wing tips and neck of eagle.*

AU-50 ABOUT UNCIRCULATED—*Trace of wear on hair above eye and on coronet.*

AU-55 CHOICE ABOUT UNCIRCULATED—*Evidence of friction on design high points. Most of mint luster remains.*

MS-60 UNCIRCULATED—*No trace of wear. Light blemishes.*

MS-63 SELECT UNCIRCULATED—*Some distracting contact marks or blemishes in prime focal areas. Luster may be impaired.*

PF-63—*Choice Brilliant surfaces with no noticeable blemishes or flaws. May have a few scatered barely noticeable marks or hairlines.*

EAGLES

	Mintage	VF-20	EF-40	AU-50	AU-55	MS-60	MS-63	PF-63
1866 . . . . (30)	3,780	$450.	$1,020.	$2,720.	$3,260.	$14,500.		$21,500.
1866S	11,500	885.	2,025.	4,085.	4,900.	16,500.		
1867 . . . . (50)	3,140	920.	1,475.	2,920.	3,600.	19,000.		22,500.
1867S	9,000	1,360.	3,490.	5,100.	6,200.	29,750.		
1868 . . . . (25)	10,655	300.	450.	945.	1,120.	9,100.		23,800.
1868S	13,500	800.	1,275.	2,200.	3,450.	17,000.		
1869 . . . . (25)	1,855	925.	1,485.	2,880.	3,460.	23,400.		21,500.
1869S	6,430	830.	1,380.	3,385.	4,025.	16,000.		
1870 . . . . (35)	4,025	490.	615.	1,250.	1,460.	12,300.		21,500.
1870CC	5,908	4,480.	13,600.	29,000.	33,000.	68,000.	$112,000.	
1870S	8,000	525.	1,360.	3,620.	4,200.	24,600.		
1871 . . . . (30)	1,820	875.	1,570.	2,485.	2,750.	12,750.		22,800.
1871CC	8,085	1,160.	2,950.	9,400.	11,260.	42,900.	54,000.	
1871S	16,500	580.	860.	3,425.	4,040.	18,800.		
1872 . . . . (30)	1,650	1,295.	1,975.	6,000.	7,250.	10,200.	23,000.	21,500.
1872CC	4,600	1,160.	4,600.	14,000.	16,900.	43,000.	54,000.	
1872S	17,300	300.	495.	1,060.	1,260.	14,400.		
1873 . . . . (25)	825	2,240.	5,620.	9,800.	11,600.	33,800.		21,500.
1873CC	4,543	1,825.	5,120.	14,400.	17,800.	45,000.	54,000.	
1873S	12,000	525.	910.	2,595.	3,100.	18,000.		
1874 . . . . (20)	53,160	150.	160.	175.	210.	1,200.	5,000.	23,800.
1874CC	16,767	480.	1,310.	4,800.	5,800.	30,000.	53,000.	
1874S	10,000	560.	1,780.	4,000.	5,600.	30,000.		
1875 . . . . (20)	120	22,500.	28,000.	39,000.				60,000.
1875CC	7,715	1,750.	5,025.	14,000.	16,750.	47,000.	63,000.	
1876 . . . . (45)	732	1,525.	3,600.	7,600.	8,900.	38,000.		19,000.
1876CC	4,696	1,580.	4,140.	11,200.	13,000.	38,000.	50,000.	
1876S	5,000	720.	900.	3,225.	3,800.	27,600.		
1877 . . . . (20)	817	1,360.	3,000.	4,500.	5,300.	20,400.		19,000.
1877CC	3,332	1,275.	3,000.	8,000.	9,860.	34,000.		
1877S	17,000	280.	425.	1,160.	1,380.	16,600.		
1878 . . . . (20)	73,800	150.	165.	210.	240.	525.	3,400.	19,000.
1878CC	3,244	1,700.	5,000.	11,200.	14,500.	34,000.		
1878S	26,100	250.	320.	965.	1,125.	8,500.	20,000.	
1879 . . . . (30)	384,770	150.	165.	195.	220.	325.	2,680.	16,600.
1879CC	1,762	2,940.	6,180.	14,000.	16,600.	47,000.		
1879O	1,500	975.	2,285.	5,125.	6,200.	21,750.		
1879S	224,000	150.	165.	195.	225.	675.	3,960.	
1880 . . . . (36)	1,644,876	150.	165.	180.	190.	210.	1,900.	15,200.
1880CC	11,190	275.	450.	925.	1,085.	8,920.		
1880O	9,200	200.	395.	820.	975.	5,100.		
1880S	506,250	150.	165.	190.	210.	250.	2,500.	
1881 . . . . (40)	3,877,260	150.	165.	175.	180.	210.	800.	15,200.
1881CC	24,015	265.	375.	580.	685.	3,900.	14,400.	
1881O	8,350	220.	430.	675.	800.	4,700.		
1881S	970,000	150.	165.	175.	180.	210.	2,400.	
1882 . . . . (40)	2,324,480	150.	165.	175.	180.	210.	700.	13,300.
1882CC	6,764	345.	640.	1,800.	2,100.	9,900.	27,000.	
1882O	10,820	215.	300.	720.	850.	3,900.	12,900.	
1882S	132,000	150.	170.	215.	235.	320.	1,600.	
1883 . . . . (40)	208,740	150.	165.	170.	175.	210.	1,650.	13,300.
1883CC	12,000	275.	450.	1,320.	1,460.	8,900.	27,000.	
1883O	800	1,260.	4,460.	6,340.	7,500.	22,500.		
1883S	38,000	150.	165.	210.	235.	560.	7,200.	
1884 . . . . (45)	76,905	150.	165.	180.	195.	325.	2,500.	13,300.
1884CC	9,925	285.	600.	1,350.	1,575.	7,860.	25,000.	
1884S	124,250	150.	165.	210.	225.	320.	3,380.	
1885 . . . . (65)	253,527	150.	165.	200.	215.	235.	2,650.	11,400.
1885S	228,000	150.	165.	200.	215.	235.	2,800.	

	Mintage	VF-20	EF-40	AU-50	AU-55	MS-60	MS-63	PF-63
1886 . . . .(60)	236,160	$150.	$165.	$200.	$210.	$230.	$1,700.	$11,400.
1886S	826,000	150.	160.	175.	180.	210.	900.	
1887 . . . .(80)	53,680	155.	170.	195.	210.	425.	2,600.	10,900.
1887S	817,000	150.	160.	175.	180.	200.	1,600.	
1888 . . . .(75)	132,996	150.	165.	190.	205.	375.	3,160.	9,000.
1888O	21,335	150.	165.	195.	210.	350.	3,160.	
1888S	648,700	150.	160.	175.	180.	215.	1,980.	
1889 . . . .(45)	4,485	210.	295.	600.	685.	1,525.	4,960.	10,200.
1889S	425,400	150.	160.	175.	180.	215.	1,395.	
1890 . . . .(63)	58,043	150.	160.	185.	200.	400.	3,160.	9,700.
1890CC	17,500	235.	275.	400.	460.	1,175.	9,000.	
1891 . . . .(48)	91,868	150.	160.	175.	180.	205.	2,650.	8,550.
1891CC	103,732	235.	270.	340.	375.	475.	3,160.	
1892 . . . .(72)	797,552	150.	160.	175.	180.	200.	1,125.	9,750.
1892CC	40,000	235.	280.	400.	485.	2,125.	5,860.	
1892O	28,688	150.	160.	175.	180.	215.	3,600.	
1892S	115,500	150.	160.	190.	200.	250.	2,600.	
1893 . . . .(55)	1,840,895	150.	160.	175.	180.	200.	720.	9,750.
1893CC	14,000	235.	430.	900.	1,020.	2,500.	11,250.	
1893O	17,000	165.	205.	260.	285.	410.	3,780.	
1893S	141,350	150.	160.	180.	185.	210.	2,935.	
1894 . . . .(43)	2,470,778	150.	160.	175.	180.	200.	700.	10,900.
1894O	107,500	150.	160.	205.	230.	575.	3,500.	
1894S	25,000	160.	225.	460.	540.	2,340.	7,200.	
1895 . . . .(56)	567,826	150.	160.	175.	180.	200.	750.	8,500.
1895O	98,000	150.	160.	205.	215.	325.	2,750.	
1895S	49,000	150.	160.	290.	325.	1,530.	6,750.	
1896 . . . .(78)	76,348	150.	160.	180.	185.	220.	1,395.	8,500.
1896S	123,750	150.	160.	295.	320.	1,495.	7,500.	
1897 . . . .(69)	1,000,159	150.	160.	175.	180.	200.	700.	10,200.
1897O	42,500	155.	170.	200.	210.	445.	2,675.	
1897S	234,750	150.	160.	200.	215.	485.	2,500.	
1898 . . . .(67)	812,197	150.	160.	175.	180.	200.	1,120.	8,300.
1898S	473,600	150.	160.	175.	180.	220.	2,700.	
1899 . . . .(86)	1,262,305	150.	160.	175.	180.	200.	740.	8,300.
1899O	37,047	155.	170.	185.	195.	350.	2,975.	
1899S	841,000	150.	160.	175.	180.	220.	1,650.	
1900 . . . .(120)	293,960	150.	160.	175.	180.	220.	740.	8,300.
1900S	81,000	155.	180.	240.	250.	525.	3,000.	
1901 . . . .(85)	1,718,825	150.	160.	175.	180.	200.	700.	8,300.
1901O	72,041	150.	160.	185.	190.	220.	1,950.	
1901S	2,812,750	150.	160.	175.	180.	200.	700.	
1902 . . . .(113)	82,513	150.	160.	175.	180.	205.	700.	8,300.
1902S	469,500	150.	160.	175.	180.	200.	700.	
1903 . . . .(96)	125,926	150.	160.	180.	185.	220.	700.	8,300.
1903O	112,771	150.	160.	190.	195.	225.	2,130.	
1903S	538,000	150.	160.	175.	180.	200.	775.	
1904 . . . .(108)	162,038	150.	160.	175.	180.	200.	700.	8,300.
1904O	108,950	150.	160.	180.	185.	230.	2,040.	
1905 . . . .(86)	201,078	150.	160.	175.	180.	200.	860.	8,300.
1905S	369,250	150.	160.	185.	200.	650.	2,975.	
1906 . . . .(77)	165,497	150.	160.	175.	180.	200.	1,000.	8,300.
1906D	981,000	150.	160.	175.	180.	200.	750.	
1906O	86,895	150.	160.	195.	200.	240.	2,190.	
1906S	457,000	150.	160.	205.	215.	320.	2,000.	
1907 . . . .(74)	1,203,973	150.	160.	175.	180.	200.	700.	8,300.
1907D	1,030,000	150.	160.	175.	180.	200.	900.	
1907S	210,500	150.	160.	195.	210.	350.	2,135.	

INDIAN HEAD TYPE 1907-1933

No Motto

With Motto
IN GOD WE TRUST

Mint mark location is above left tip of branch on 1908 D no motto, and at left of arrow points thereafter.

VF-20 VERY FINE—*Bonnet feathers worn near band. Hair high points show wear.*
EF-40 EXTREMELY FINE—*Slight wear on cheekbone and headdress feathers. Eagle's eye and left wing will show slight wear.*
AU-50 ABOUT UNCIRCULATED—*Trace of wear on hair above eye and on forehead.*
AU-55-CHOICE ABOUT UNCIRCULATED—*Evidence of friction on design high points. Most of mint luster remains.*
MS-60 UNCIRCULATED—*No trace of wear. Light blemishes.*
MS-63 SELECT UNCIRCULATED—*Some distracting contact marks or blemishes in prime focal areas. Luster may be impaired.*
PF-63—*Reflective surfaces with only a few blemishes in secondary focal places. No major flaws.*

Uncirculated (MS-65) coins are worth substantial premiums.

No Motto on Reverse 1907-1908

	Mintage	VF-20	EF-40	AU-50	AU-55	MS-60	MS-63	PF-63
1907 Wire rim, periods	500	$7,400.	$7,900.	$9,000.	$9,600.	$12,000.	$16,000.	
1907, Rounded rim, periods before and after E PLURIBUS UNUM	42	14,800.	16,000.	18,000.	18,800.	22,000.	$36,000.	
1907 No periods	239,406	260.	270.	290.	300.	335.	1,650.	
1908 No motto	33,500	270.	280.	300.	310.	560.	2,000.	
1908D No motto	210,000	260.	270.	290.	300.	510.	3,800.	

Motto on Reverse 1908-1933

	Mintage	VF-20	EF-40	AU-50	AU-55	MS-60	MS-63	Matte PF-63
1908 (116)	341,486	$240.	$250.	$285.	$295.	$335.	$1,120.	$10,500.
1908D	836,500	240.	250.	300.	320.	500.	4,050.	
1908S	59,850	270.	280.	350.	385.	1,000.	5,600.	
1909 (74)	184,863	240.	250.	285.	295.	345.	1,500.	10,500.
1909D	121,540	240.	250.	285.	295.	360.	2,340.	
1909S	292,350	240.	250.	285.	295.	410.	2,600.	
1910 (204)	318,704	240.	250.	285.	295.	310.	760.	10,500.
1910D	2,356,640	240.	250.	285.	295.	325.	740.	
1910S	811,000	240.	250.	285.	295.	400.	1,080.	
1911 (95)	505,595	240.	250.	285.	295.	325.	775.	10,500.
1911D	30,100	400.	500.	560.	675.	2,400.	11,000.	
1911S	51,000	360.	375.	435.	460.	725.	4,500.	
1912 (83)	405,083	240.	250.	285.	295.	325.	750.	10,500.
1912S	300,000	240.	250.	285.	300.	500.	3,500.	
1913 (71)	442,071	240.	250.	285.	295.	325.	650.	10,500.
1913S	66,000	400.	425.	560.	660.	2,300.	17,500.	
1914 (50)	151,050	240.	250.	285.	300.	375.	1,260.	10,500.
1914D	343,500	240.	250.	285.	300.	385.	1,280.	
1914S	208,000	240.	250.	285.	305.	450.	1,400.	
1915 (75)	351,075	240.	250.	285.	300.	385.	840.	10,900.
1915S	59,000	375.	485.	560.	625.	1,900.	6,300.	
1916S	138,500	240.	250.	300.	320.	495.	2,600.	
1920S	126,500	4,000.	4,800.	5,400.	6,000.	12,000.	37,000.	
1926	1,014,000	240.	250.	285.	295.	320.	650.	
1930S	96,000	3,200.	4,000.	5,300.	5,600.	6,850.	11,500.	
1932	4,463,000	240.	250.	285.	295.	320.	650.	
1933	312,500	17,000.	20,000.	30,000.	31,500.	42,000.	72,000.	

— DOUBLE EAGLES ($20.00 Gold Pieces) — 1850-1933 —

This largest denomination of all regular United States issues was authorized to be coined by the Act of March 3, 1849. Its weight was 516 grains, .900 fine.

Mint mark location is below the eagle

VF-20 VERY FINE—*LIBERTY is bold. Prongs on crown defined. Lower half worn flat. Hair worn about ear.*
EF-40 EXTREMELY FINE—*Trace of wear on rounded prongs of crown and down hair curls. Minor bag marks.*
AU-50 ABOUT UNCIRCULATED—*Trace of wear on hair over eye and on coronet.*
AU-55-CHOICE ABOUT UNCIRCULATED—*Evidence of friction on design high points. Most of mint luster remains.*
MS-60 UNCIRCULATED—*No trace of wear. Light blemishes.*
MS-63 SELECT UNCIRCULATED—*Some distracting contact marks or blemishes in prime focal areas. Luster may be impaired.*
PF-63—*Reflective surfaces with only a few blemishes in secondary focal places. No major flaws.*

Without Motto on Reverse 1850-1866

	Mintage	VF-20	EF-40	AU-50	AU-55	MS-60	MS-63	PF-63
1850	1,170,261	$385.	$635.	$1,525.	$1,800.	$4,100.	$30,000.	
1850O	141,000	470.	775.	4,400.	5,250.	20,000.		
1851	2,087,155	365.	385.	540.	650.	1,950.	12,500.	
1851O	315,000	400.	500.	960.	1,150.	10,600.		
1852	2,053,026	365.	390.	520.	635.	2,000.	8,600.	
1852O	190,000	420.	500.	1,075.	1,250.	9,300.		
1853	1,261,326	365.	390.	540.	650.	2,700.	13,800.	
1853O	71,000	400.	650.	1,500.	1,780.	15,000.		
1854	757,899	375.	400.	540.	680.	3,600.	13,800.	
1854O	3,250	17,000.	34,000.	64,000.	72,000.	150,000.		
1854S	141,468	385.	450.	710.	850.	2,200.	7,400.	
1855	364,666	375.	400.	635.	800.	4,800.		
1855O	8,000	1,275.	3,150.	9,600.	10,800.	44,000.		
1855S	879,675	375.	400.	600.	790.	4,250.	8,000.	
1856	329,878	380.	410.	610.	825.	5,200.	14,000.	
1856O	2,250	22,000.	41,000.	65,000.	74,000.	128,000.	260,000.	
1856S	1,189,750	375.	400.	650.	785.	3,400.	7,400.	
1857	439,375	375.	400.	540.	675.	2,000.	16,100.	
1857O	30,000	580.	960.	2,300.	2,600.	16,000.	72,000.	
1857S	970,500	375.	400.	560.	695.	2,400.	4,400.	
1858	211,714	400.	500.	680.	780.	2,900.	22,000.	
1858O	35,250	750.	1,150.	2,700.	3,100.	15,400.		
1858S	846,710	375.	400.	550.	780.	5,600.		
1859 (80)	43,677	525.	1,160.	2,300.	2,800.	18,000.		$52,000.
1859O	9,100	1,850.	3,800.	9,400.	10,800.	46,000.		
1859S	636,445	375.	400.	560.	760.	2,900.		
1860 (59)	577,729	375.	400.	535.	585.	2,260.	12,000.	43,000.
1860O	6,600	1,750.	3,200.	9,600.	10,860.	50,000.		
1860S	544,950	375.	400.	575.	680.	3,750.	12,300.	
1861 (66)	2,976,519	375.	400.	535.	625.	1,450.	5,800.	43,000.
1861O	17,741	1,300.	2,200.	7,600.	8,800.	52,000.		
1861S	768,000	375.	400.	880.	975.	4,900.	19,000.	
1862 (35)	92,168	500.	800.	1,600.	1,760.	9,200.	20,600.	36,000.
1862S	854,173	375.	425.	880.	940.	6,200.		

	Mintage	VF-20	EF-40	AU-50	AU-55	MS-60	MS-63	PF-63
1863 . . . .(30)	142,820	$385.	$485.	$1,020.	$1,100.	$10,000.	$22,000.	
1863S	966,570	375.	430.	750.	860.	4,500.	19,000.	
1864 . . . .(50)	204,285	425.	565.	1,000.	1,160.	8,000.		$36,000.
1864S	793,660	375.	400.	920.	1,000.	3,800.	13,600.	
1865 . . . .(25)	351,200	375.	400.	525.	585.	3,600.	15,800.	36,000.
1865S	1,042,500	375.	400.	525.	580.	3,200.	3,800.	
1866S	12,000	900.	1,600.	6,000.	7,400.	27,000.		

Motto Above Eagle, Value TWENTY D. 1866-1876

	Mintage	VF-20	EF-40	AU-50	AU-55	MS-60	MS-63	PF-63
1866 . . . .(30)	698,775	$375.	$460.	$700.	$800.	$2,900.	$18,000.	$29,000.

	Mintage	VF-20	EF-40	AU-50	AU-55	MS-60	MS-63	PF-63
1866S	842,250	375.	380.	690.	840.	9,200.		
1867 . . . .(50)	251,065	375.	380.	500.	575.	1,460.	12,400.	29,000.
1867S	920,750	375.	400.	880.	960.	8,400.		
1868 . . . .(25)	98,600	500.	640.	1,080.	1,200.	5,900.	24,700.	29,000.
1868S	837,500	375.	400.	675.	760.	5,200.		
1869 . . . .(25)	175,155	375.	525.	690.	820.	3,600.	13,200.	29,000.
1869S	686,750	375.	380.	600.	800.	3,100.	19,000.	
1870 . . . .(35)	155,185	400.	535.	925.	1,020.	5,200.		29,000.
1870CC	3,789	46,000.	62,000.	128,000.	150,000.	200,000.		
1870S	982,000	375.	380.	500.	650.	3,000.	18,000.	
1871 . . . .(30)	80,150	375.	525.	860.	980.	2,400.	16,000.	29,000.
1871CC	17,387	2,800.	4,500.	11,000.	13,400.	30,000.		
1871S	928,000	375.	380.	410.	480.	2,600.	13,600.	
1872 . . . .(30)	251,880	375.	380.	410.	460.	1,560.	15,800.	29,000.
1872CC	26,900	1,000.	1,300.	3,000.	4,200.	16,000.		
1872S	780,000	375.	380.	410.	460.	1,680.	15,200.	
1873 . . . .(25)	1,709,825	375.	380.	400.	440.	575.	6,800.	29,000.
1873CC	22,410	1,250.	2,000.	3,600.	4,260.	18,000.	66,000.	
1873S	1,040,600	375.	380.	400.	445.	925.	13,200.	
1874 . . . .(20)	366,800	375.	380.	400.	440.	680.	12,300.	29,000.
1874CC	115,085	600.	825.	1,300.	1,420.	5,200.		
1874S	1,214,000	375.	380.	400.	435.	800.	16,000.	
1875 . . . .(20)	295,740	375.	380.	400.	430.	590.	6,800.	45,000.
1875CC	111,151	600.	700.	860.	925.	1,350.	11,000.	
1875S	1,230,000	375.	380.	400.	430.	590.	10,000.	
1876 . . . .(45)	583,905	375.	380.	400.	430.	580.	7,300.	29,000.
1876CC	138,441	600.	700.	900.	980.	2,700.	22,000.	
1876S	1,597,000	375.	380.	400.	430.	580.	7,300.	

TWENTY DOLLARS 1877-1907

	Mintage	VF-20	EF-40	AU-50	AU-55	MS-60	MS-63	PF-63
1877 . . . .(20)	397,670	$375.	$380.	$400.	$420.	$480.	$3,400.	$21,500.
1877CC	42,565	695.	860.	1,300.	1,380.	9,600.		
1877S	1,735,000	375.	380.	400.	420.	435.	7,750.	
1878 . . . .(20)	543,645	375.	380.	400.	410.	425.	3,500.	23,500.
1878CC	13,180	1,080.	1,600.	2,500.	2,800.	15,000.		
1878S	1,739,000	375.	380.	400.	420.	435.	13,750.	
1879 . . . .(30)	207,630	375.	380.	400.	425.	600.	7,950.	25,000.
1879CC	10,708	1,120.	1,780.	3,200.	3,600.	18,000.		
1879O	2,325	2,560.	3,800.	8,400.	9,800.	45,000.	75,000.	
1879S	1,223,800	375.	380.	400.	430.	800.		
1880 . . . .(36)	51,456	375.	380.	400.	450.	1,780.	10,400.	22,500.
1880S	836,000	375.	380.	400.	425.	585.	9,400.	
1881 . . . .(61)	2,260	2,500.	3,700.	7,500.	8,400.	26,000.		22,500.
1881S	727,000	375.	380.	400.	425.	525.	11,000.	
1882 . . . .(59)	630	3,920.	8,200.	15,800.	16,200.	39,000.	84,000.	22,500.
1882CC	39,140	635.	750.	1,060.	1,180.	3,960.		
1882S	1,125,000	375.	380.	400.	420.	435.	9,400.	
1883, Pfs only . . .(92)	92							40,000.
1883CC	59,962	625.	725.	900.	985.	2,400.	13,000.	
1883S	1,189,000	375.	380.	400.	420.	425.	5,300.	
1884, Pfs only . . .(71)	71							40,000.
1884CC	81,139	600.	710.	880.	975.	1,600.		
1884S	916,000	375.	380.	400.	410.	425.	4,260.	
1885 . . . .(77)	828	3,700.	4,750.	6,200.	7,060.	21,000.	39,000.	20,500.
1885CC	9,450	1,175.	1,680.	3,000.	3,260.	6,100.		
1885S	683,500	375.	380.	400.	410.	425.	4,200.	
1886 . . . .(106)	1,106	4,500.	6,300.	17,000.	18,900.	27,000.	47,000.	20,000.
1887, Pfs only . .(121)	121							29,000.
1887S	283,000	375.	380.	400.	410.	425.	8,900.	
1888 . . . .(105)	226,266	375.	380.	400.	410.	430.	2,975.	16,500.
1888S	859,600	375.	380.	400.	410.	425.	3,400.	
1889 . . . .(41)	44,111	375.	380.	400.	410.	435.	6,860.	16,700.
1889CC	30,945	650.	800.	1,150.	1,220.	2,000.	9,800.	
1889S	774,700	375.	380.	400.	410.	425.	4,260.	
1890 . . . .(55)	75,995	375.	380.	400.	410.	425.	3,480.	15,500.
1890CC	91,209	600.	650.	760.	825.	1,350.	17,000.	
1890S	802,750	375.	380.	400.	410.	425.	5,340.	
1891 . . . .(52)	1,442	1,800.	2,800.	4,900.	5,600.	21,000.		15,800.
1891CC	5,000	1,920.	2,975.	4,400.	4,780.	9,250.	28,000.	
1891S	1,288,125	375.	380.	400.	410.	425.	2,080.	
1892 . . . .(93)	4,523	625.	900.	1,420.	1,540.	3,200.	11,500.	15,500.
1892CC	27,265	635.	750.	1,080.	1,160.	1,940.	15,750.	
1892S	930,150	375.	380.	400.	410.	425.	2,500.	
1893 . . . .(59)	344,339	375.	380.	400.	410.	425.	1,500.	15,800.
1893CC	18,402	750.	900.	1,020.	1,100.	1,750.	9,400.	

	Mintage	VF-20	EF-40	AU-50	AU-55	MS-60	MS-63	PF-63
1893S	996,175	$375.	$380.	$400.	$410.	$425.	$2,400.	
1894 (50)	1,368,990	375.	380.	400.	410.	425.	980.	$15,500.
1894S	1,048,550	375.	380.	400.	410.	425.	1,500.	
1895 (51)	1,114,656	375.	380.	400.	410.	425.	810.	15,500.
1895S	1,143,500	375.	380.	400.	410.	425.	1,500.	
1896 (128)	792,663	375.	380.	400.	410.	425.	1,260.	15,500.
1896S	1,403,925	375.	380.	400.	410.	425.	1,400.	
1897 (86)	1,383,261	375.	380.	400.	410.	425.	850.	16,000.
1897S	1,470,250	375.	380.	400.	410.	425.	920.	
1898 (75)	170,470	375.	380.	400.	410.	425.	3,000.	15,500.
1898S	2,575,175	375.	380.	400.	410.	425.	830.	
1899 (84)	1,669,384	375.	380.	400.	410.	425.	640.	15,500.
1899S	2,010,300	375.	380.	400.	410.	425.	1,150.	
1900 (124)	1,874,584	375.	380.	400.	410.	425.	550.	15,500.
1900S	2,459,500	375.	380.	400.	410.	425.	1,450.	
1901 (96)	111,526	375.	380.	400.	410.	425.	600.	15,500.
1901S	1,596,000	375.	380.	400.	410.	425.	2,400.	
1902 (114)	31,254	375.	380.	400.	410.	525.	6,500.	15,500.
1902S	1,753,625	375.	380.	400.	410.	425.	2,400.	
1903 (158)	287,428	375.	380.	400.	410.	425.	550.	15,500.
1903S	954,000	375.	380.	400.	410.	425.	1,120.	
1904 (98)	6,256,797	375.	380.	400.	410.	425.	525.	15,500.
1904S	5,134,175	375.	380.	400.	410.	425.	600.	
1905 (92)	59,011	375.	380.	400.	425.	575.	8,900.	15,500.
1905S	1,813,000	375.	380.	400.	410.	425.	2,380.	
1906 (94)	69,690	375.	380.	400.	410.	425.	4,000.	15,500.
1906D	620,250	375.	380.	400.	410.	425.	1,200.	
1906S	2,065,750	375.	380.	400.	410.	425.	1,450.	
1907 (78)	1,451,864	375.	380.	400.	410.	425.	580.	15,500.
1907D	842,250	375.	380.	400.	410.	425.	1,275.	
1907S	2,165,800	375.	380.	400.	410.	425.	1,460.	

SAINT-GAUDENS TYPE 1907-1933

The $20 gold piece designed by Augustus Saint-Gaudens is considered to be the most beautiful United States coin. The first coins issued were 11,250 high relief pieces struck for general circulation. The relief is much higher than later issues and the date 1907 is in Roman numerals. A few of the proof coins were made using the lettered edge collar from the extremely high relief version. These can be distinguished by a pronounced bottom left serif on the N in UNUM, and other minor differences. Flat-relief double eagles were issued later in 1907 with Arabic numerals, and continued through 1933.

The field of the rare extremely high relief experimental pieces is excessively concave and connects directly with the edge without any border, giving it a sharp knifelike appearance; Liberty's skirt shows two folds on the side of her right leg; the Capitol building in the background at left is very small; the sun, on the reverse side, has 14 rays, as opposed to the regular high relief coins that have only 13 rays extending from the sun. High relief proofs are trial or experimental pieces.

VF-20 VERY FINE—*Minor wear on legs and toes. Eagle's left wing and breast feathers worn.*
EF-40 EXTREMELY FINE—*Drapery lines on chest visible. Wear on left breast, knee and below. Eagle's feathers on breast and right wing are bold.*
AU-50 ABOUT UNCIRCULATED—*Trace of wear on nose, breast, and knee. Wear visible on eagle's wings.*
AU-55-CHOICE ABOUT UNCIRCULATED—*Evidence of friction on design high points. Most of mint luster remains.*
MS-60 UNCIRCULATED—*No trace of wear. Light marks or blemishes.*
MS-63 SELECT UNCIRCULATED—*Some distracting contact marks or blemishes in prime focal areas. Luster may be impaired.*

	PF
1907, Ex. high relief, plain edge (*Unique*)	—
1907, Ex. high relief, lettered edge	—

	Mintage	VF-20	EF-40	AU-50	AU-55	MS-60	MS-63	PF
1907 High relief, Roman numerals (MCMVII),	11,250	$3,800.	$4,600.	$5,400.	6,400	$7,200.	$14,000.	—

Arabic Numerals

No Motto

Motto IN GOD WE TRUST. 1908-1933

Mint mark location is on obverse above date.

	Mintage	VF-20	EF-40	AU-50	AU-55	MS-60	MS-63	Matte PF-63
1907	361,667	$400.	$420.	$435.	$440.	$460.	$620.	
1908, No Motto	4,271,551	400.	420.	435.	440.	460.	540.	
1908D, No Motto	663,750	400.	420.	475.	480.	500.	640.	
1908, With Motto (101)	156,359	400.	420.	435.	445.	475.	960.	$14,000.
1908, With Motto	349,500	400.	420.	475.	480.	510.	840.	
1908S, With Motto	22,000	800.	1,100.	1,200.	1,280.	3,000.	9,000.	

1909, 9 over 8

	Mintage	VF-20	EF-40	AU-50	AU-55	MS-60	MS-63	Matte PF-63
1909, 9/8	} 161,282	$400.	$420.	$500.	$550.	$700.	$4,500.	
1909 (67)		400.	420.	475.	480.	510.	2,000.	$14,500.
1909D	52,500	400.	420.	600.	620.	875.	5,000.	
1909S	2,774,925	400.	420.	475.	480.	500.	550.	
1910 (167)	482,167	400.	420.	475.	480.	500.	535.	14,000.
1910D	429,000	400.	420.	475.	480.	500.	570.	
1910S	2,128,250	400.	420.	475.	480.	510.	640.	
1911 (100)	197,350	400.	420.	475.	480.	510.	1,360.	14,000.
1911D	846,500	400.	420.	475.	480.	500.	535.	
1911S	775,750	400.	420.	475.	480.	500.	535.	
1912 (74)	149,824	400.	420.	475.	480.	500.	850.	14,000.
1913 (58)	168,838	400.	420.	475.	480.	500.	1,900.	14,000.
1913D	393,500	400.	420.	475.	480.	500.	625.	
1913S	34,000	400.	410.	625.	635.	850.	2,500.	
1914 (70)	95,320	400.	420.	475.	480.	500.	1,200.	14,000.
1914D	453,000	400.	420.	475.	480.	500.	535.	
1914S	1,498,000	400.	420.	475.	480.	500.	525.	
1915 (50)	152,050	400.	420.	475.	480.	500.	1,500.	14,000.

DOUBLE EAGLES

	Mintage	VF-20	EF-40	AU-50	AU-55	MS-60	MS-63
1915S	567,500	$400.	$420.	$475.	$480.	$500.	$525.
1916S	796,000	400.	420.	475.	480.	500.	640.
1920	228,250	400.	420.	475.	480.	500.	620.
1920S	558,000	6,500.	9,000.	10,000.	11,400.	17,000.	36,000.
1921	528,500	8,500.	13,000.	14,500.	15,800.	26,000.	84,000.
1922	1,375,500	400.	420.	450.	455.	475.	525.
1922S	2,658,000	425.	450.	485.	490.	600.	900.
1923	566,000	400.	420.	450.	455.	475.	525.
1923D	1,702,250	400.	420.	480.	485.	500.	540.
1924	4,323,500	400.	420.	450.	455.	475.	510.
1924D	3,049,500	700.	900.	1,000.	1,080.	1,300.	4,800.
1924S	2,927,500	700.	900.	1,000.	1,080.	1,300.	4,800.
1925	2,831,750	400.	420.	450.	455.	475.	510.
1925D	2,938,500	800.	1,000.	1,360.	1,400.	2,200.	6,000.
1925S	3,776,500	720.	1,000.	1,240.	1,360.	3,900.	14,000.
1926	816,750	400.	420.	450.	455.	475.	510.
1926D	481,000	1,300.	1,800.	2,450.	2,760.	5,600.	15,000.
1926S	2,041,500	560.	900.	1,080.	1,095.	1,200.	2,800.
1927	2,946,750	400.	420.	450.	455.	475.	510.
1927D	180,000	90,000.	140,000.	160,000.	165,000.	185,000.	270,000.
1927S	3,107,000	2,600.	4,000.	4,600.	4,900.	7,800.	36,000.
1928	8,816,000	400.	420.	450.	455.	475.	510.
1929	1,779,750	3,640.	5,840.	6,280.	6,420.	7,400.	13,800.
1930S	74,000	8,450.	13,420.	14,860.	15,400.	17,600.	32,000.
1931	2,938,250	4,860.	7,850.	8,420.	8,640.	11,500.	19,800.
1931D	106,500	4,675.	7,850.	8,760.	9,800.	17,000.	21,600.
1932	1,101,750	4,950.	9,000.	10,400.	10,860.	11,600.	19,400.
1933	445,500	None placed in circulation					

COMMEMORATIVE SILVER COINS

Isabella Quarter

In 1892, to commemorate the World's Columbian Exposition in Chicago, Congress authorized the coinage of a special half dollar and quarter dollar, thus starting a long line of United States commemorative coins. Nearly all commemorative coins have been distributed by private individuals or commissions; they paid the mint the face value of the coins and in turn sold the pieces at a premium to collectors. There are a few instances in which some of the very large issues were later released to circulation at face value.

	Mintage	AU-50	MS-60	MS-63	MS-65
1893, Columbian Exposition, Chicago	24,214	$220.	$300.	$350.	$1,000.

Alabama, Albany, Antietam, Arkansas

2x2 in Field

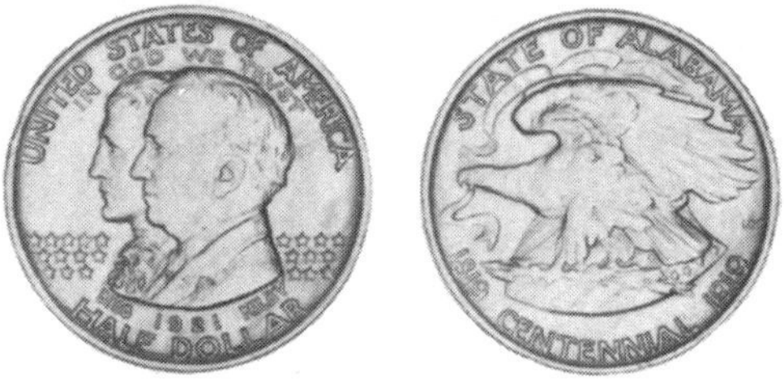

	Mintage	AU-50	MS-60	MS-63	MS-65
1921, Alabama Centennial, with "2X2" in field of obverse	6,006	$100.	$150.	$225.	$900.
1921, Alabama Centennial, no "2X2"	59,038	70.	100.	200.	900.

1936, Albany, New York	17,671	115.	125.	150.	175.

1937, Battle of Antietam	18,028	200.	250.	275.	300.

1935, Arkansas Centennial	13,012	Set	100.	125.	300.
1935D	5,505				
1935S	5,506				

Arkansas, Bay Bridge, Boone

		Mintage	AU-50	MS-60	MS-63	MS-65
1936,	Arkansas Centennial, same as 1935-date 1936 on rev					
1936D	Same	9,660		$100.	$125.	$300.
1936S	Same					
1937,	Arkansas Centennial (same as 1935)					
1937D	Same	5,505		100.	125.	400.
1937SD	Same					
1938,	Arkansas Centennial (same as 1935)					
1938,	Same	3,155		125.	200.	700.
1938S	Same					
1939,	Arkansas Centennial (same as 1935)	2,104				
1939D	Same			325.	400.	1,400.
1939S	Same					
	Single, type coin		$30.	35.	45.	100.

	Mintage	AU-50	MS-60	MS-63	MS-65
1936S, San Francisco Oakland Bay Bridge	71,424	60.	65.	70.	125.

1934 added on reverse

		Mintage	AU-50	MS-60	MS-63	MS-65
1934,	Daniel Boone Bicentennial	10,007	40.	45.	50.	90.
1935,	Same	10,010				
1935D,	Same	5,005	Set	135.	150.	270.
1935S,	Same	5,005				
1935,	Daniel Boone Bicentennial, same as 1934 but small 1934 added on reverse	10,008				
1935D,	Same	2,003	Set	300.	350.	800.
1935S,	Same	2,004				
1936,	D. Boone Bicentennial, same as above	12,012				
1936D,	Same	5,005	Set	135.	150.	270.
1936S,	Same	5,006				
1937,	D. Boone Bicentennial, same as above	9,810				
1937D,	Same	2,506	Set	250.	300.	500.
1937S,	Same	2,506				
1938,	Daniel Boone, same as above	2,100				
1938D,	Same	2,100	Set	375.	450.	750.
1938S,	Same	2,100				
	Single type coin		40.	45.	50.	90.

	Mintage	AU-50	MS-60	MS-63	MS-65
1936, Bridgeport, Conn., Centennial	25,015	$60.	$70.	$80.	$100.

1925S, California Diamond Jubilee	86,394	60.	70.	80.	500.

1951, Carver-Washington	110,018	Set	25.	50.	200.
1951D	10,0044				
1951S	10,004				
1952	2,006,292	Set	25.	50.	150.
1952D	8,006				
1952S	8,006				
1953	8,003	Set	25.	50.	200.
1953D	8,003				
1953S	108,020				
1954	12,006	Set	25.	50.	150.
1954D	12,006				
1954S	122,024				
Single type coin				9.	20.
1936, Cincinnati Music Center	5,005	Set	300.	330.	1,200.
1936D, Same	5,005				
1936S, Same	5,006				
Single type coin		90.	100.	110.	300.

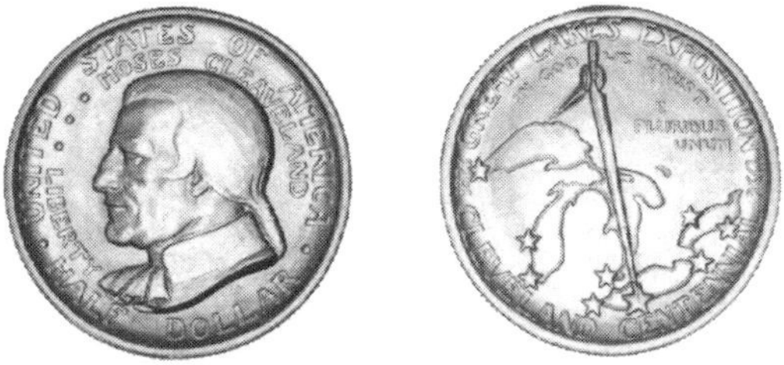

	Mintage	AU-50	MS-60	MS-63	MS-65
1936, Cleveland, Great Lakes Exposition	50,030	$30.	$40.	$45.	$90.

	Mintage	AU-50	MS-60	MS-63	MS-65
1936, Columbia, S.C., Sesquicentennial	9,007				
1936D, Same	8,009	Set	340.	380.	450.
1936S, Same	8,007				
Single type coin		100.	110.	120.	150.

	Mintage	AU-50	MS-60	MS-63	MS-65
1892, Columbian Exp. Chicago	950,000	8.	14.	30.	350.
1893, Same Type	1,550,405	7.	14.	30.	400.

	Mintage	AU-50	MS-60	MS-63	MS-65
1935, Connecticut Tercentenary	25,018	75.	100.	120.	250.

	Mintage	AU-50	MS-60	MS-63	MS-65
1936, Delaware Tercentenary	20,993	$100.	$125.	$150.	$175.

	Mintage	AU-50	MS-60	MS-63	MS-65
1936, Elgin, Illinois, Centennial	20,015	75.	100.	110.	125.

	Mintage	AU-50	MS-60	MS-63	MS-65
1936, Battle of Gettysburg	26,928	125.	150.	175.	300.

	Mintage	AU-50	MS-60	MS-63	MS-65
1922, Grant Memorial, small star above word "Grant" in obv. field	4,256	300.	500.	600.	3,000.
1922, Same, no star in obverse field	67,405	30.	40.	75.	350.

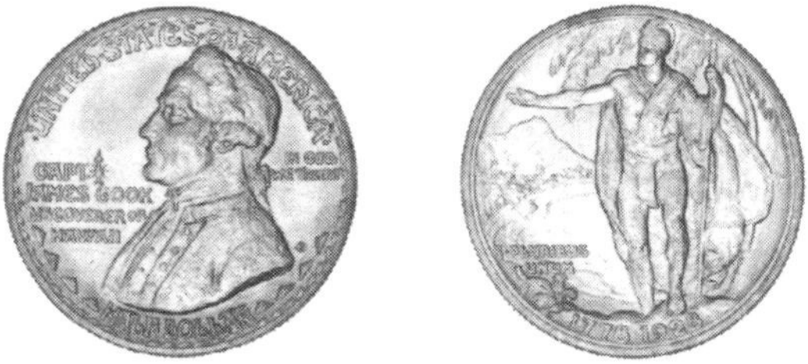

	Mintage	AU-50	MS-60	MS-63	MS-65
1928, Hawaiian Sesquicentennial	9,958	$600.	$750.	$900.	$2,500.
1928, Hawaiian Sesquicentennial sandblast Proof presentation piece	50				

	Mintage	AU-50	MS-60	MS-63	MS-65
1935, Hudson, N.Y. Sesquicentennial	10,008	200.	250.	275.	600.

	Mintage	AU-50	MS-60	MS-63	MS-65
1924, Huguenot-Walloon Tercentenary	142,080	40.	50.	75.	250.

	Mintage	AU-50	MS-60	MS-63	MS-65
1918, Illinois Centennial	100,058	30.	40.	50.	200.

	Mintage	AU-50	MS-60	MS-63	MS-65
1946, Iowa Centennial	100,057	$30.	$35.	$40.	$50.

1925, Lexington-Concord Sesquicentennial	162,013	25.	30.	50.	250.

1936, Long Island Tercentenary	81,826	25.	30.	35.	150.

1936, Lynchburg, Va., Sesquicentennial	20,013	75.	80.	90.	125.

2 ★ 4 in field

	Mintage	AU-50	MS-60	MS-63	MS-65
1920, Maine Centennial	50,028	$35.	$50.	$75.	$250.
1934, Maryland Tercentenary	25,015	50.	60.	70.	125.
1921, Missouri Centennial "2*4" above "1821"	5,000	200.	225.	400.	2,500.
1921, Missouri Centennial, no "2*4"	5,428	100.	175.	350.	2,500.
1923S, Monroe Doctrine Centennial	274,077	10.	20.	60.	1,200.

	Mintage	AU-50	MS-60	MS-63	MS-65
1938, New Rochelle, N.Y. 1688-1938	15,266	$100.	$125.	$150.	$200.

	Mintage	AU-50	MS-60	MS-63	MS-65
1936, Norfolk, Va. Bicentennial	16,936	150.	160.	175.	200.

	Mintage	MS-60	MS-65
1926, Oregon Trail Memorial	47,955	$60.	$125.
1926S, Same	83,055	60.	125.
1928, Same	6,028	75.	150.
1933D, Same	5,008	100.	250.
1934D, Same	7,006	70.	140.
1936, Same	10,006	60.	125.
1936S, Same	5,006	60.	150.
1937D, Same	12,008	60.	125.

	Mintage	AU-50	MS-60	MS-65
1938, Same	6,006	Set	$250.	$400.
1938D, Same	6,005			
1938S, Same	6,006			
1939, Same	3,004	Set	500.	900.
1939D, Same	3,004			
1939S, Same	3,005			
Single type coin		50.	60.	125.

	Mintage	AU-50	MS-60	MS-63	MS-65
1915S, Panama-Pacific Exposition	27,134	$125.	$150.	$300.	$1,000.

	Mintage	AU-50	MS-60	MS-63	MS-65
1920, Pilgrim Tercentenary	152,112	$25.	$30.	$40.	$175.
1921, Same, with 1921 date added in field	20,053	40.	50.	70.	250.

	Mintage	AU-50	MS-60	MS-63	MS-65
1936, Rhode Island Tercentenary	20,013	Set	100.	115.	300.
1936D, Same	15,010				
1936S, Same	15,011				
Single type coin		25.	30.	35.	100.

	Mintage	AU-50	MS-60	MS-63	MS-65
1937, Roanoke Island, N.C.	29,030	75.	90.	100.	125.

	Mintage	AU-50	MS-60	MS-63	MS-65
1936, Arkansas Centennial (Robinson)	25,265	40.	50.	60.	150.

	Mintage	AU-50	MS-60	MS-63	MS-65
1935S, San Diego, California-Pacific Exp.	70,132	$25.	$35.	$40.	$50.
1936D, D mint (same as 1935)	30,092	25.	40.	45.	60.

	Mintage	AU-50	MS-60	MS-63	MS-65
1926, Sesquicentennial of American Independence	141,120	25.	30.	60.	2,000.

	Mintage	AU-50	MS-60	MS-63	MS-65
1935, Old Spanish Trail	10,008	350.	400.	450.	500.

	Mintage	AU-50	MS-60	MS-63	MS-65
1925, Stone Mountain Memorial	1,314,709	20.	25.	30.	100.

	Mintage	AU-50	MS-60	MS-63	MS-65
1934, Texas Centennial	61,463	$40.	$45.	$50.	$80.
1935, Texas Centennial, same as 1934	9,996				
1935D, Same	10,007	Set	135.	150.	240.
1935S, Same	10,008				
1936, Texas Centennial, same as 1934	8,911				
1936D, Same	9,039	Set	135.	150.	240.
1936S, Same	9,055				
1937, Texas Centennial, same as 1934	6,571				
1937D, Same	6,605	Set	135.	150.	240.
1937S, Same	6,637				
1938, Texas Centennial, same as 1934	3,780				
1938D, Same	3,775	Set	250.	300.	600.
1938S, Same	3,814				
Single type coin		40.	45.	50.	80.

	Mintage	AU-50	MS-60	MS-63	MS-65
1925S, Fort Vancouver Centennial	14,994	$100.	$135.	$160.	$600.

	Mintage	AU-50	MS-60	MS-63	MS-65
1927, Vermont Sesquicentennial (Bennington)	28,142	$60.	$75.	$90.	$400.

B.T. Washington, Wisconsin, York County

	Mintage		MS-60	MS-65
1946, Booker T. Washington Memorial	1,000,546	Set	$25.	$60.
1946D	200,113			
1946S	500,279			
1947	100,017	Set	30.	100.
1947D	100,017			
1947S	100,017			
1948	8,005	Set	60.	80.
1948D	8,005			
1948S	8,005			
1949	6,004	Set	$90.	$140.
1949D	6,004			
1949S	6,004			
1950	6,004	Set	50.	80.
1950D	6,004			
1950S	512,091			
1951	510,082	Set	40.	80.
1951D	7,004			
1951S	7,004			
Single type coin			8.	20.

	Mintage	AU-50	MS-60	MS-63	MS-65
1936, Wisconsin Centennial	25,015	$60.	$75.	$85.	$120.

	Mintage	AU-50	MS-60	MS-63	MS-65
1936, York County, Maine Tercentenary	25,015	60.	65.	70.	100.

COMMEMORATIVE SILVER

Lafayette

	Mintage	AU-50	MS-60	MS-63	MS-65
1900, Lafayette Dollar	36,026	$175.	$250.	$650.	$4,000.

COMMEMORATIVE GOLD

Grant, Lewis & Clark, Louisiana Purchase, McKinley, Panama-Pacific

	Mintage	AU-50	MS-60	MS-63	MS-65
1922, Grant Memorial Dollar, star above word "Grant"	5,016	$450.	$500.	$800.	$1,500.
1922, Same, without star	5,000	425.	450.	800.	1,500.
1904, Lewis and Clark Exposition Dollar	10,025	250.	300.	800.	4,000.
1905, Lewis and Clark Exposition Dollar	10,041	250.	350.	1,200.	6,000.

	Mintage	AU-50	MS-60	MS-63	MS-65
1903, Louisiana Purchase Jefferson Dollar	17,500	150.	175.	350.	1,000.
1903, Louisiana Purchase McKinley Dollar	17,500	150.	175.	350.	1,000.
1916, McKinley Memorial Dollar	15,000	125.	150.	300.	900.
1917, McKinley Memorial Dollar	5,000	150.	225.	450.	1,250.

	Mintage	AU-50	MS-60	MS-63	MS-65
1915S, Panama-Pacific Exposition Dollar	15,000	125.	150.	300.	900.
1915S, Panama-Pacific Exposition $2.50	6,749	500.	600.	1,200.	2,500.

	Mintage	AU-50	MS-60	MS-63	MS-65
1915S, Panama-Pacific $50 Round	483	$16,500.	$18,500.	$30,000.	$75,000.

	Mintage	AU-50	MS-60	MS-63	MS-65
1915S, Panama-Pacific $50 Octagonal	645	15,500.	16,500.	27,000.	70,000.
1926, United States Sequicentennial $2.50	46,019	125.	150.	250.	1,900.

	Mintage	MS-65	PF-65
1982D, George Washington-250th Anniversary	2,210,458	$2.50	
1982S, Same, Proof	(4,894,044)		$3.00

	Mintage	MS-65	PF-65
1983P, Discus Thrower Silver Dollar	294,543	5.00	
1983D, Same type D mint	174,014	5.00	
1983S, Same type S mint (1,577,025)	174,014	5.00	5.00

	Mintage	MS-65	PF-65
1984P, Olympic Coliseum Silver Dollar	217,954	5.00	
1984D, Same type D mint	116,675	6.00	
1984S, Same type S mint (1,801,210)	116,675	7.00	6.00

		Mintage	MS-65	PF65
1984P, Olympic Gold Eagle	(33,309)			$175.00
1984D, Olympic Gold Eagle	(34,533)			175.00
1984S, Olympic Gold Eagle	(48,551)			160.00
1984W, Olympic Gold Eagle	(381,085)	75,886	$160.00	160.00

		Mintage	MS-65	PF65
1986D, Statue of Liberty Half Dollar		928,008	3.75	
1986S, Same type S mint Proof	(6,925,627)			3.75

		Mintage	MS-65	PF65
1986P, Statue of Liberty Silver Dollar		723,635	7.00	
1986S, Same type S mint Proof	(6,414,638)			7.00

		Mintage	MS-65	PF65
1986W, Statue of Liberty Gold $5.00	(404,013)	95,248	80.00	80.00

	Mintage	MS-65	PF65
1987P, U.S. Constituton Silver Dollar	451,629	$6.00	
1987S, Same type S mint Proof . . . .(2,747,116)			$6.00

1987W, U.S. Constitution Gold $5.00 . . . .(651,659)	214,225	80.00	80.00

1988D, Olympic Silver Dollar	191,368	6.00	
1988S, Same type S mint, Proof . . . .(1,359,366)			6.00

1988W, Olympic Gold $5.00 . . . .(281,465)	62,913	80.00	80.00

	Mintage	MS-65	PF65
1989D, Congress Bicentennial Half Dollar	163,753	$4.00	
1989S, Congress Bicentennial Half Dollar (767,897)			$4.00

	Mintage	MS-65	PF65
1989D, Congress Silver Dollar	135,203	7.00	
1989S, Congress Silver Dollar (762,198)			8.00

	Mintage	MS-65	PF65
1989W, Congress Bicentennial Gold $5.00 (164,690)	46,899	80.00	80.00

	Mintage	MS-65	PF65
1990W, Eisenhower Silver Dollar	241,669	8.00	
1990P, Same type P mint, Proof (1,144,461)			10.00

	Mintage	MS-65	PF65
1991D, Mount Rushmore Half Dollar	172,754	$7.00	
1991S, Same type S mint, Proof (753,257)			$8.00

	Mintage	MS-65	PF65
1991P, Mount Rushmore Silver Dollar	133,139	15.00	
1991S, Same type S mint, Proof (738,419)			17.00

	Mintage	MS-65	PF65
1991W, Mount Rushmore Gold $5.00 (111,991)	31,959	100.00	90.00

	Mintage	MS-65	PF65
1991D, Korean War Silver Dollar	213,049	12.00	
1991P, Same type P mint, Proof (618,488)			15.00

	Mintage	MS-65	PF65
1991D, U.S.O. Silver Dollar	124,958	$7.00	
1991S, Same type S mint Proof (321,275)			$8.00

	Mintage	MS-65	PF65
1992P, Olympic Clad Half Dollar	161,619	4.00	
1992S, Same type S mint Proof (519,699)			4.00

	Mintage	MS-65	PF65
1992D, Olympic Silver Dollar	187,562	10.00	
1992S, Same type S mint Proof (504,544)			12.00

	Mintage	MS-65	PF65
1992W, Olympic Gold $5.00 (77,313)	27,732	80.00	80.00

	Mintage	MS-65	PF-65
1992D, White House Silver Dollar	123,803	$15.00	
1992W, Same type W mint Proof	(375,849)		$20.00

	Mintage	MS-65	PF-65
1992D, Columbus Half Dollar	135,718	5.00	
1992S, Same type S mint Proof	(390,255)		5.00

	Mintage	MS-65	PF-65
1992D, Columbus Silver Dollar	106,962	15.00	
1992P, Same type P mint Proof	(385,290)		17.00

		Mintage	MS-65	PF-65
1992W, Columbus Gold $5.00	(79,734)	24,331	$110.00	$100.00

		Mintage	MS-65	PF-65
1993W, Bill of Rights Silver Half Dollar		173,224	9.00	
1993S, Same type S mint Proof	(559,758)			7.00

		Mintage	MS-65	PF-65
1993D, Bill of Rights Silver Dollar		92,415	10.00	
1993S, Same type S mint Proof	(515,038)			9.00

		Mintage	MS-65	PF-65
1993W, Bill of Rights Gold $5.00	(79,422)	22,897	110.00	100.00

	Mintage	MS-65	PF-65
(1993) 1991-1995P, World War II Clad Half Dollar . . . . (290,3430)	192,968	$14.00	$15.00

	Mintage	MS-65	PF-65
(1993) 1991-1995D, World War II Silver Dollar	94,700	15.00	
(1993) Same type W mint Proof . . . . (322,422)			18.00

	Mintage	MS-65	PF-65
(1993) 1991-1995W, World War II Gold $5 . . . . (65,461)	23,089	110.00	100.00

	Mintage	MS-65	PF-65
1994D, World Cup Tournament Clad Half Dollar	52,836	4.50	
1994P, Same type P mint Proof . . . . (122,412)			4.50

	Mintage	MS-65	PF-65
1994D, World Cup Tournament Silver Dollar	81,698	$12.00	
1994S, Same type S mint Proof . . . .(576,978)			$15.00

	Mintage	MS-65	PF-65
1994W, World Cup Tournament Gold $5 . . . .(89,619)	22,464	110.00	100.00

	Mintage	MS-65	PF-65
1993, (1994) P Thomas Jefferson Silver Dollar	266,927	12.00	
1993, (1994) S Same type S mint Proof . . . .(332,891)			15.00

Vietnam War Memorial, POWs, Women Veterans

	Mintage	MS-65	PF-65
1994W, Vietnam War Memorial Silver Dollar	57,317	$35.00	
1994P, Same type P mint Proof . . . .(226,262)			$40.00

	Mintage	MS-65	PF-65
1994W, U.S. POW Silver Dollar	54,790	40.00	
1994P, Same type P mint Proof . . . .(220,100)			35.00

	Mintage	MS-65	PF-65
1994W, Women Veterans Silver Dollar	53,054	25.00	
1994P, Same type P mint Proof . . . .(213,201)			20.00

	Mintage	MS-65	PF-65
1994D, U.S. Capitol Silver Dollar	68,352	$10.00	
1994S, Same type S mint Proof	(279,416)		$11.00

	Mintage	MS-65	PF-65
1995S, Civil War Battlefield Clad Half Dollar	119,510	18.00	
1995S, Same type S mint Proof	(330,099)		18.00

	Mintage	MS-65	PF-65
1995P, Civil War Battlefield Silver Dollar	45,866	30.00	
1995S, Same type S mint Proof	(55,246)		35.00

	Mintage	MS-65	PF-65
1995W, Civil War Battlefield Gold $5	12,735	$250.00	
1995W, Same type W mint Proof	(55,246)		$200.00

	Mintage	MS-65	PF-65
1995D, Olympic Games. Basketball Clad Half Dollar	171,001	10.00	
1995S, Same type S Mint Proof	(169,655)		8.00
1995D, Olympic Games. Baseball Clad Half Dollar	164,605	10.00	
1995S, Same type S Mint Proof	(118,087)		8.00
1996D, Olympic Games. Swimming Clad Half Dollar	49,533	60.00	
1996S, Same type S Mint Proof	(114,315)		12.00
1996D, Olympic Games. Soccer Clad Half Dollar	52,836	30.00	
1996S, Same type S Mint Proof	(112,412)		45.00

	Mintage	MS-65	PF-65
1995D, Olympic Games. Gymnastics Silver Dollar	42,497	35.00	
1995P, Same type P Mint Proof	(182,676)		22.00
1995D, Olympic Games. Paralympics Silver Dollar	28,649	40.00	
1995P, Same type P Mint Proof	(138,337)		20.00
1995D, Olympic Games. Track and Field Silver Dollar	24,796	35.00	
1995P, Same type P Mint Proof	(136,935)		15.00
1995D, Olympic Games. Cycling Silver Dollar	19,662	55.00	
1995P, Same type P Mint Proof	(118,795)		20.00

Olympic Games, Special Olympics, Community Service

	Mintage	MS-65	PF-65
1996D, Olympic Games. Tennis Silver Dollar	15,983	$100.00	
1996P, Same type P Mint Proof (92,016)			$35.00
1996D, Olympic Games. Paralympics Silver Dollar	14,497	140.00	
1996P, Same type P Mint Proof (84,280)			35.00
1996D, Olympic Games. Rowing Silver Dollar	16,258	125.00	
1996P, Same type P Mint Proof (151,890)			25.00
1996D, Olympic Games. High Jump Silver Dollar	15,697	140.00	
1996P, Same type P Mint Proof (124,502)			20.00

	Mintage	MS-65	PF-65
1995W, Olympic Games. Torch Runner Gold $5	14,675	165.00	
1995W, Same type W Mint Proof (57,442)			125.00
1995W, Olympic Games. Stadium Gold $5	10,579	200.00	
1995W, Same type W Mint Proof (43,124)			150.00
1996W, Olympic Games. Flag Bearer Gold $5	9,174	250.00	
1996W, Same type W Mint Proof (32,886)			180.00
1996W, Olympic Games. Cauldron Gold $5	9,210	250.00	
1996W, Same type W Mint Proof (38,555)			180.00

	Mintage	MS-65	PF-65
1995W, Special Olympics Silver Dollar	89,301	10.00	
1995P, Same type P mint Proof (351,764)			10.00

	Mintage	MS-65	PF-65
1996S, Community Service Silver Dollar	23,468	125.00	
1996S, Same type S mint Proof (100,787)			35.00

SMITHSONIAN INSTITUTION

	Mintage	MS-65	PF-65
1996D, Smithsonian Silver Dollar	30,593	$55.00	
1996P, Same type P Mint Proof (126,616)			$27.00
1996W, Smithsonian Gold $5	21,840	300.00	
1996W, Same type W Mint Proof (8,948)			175.00

BOTANIC GARDENS

	Mintage	MS-65	PF-65
1997P, Botanic Gardens Silver Dollar	57,272	18.00	
1997P, Same type P mint Proof (264,528)			20.00

JACKIE ROBINSON

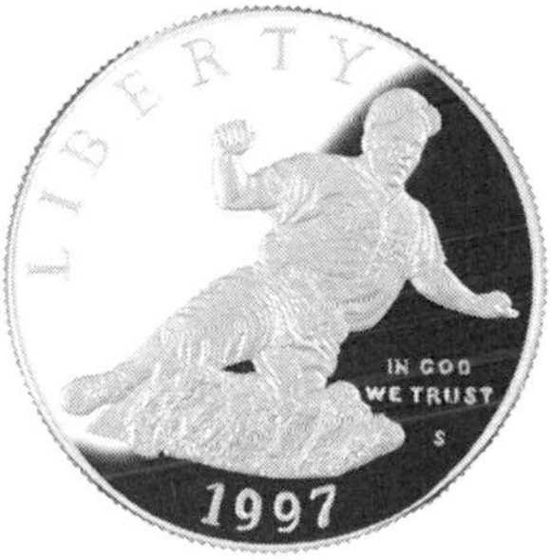

	Mintage	MS-65	PF-65
1997S, Jackie Robinson Silver Dollar	30,180	$30.00	
1997S, Same type S Mint Proof (110,002)			$30.00
1997W, Jackie Robinson Gold $5	5,174	900.00	
1997W, Same type W Mint Proof (24,072)			250.00

JACKIE ROBINSON

FRANKLIN D. ROOSEVELT

	Mintage	MS-65	PF-65
1997W, Franklin D. Roosevelt Gold $5	11,805	$150.00	
1997W, Same type W mint Proof . . . . (29,233)			$140.00

NATIONAL LAW ENFORCEMENT OFFICERS MEMORIAL

	Mintage	MS-65	PF-65
1997P, Law Enforcement Silver Dollar	28,575	70.00	
1997P, Same type P mint Proof . . . . (110,428)			60.00

ROBERT F. KENNEDY

	Mintage	MS-65	PF-65
1998S, Robert F. Kennedy Silver Dollar	106,422	15.00	
1998S, Same type S mint Proof . . . . (99,020)			20.00

BLACK REVOLUTIONARY WAR PATRIOTS

	Mintage	MS-65	PF-65
1998S, Black Patriots Silver Dollar	37,210	$60.00	
1998S, Same type S mint Proof	(75,070)		$50.00

DOLLEY MADISON COMMEMORATIVE

	Mintage	MS-65	PF-65
1999P, Dolley Madison Silver Dollar	89,100	20.00	
1999P, Same type P mint Proof	(224,400)		25.00

GEORGE WASHINGTON COMMEMORATIVE GOLD

	Mintage	MS-65	PF-65
1999W, George Washington Gold $5	22,511	150.00	
1999W, Same type W mint Proof	(41,693)		160.00

YELLOWSTONE NATIONAL PARK

	Mintage	MS-65	PF-65
1999P, Yellowstone Silver Dollar	62,000	$20.00	
1999P, Same type P mint Proof	(144,900)		$20.00

LIBRARY OF CONGRESS BICENTENNIAL

2000P, Library of Congress Silver Dollar		15.00	
2000P, Same type P Mint Proof			17.00
2000W, Library of Congress bimetallic $10		600.00	
2000W, Same type W Mint Proof			325.00

LEIF ERICSON MILLENNIUM

2000P, Leif Ericson Silver Dollar	28,100	35.00	
2000P, Same type P mint Proof	(142,900)		25.00

MODERN COMMEMORATIVES

AMERICAN BUFFALO COMMEMORATIVE

	Mintage	MS-65	PF-65
2001D, Buffalo/Indian Silver Dollar	227,131	$75.00	
2001P, Same Type P mint Proof	(272,869)		$75.00

CAPITOL VISITORS CENTER

	Mintage	MS-65	PF-65
2001P, Capitol Clad Half Dollar	99,157	6.00	
2001P, Same type P mint Proof	(77,962)		6.50

	Mintage	MS-65	PF-65
2001P, Capitol Silver Dollar	35,380	18.00	
2001P, Same type P mint Proof	(143,793)		18.00

	Mintage	MS-65	PF-65
2001P, Capitol Gold $5	6,761	300.00	
2001P, Same type P mint Proof	(27,652)		150.00

SALT LAKE OLYMPIC GAMES

	Mintage	MS-65	PF-65
2002P, Salt Lake Olympic Silver Dollar	35,287	$18.00	
2002P, Same type P mint Proof (142,813)			$20.00

	Mintage	MS-65	PF-65
2002W, Salt Lake Olympic $5	5,727	150.00	
2002W, Same type W mint Proof (8,882)			125.00

UNITED STATES MILITARY ACADEMY

	Mintage	MS-65	PF-65
2002W, West Point Silver Dollar	101,236	18.00	
2002W, Same type W mint Proof (282,743)			19.00

FIRST FLIGHT CENTENNIAL

	Mintage	MS-65	PF-65
2003P, First Flight Clad Half-Dollar		10.	
2003P, Same Type P Mint Proof			13.
2003P, First Flight Silver Dollar		33.	
2003P, Same Type P Mint Proof			37.
2003W, First Flight $10.00		365.	
2003W, Same Type W Mint Proof			375.

THOMAS A. EDISON

	Mintage	MS-65	PF-65
2004P, Thomas A. Edison Silver Dollar		33.	
2004P, Same Type P Mint Proof			37.

Government Sets–In Original Holders

1983-84 OLYMPICS

Date	Price
1983 and 1984, Proof dollars	$12.00
1983 and 1984, 6 coin set. One 1983 and one 1984 uncirculated and Proof dollar. One uncirculated and one Proof gold $10	280.00
1983, Collector set. 1983 PDS uncirculated dollars	15.00
1984, Collector set. 1984 PDS uncirculated dollars	18.00
1983 and 1984, gold and silver uncirculated set. One 1983 and one 1984 uncirculated dollar and one 1984 uncirculated gold $10	140.00
1983 and 1984, gold and silver Proof set. One 1983 and one 1984 Proof dollar and one 1984 Proof $10.*	140.00

1986 STATUE OF LIBERTY

1986, 2 coin set: Proof silver dollar and clad half dollar	10.00
1986, 3 coin set: Proof silver dollar, clad half dollar and gold $5	95.00
1986, 2 coin set: uncirculated silver dollar and clad half dollar	10.00
1986, 3 coin set: uncirculated silver dollar, clad half dollar and gold $5	95.00
1986, 6 coin set: 1 each of Proof and uncirculated*	190.00

1987 CONSTITUTION

1988, 2 coin set: uncirculated silver dollar and gold $5	90.00
1988, 2 coin set: Proof silver dollar and gold $5	90.00
1988, 4 coin set: 1 each of Proof and uncirculated	180.00

1988 OLYMPIAD

1988, 2 coin set: uncirculated silver dollar and gold $5	85.00
1988, 2 coin set: Proof silver dollar and gold $5	85.00
1988, 4 coin set: 1 each of Proof and uncirculated*	170.00

1989 CONGRESS

1989, 2 coin set: Proof silver dollar and clad half dollar	10.00
1989, 3 coin set: Proof silver dollar, clad half dollar and gold $5	85.00
1989, 2 coin set: uncirculated silver dollar and clad half dollar	10.00
1989, 3 coin set: uncirculated silver dollar, clad half dollar and gold $5	85.00
1989, 6 coin set: 1 each of Proof and uncirculated*	170.00

1991 MOUNT RUSHMORE

1991, 2 coin set: uncirculated half dollar and dollar	20.00
1991, 2 coin set: Proof half dollar and silver dollar	25.00
1991, 3 coin set: uncirculated half dollar, silver dollar and gold $5	110.00
1991, 3 coin set: Proof half dollar, silver dollar and gold $5	110.00
1991, 6 coin set: 1 each of Proof and uncirculated*	230.00

1992 XXV OLYMPIAD

1992, 2 coin set: uncirculated half dollar and dollar	15.00
1992, 2 coin set: Proof half dollar and dollar	17.00
1992, 3 coin set: uncirculated half dollar, dollar and gold $5	90.00
1992, 3 coin set: Proof half dollar, dollar and gold $5	85.00
1992, 6 coin set: 1 each Proof and uncirculated*	200.00

1992 COLUMBUS

1992, 2 coin set: uncirculated half dollar and dollar	15.00
1992, 2 coin set: Proof half dollar and silver dollar	20.00
1992, 3 coin set: uncirculated half dollar, silver dollar and gold $5	120.00
1992, 3 coin set: Proof half dollar, silver dollar and gold $5	110.00
1992, 6 coin set: 1 each of Proof and uncirculated*	230.00

**Packaged in cherrywood box.*

Government Sets–In Original Holders

1993 BILL OF RIGHTS

Date	Price
1993, 2 coin set: uncirculated half dollar and dollar	$15.00
1993, 2 coin set: Proof half dollar and silver dollar	16.00
1993, 3 coin set: uncirculated half dollar, silver dollar and gold $5	120.00
1993, 3 coin set: Proof half dollar, silver dollar and gold $5	110.00
1993, 6 coin set: 1 each of Proof and uncirculated*	230.00
1993, "Young Collector" set: silver half dollar	10.00
1993, "Educational" set: silver half dollar and Madison medal	8.00

1993 THOMAS JEFFERSON

1993, 3 piece set: Jefferson dollar, nickel and $2 note	40.00

1993 WORLD WAR II

1993, 2 coin set: uncirculated half dollar and dollar	15.00
1993, 2 coin set: Proof half dollar and silver dollar	17.00
1993, 3 coin set: uncirculated half dollar, silver dollar and gold $5	130.00
1993, 3 coin set: Proof half dollar, silver dollar and gold $5	125.00
1993, 6 coin set: 1 each of Proof and uncirculated*	265.00
1993, "Young Collector" set: silver half dollar	10.00
1993, "Victory" set: silver dollar, French franc	9.00

1994 WORLD SOCCER CUP

1994, 2 coin set: uncirculated half dollar and dollar	15.00
1994, 2 coin set: Proof half dollar and silver dollar	17.00
1994, 3 coin set: uncirculated half dollar, silver dollar and gold $5	115.00
1994, 3 coin set: Proof half dollar, silver dollar and gold $5	110.00
1994, 6 coin set: 1 each of Proof and uncirculated*	225.00
1994, "Young Collector" set: uncirculated silver half dollar	8.00
1994, "Special Edition" set: Proof clad half dollar and silver dollar	17.00

1994 U.S. VETERANS

1994, 3 coin set: Unc. POW, Vietnam and Women dollar	100.00
1994, 3 coin set: Proof POW, Vietnam and Women dollar	75.00

1995 SPECIAL OLYMPICS

1995, 2 coin set: Proof Schriver Dollar, 1995S Kennedy Half Dollar.	42.00

1995 CIVIL WAR BATTLEFIELD PRESERVATION

1995, 2 coin set: uncirculated half dollar and dollar	35.00
1995, 2 coin set: Proof half dollar and silver dollar	45.00
1995, 3 coin set: uncirculated half dollar, dollar and gold $5	300.00
1995, 3 coin set: Proof half dollar, dollar and gold $5	250.00
1995, 6 coin set: 1 each of Proof and uncirculated.*	550.00
1995, "Young Collector" set: uncirculated half dollar	10.00
1995, 2 coin "Union Set": half dollar and dollar	20.00
1995, 3 coin "Union Set": half dollar, dollar and $5	150.00

1995–96 CENTENNIAL OLYMPIC GAMES

1995, 4 coin set #1: uncirculated 50¢ Basketball, $1 Gymnast, $1 Blind, $5 Torch	200.00
1995, 4 coin set #1: Proof 50¢ Basketball, $1 Gymnast, $1 Blind, $5 Torch	125.00
1995, 2 coin set #1: Proof $1 Gymnast, $1 Blind	35.00
1995, "Young Collector" set: uncirculated Basketball half dollar	8.00
1995-96 16, coin set: 1 each all uncirculated coins*	750.00
1995-96 16, coin set: 1 each all Proof coins*	750.00
1995-96 32, coin set: 1 each all uncirculated and Proof coins*	2,600.00

**Packaged in cherrywood box.*

1996 NATIONAL COMMUNITY SERVICE

Date	Price
1996, Proof silver dollar and Saint-Gaudens stamp	$35.00

1996 SMITHSONIAN INSTITUTION 150TH ANNIVERSARY

1996, 2 coin set: Proof dollar and gold $5	170.00
1996, 4 coin set: 1 each of Proof and uncirculated. *	510.00
1996, "Young Collector" set: Proof silver dollar	20.00

1997 BOTANIC GARDENS

1997, Dollar, Jefferson nickel and $1 note	100.00

1997 JACKIE ROBINSON

1997, 2 coin set: Proof dollar and $5 gold	275.00
1997, 4 coin set: 1 each of Proof and uncirculated	1,100.00
1997, 3 piece legacy set: Baseball card, pin and $5 gold	275.00

1997 NATIONAL LAW ENFORCEMENT OFFICERS MEMORIAL

1997, Insignia set: dollar, lapel pin and patch	80.00

1998 ROBERT F. KENNEDY

1998, 2 coin set: RFK dollar and JFK silver half dollar	240.00
1998, 2 coin set: RFK dollar, Proof and uncirculated	50.00

1998 BLACK REVOLUTIONARY WAR PATRIOTS

1998, 2 coin set: uncirculated and Proof dollar	100.00
1998, "Young Collector" set: uncirculated dollar	55.00
1998, Coin and 4 stamps set	55.00

1999 DOLLEY MADISON COMMEMORATIVE

1999, 2 coin set: Proof and uncirculated dollars	40.00

1999 GEORGE WASHINGTON

1999, 2 coin set: 1 each Proof and uncirculated $5 gold	300.00

1999 YELLOWSTONE NATIONAL PARK

1999, 2 coin set: 1 each Proof and uncirculated dollars	40.00

2000 LEIF ERICSON MILLENNIUM

2000, 2 coin set. Proof $1 and Islandic 1,000 kronur	50.00

2001 AMERICAN BUFFALO

2001, 2 coin set: Proof and uncirculated dollars	170.00
2001, coinage and currency set	90.00

2001 CAPITOL VISITORS CENTER

2001, 3 coin Proof set: 50¢, $1, $5	170.00

2002 SALT LAKE OLYMPIC GAMES

2002, 2 coin Proof set: $1 and $5	150.00
2002, 4 coin Proof and uncirculated set	300.00

** Packaged in cherrywood box.*

Private coins were circulated in most instances because of a shortage of regular coinage. The words "Private Gold," used with reference to coins struck outside of the United States Mint, are a general term. In the sense that no state or territory had authority to coin money, private gold simply refers to those interesting necessity pieces of various shapes, denominations and degrees of intrinsic worth which were circulated in isolated areas of our country by individuals, assayers, bankers, etc. Some will use the words "Territorial" and "State" to cover certain issues because they were coined and circulated in a territory or state. While the state of California properly sanctioned the ingots stamped by F. D. Kohler as state assayer, in no instance were any of the gold pieces struck by authority of any of the territorial governments.

The stamped ingots put out by Augustus Humbert, the United States assayer of gold, were not recognized at the United States Mint as an official issue of coins, but simply as ingots, though Humbert placed the value and fineness on the pieces as an official agent of the federal government.

TEMPLETON REID
Georgia 1830

The first private gold coinage under the Constitution was struck by Templeton Reid, a jeweler and gunsmith, in Milledgeville, Georgia in July, 1830. To be closer to the mines, he moved to Gainesville where most of his coins were made. Although weights were accurate, Reid's assays were not and his coins were slightly short of claimed value. Accordingly, he was severely attacked in the newspapers and soon lost the public's confidence.

	VF
1830, $2.50	$26,000.
1830, $5	60,000.

	VG
1830, TEN DOLLARS	$60,000.
(No Date), TEN DOLLARS	50,000.

TEMPLETON REID
"California Gold 1849"

1849, TEN DOLLAR CALIFORNIA GOLD (Smithsonian Collection) . . . . (*Unique*)

THE BECHTLERS
Rutherford County, N. C. 1830-1852

Two skilled German metallurgists, Christopher Bechtler and his son August, and later Christopher Bechtler, Junior, a nephew of Christopher the elder, operated a "private" mint at Rutherfordton, North Carolina. Rutherford county in which Rutherfordton is located was the principal source of the nation's gold supply from 1790 to 1848.

CHRISTOPHER BECHTLER

	VF	EF	AU	UNC
ONE DOLLAR N. CAROLOLINA, 28 gr. N reversed	$850.	$1,500.	$2,000.	$4,000.
ONE DOLLAR N. CAROLINA, 28 gr., no star	1,400.	2,700.	3,900.	6,000.

	VF	EF	AU	UNC
ONE DOLLAR CAROLINA, 30 gr.	900.	1,600.	2,000.	3,500.
$2.50 CAROLINA, 67 gr. 21 carats	2,000.	3,000.	4,000.	6,200.

	VF	EF	AU	UNC
$2.50 CAROLINA, 70 gr. 20 carats	2,000.	3,300.	4,100.	6,500.
$2.50 GEORGIA, 64 gr. 22 carats	2,100.	3,500.	4,200.	6,500.

	VF	EF	AU	UNC
$2.50 NORTH CAROLINA, 75 gr. 20 carats				
RUTHERFORD in a circle. BORDER of lg. BEADS	$4,000.	$6,000.	$7,500.	$12,000.
$2.50 NORTH CAROLINA, without 75 G	4,000.	6,500.	7,500.	12,000.

	VF	EF	AU	UNC
5 DOLLARS CAROLINA, RUTHERFORD,				
140 gr. 20 carats. AUGUST 1, 1834,				
Plain edge	2,300.	3,750.	5,500.	7,000.
Reeded edge	2,750.	4,500.	6,000.	7,750.
BECHTLER without star and C	—			
5 DOLLARS CAROLINA, 134 gr. 21 carats, with star	2,000.	3,250.	5,000.	6,500.
(Obverse of A.BECHTLER as shown)				

	VF	EF	AU	UNC
5 DOLLARS GEORGIA, RUTHERFORD, 128 gr. 22 carats ..	2,250.	3,500.	5,000.	7,500
5 DOLLARS GEORGIA, RUTHERF., 128 gr. 22 carats	2,250.	3,500.	5,000.	7,500.

Without 150 G

	VF	EF	AU	UNC
5 DOLLARS CAROLINA, RUTHERF.,				
140 gr. 20 carats, AUGUST 1, 1834	2,750.	4,250.	5,200.	7,500.
5 DOLLARS CAROLINA, RUTHERF.,				
Similar, 20 distant from carats	3,500.	5,000.	7,000.	—
5 DOLLARS NORTH CAROLINA, 150 gr. 20 carats	4,000.	6,000.	9,000.	14,000.
5 DOLLARS NORTH CAROLINA, 20 carats, without 150 G ..	4,500.	6,500.	11,000.	17,000.

THE BECHTLERS

AUGUST BECHTLER

1842-1852

1 DOLLAR CAROLINA, 27 gr. 21 carats	$550.	$850.	$1,100.	$1,900.
5 DOLLARS CAROLINA, 134 gr. 21 carats	1,800.	3,250.	4,000.	6,750.

5 DOLLARS CAROLINA, 128 gr. 22 carats	3,500.	4,500.	6,000.	9,000.
5 DOLLARS CAROLINA, 141 gr. 20 carats	3,500.	4,500.	6,000.	9,000.

NORRIS, GREGG & NORRIS

San Francisco 1849

These pieces are considered the first of the California private gold coins. A newspaper account dated May 31, 1849, described a five-dollar gold coin, struck at Benicia City, though with the imprint San Francisco, and the private stamp of Norris, Gregg and Norris.

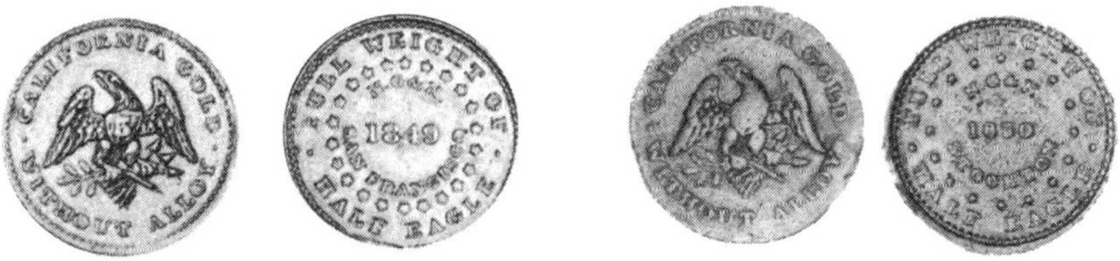

	F	V.F	E.F	AU	UNC
1849, HALF EAGLE - Plain edge	$1,750.	$2,500.	$4,500.	$7,000.	$12,000.
1849, HALF EAGLE - Reeded edge	1,750.	2,500.	4,500.	7,000.	12,000.
1850, HALF EAGLE with STOCKTON beneath date					(*Unique*)

MOFFAT & CO.

San Francisco 1849-1853

The firm of Moffat and Company was perhaps the most important of the California private coiners. The assay office they conducted was semi-official in character, and successors to this firm later established the United States branch mint of San Francisco.

In June or July, 1849, Moffat & Co. began to issue small rectangular pieces of gold in values from $9.43 to $264. The $9.43, $14.25 and $16.00 varieties are the only types known today.

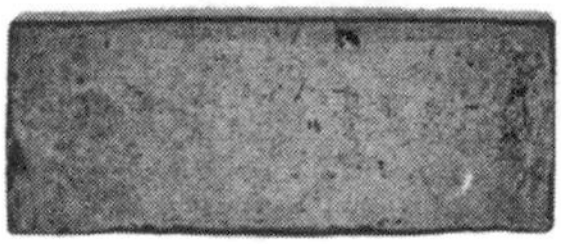

	EF
$9.43 Ingot (*Unique*)	—
$14.25 Ingot (*Unique*)	—
$16.00 Ingot	$17,000

The dies for the $10 piece were cut by Albert Kuner. The words MOFFAT & Co. appear on the coronet of Liberty instead of the word LIBERTY as in regular United States issues.

	F	VF	EF	AU	UNC
1849, FIVE DOL. (All varieties)	$650.	$900.	$1,500.	$2,500.	$4,500.
1850, FIVE DOL. (All varieties)	650.	900.	1,500.	2,500.	4,500.
1849, TEN DOL.	1,100.	1,600.	3,000.	5,000.	8,000.
1849, TEN D.	1,200.	1,650.	3,400.	5,500.	7,500.

United States Assay Office

AUGUSTUS HUMBERT

U. S. Assayer 1851

When Augustus Humbert was appointed United States Assayer, he placed his name and the government stamp on the ingots of gold issued by Moffat & Co. The assay office, a Provisional Government Mint, was a temporary expedient to accommodate the Californians until the establishment of a permanent branch mint. The fifty-dollar gold piece was accepted as legal tender on a par with standard U.S. gold coins.

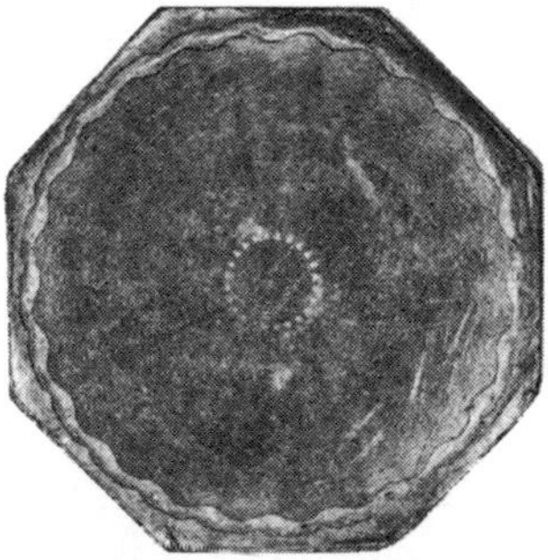

LETTERED EDGE VARIETIES

50 on reverse

	F	VF	EF	AU	UNC
1851, 50 DC 880 THOUS., no 50 on Reverse. Sunk in edge: AUGUSTUS HUMBERT UNITED STATES ASSAYER OF GOLD CALIFORNIA 1851	$4,250.	$5,500.	$9,000.	$14,000.	—
1851, 50 D C Similar to last variety, but 50 on Reverse	4,500.	5,750.	10,000.	16,000.	—
1851, Similar to last variety, but 887 THOUS	4,500.	5,750.	9,500.	15,000.	—

REEDED EDGE VARIETIES

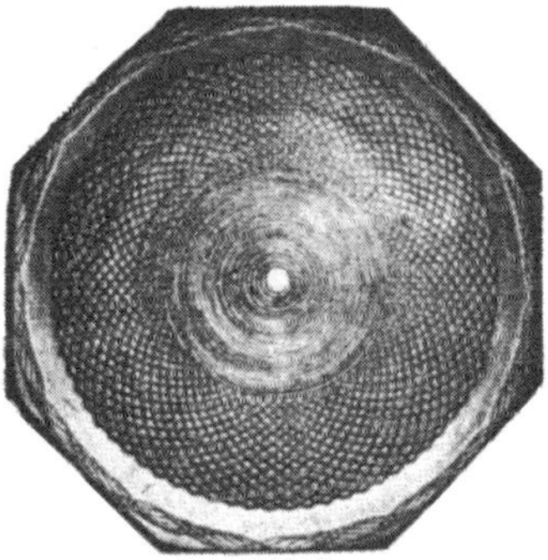

	F	VF	EF	AU	UNC
1851, FIFTY DOLLS 880 THOUS. "Target" Reverse . . .	3,250.	4,250.	6,000.	9,000.	14,500.
1851, FIFTY DOLLS 887 THOUS. "Target" Reverse . . .	3,250.	4,250.	6,000.	9,000.	14,500.
1852, FIFTY DOLLS 887 THOUS.	3,250.	4,250.	6,250.	9,500.	15,000.

Moffat & Co. proceeded in January, 1852 to issue a new ten-dollar piece bearing the stamp moffat & co.

	F	VF	EF	AU	UNC
1852, TEN D. MOFFAT & CO	950.	1,800.	3,100.	7,000.	—

	F	VF	EF	AU	UNC
1852, TWENTY DOLS. 1852, 2 over 1	$1,650.	$2,300.	$4,000.	$8,000.	—

1852, TEN DOLS. 1852, 2 over 1	650.	1,200.	2,300.	3,750.	—
1852, TEN DOLS.	600.	1,000.	1,700.	2,800.	5,250.

UNITED STATES ASSAY OFFICE OF GOLD

1852

The firm of Moffat & Co. dissolved and a new reorganized company known as the United States Assay Office of Gold, composed of Curtis, Perry and Ward took over the contract.

1852, FIFTY DOLLS. 887 THOUS.	3,500.	4,000.	6,000.	9,000.	16,000.
1852, FIFTY DOLLS. 900 THOUS.	3,500.	4,000.	6,200.	9,200.	19,000.

	F	VF	EF	AU	UNC
1852, TEN DOLS 884 THOUS.	$625.	$1,000.	$1,500.	$2,500.	$5,000.
1853, TEN D. 884 THOUS.	1,650.	2,600.	5,750.	8,500.	—
1853, TEN D. 900 THOUS.	1,300.	1,900.	3,200.	4,400.	—
1853, TWENTY D. 884 THOUS.	2,000.	4,000.	6,000.	9,000.	—
1853, TWENTY D. 900 THOUS.	750.	1,200.	1,500.	2,300.	3,750.

The last Moffat issue was the 1853 twenty dollar piece which is very similar to the U.S. double eagle of that period. It was struck after the retirement of Mr. Moffat from the Assay Office.

	F	VF	EF	AU	UNC
1853, TWENTY D.	1,300.	1,650.	2,400.	3,500.	6,250.

CINCINNATI MINING & TRADING CO.

The origin and location of this company are unknown.

	EF	UNC
1849, FIVE DOLLARS	—	—
1849, TEN DOLLARS	—	—

MASSACHUSETTS AND CALIFORNIA COMPANY

San Fransisco 1849

This company was believed to have been organized in Northampton, Mass. in May, 1849.

	F	VF	EF
1849, FIVE D.	$35,000	$50,000	$80,000

MINERS' BANK

San Francisco 1849

The institution of Wright & Co., exchange brokers located in Portsmouth Square, San Francisco, was known as the Miners' Bank.

A ten dollar piece was issued in the autumn of 1849, but the coins were not readily accepted because they were worth less than face value.

	VF	EF	AU	UNC
(1849) TEN. D.	$4,000	$7,500	$11,000	$24,000

J.S. ORMSBY

Sacramento 1849

The initials J. S. O. which appear on certain issues of California privately coined gold pieces represent the firm of J. S. Ormsby & Co. They struck both five and ten dollar denominations, all undated.

	VF
(1849) 5 DOLLS. (*Unique*)	—
(1849) 10 DOLLS.	—

PACIFIC COMPANY

San Francisco 1849

The origin of the Pacific Co. is very uncertain. All data regarding the firm is based on conjecture. Edgar H. Adams wrote that he believed that the coins bearing the stamp of the Pacific Company were produced by the coining firm of Broderick and Kohler.

	EF
1849, 1 DOLLAR	—
1849, 5 DOLLARS	$70,000.
1849, 10 DOLLARS	$90,000.

F. D. KOHLER

California State Assayer 1850

The State Assay Office was authorized April 12, 1850. Governor Burnett appointed F. D. Kohler that year who thereupon sold his assaying business to Baldwin & Co. He served at both San Francisco and Sacramento Offices. The State Assay Offices were discontinued at the time the U. S. Assay Office was established Feb. 1, 1851.

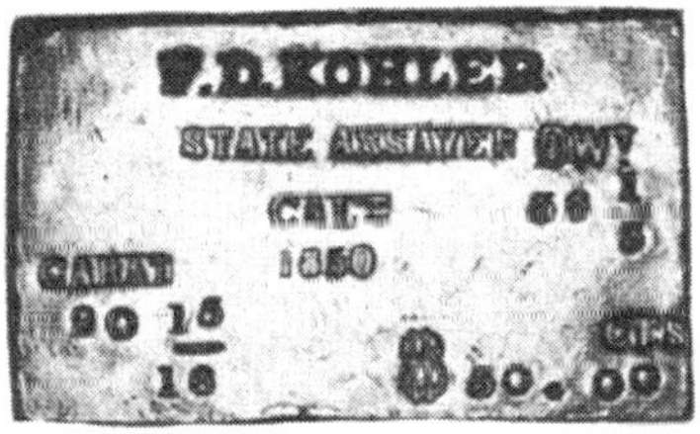

	EF
$36.55 Sacramento	—
$37.31 San Francisco	—
$40.07 San Francisco	—
$45.34 San Francisco	—
$50.00 San Francisco	—
$54.09 San Francisco	—

DUBOSQ & COMPANY

San Francisco 1850

Theodore Dubosq, a Philadelphia jeweler who took melting and coining machinery to San Francisco in 1849, produced the following pieces.

	VF
1850, FIVE D.	$25,000.
1850, TEN D.	30,000.

BALDWIN & COMPANY

San Francisco 1850

George C. Baldwin and Thomas S. Holman were in the jewelry business in San Francisco and were known as Baldwin & Co. They were the successors to F. D. Kohler & Co., taking over their machinery and other equipment in May, 1850.

	F	VF	EF	AU	UNC
1850, FIVE DOL.	$2,500.	$3,500.	$6,500.	$7,500.	$10,000.
1850, TEN DOLLARS - Horseman type	12,500.	22,500.	30,000.	40,000.	50,000.

	F	VF	EF	AU	UNC
1851, TEN D.	3,500.	5,250.	12,000.	15,000.	—

	F	VF	EF	AU	UNC
1851, TWENTY DOLLARS.		30,000	50,000	—	—

SHULTZ & COMPANY

San Francisco 1851

The firm located in back of Baldwin's establishment operated a brass foundry beginning in 1851. Judge G. W. Shultz and William T. Garratt were partners in the enterprise.

	F	VF
1851, FIVE D.	$9,500	$18,000

DUNBAR & COMPANY
San Francisco 1851

Edward E. Dunbar operated the California Bank in San Francisco. He later returned to New York and organized the famous Continental Bank Note Co.

	EF
1851, FIVE D	$55,000.

WASS, MOLITOR & COMPANY
San Francisco 1852-1855

The gold smelting and assaying plant of Wass, Molitor & Co. was operated by Count S. C. Wass and A. P. Molitor. They maintained an excellent laboratory and complete apparatus for analysis and coinage of gold.

	F	VF	EF	AU	UNC
1852, FIVE DOLLARS	$1,500.	$2,250.	$4,500.	$7,000.	$13,000.

Large Head **Small Head**

	F	VF	EF	AU	UNC
1852, TEN D. Large head	850.	1,500.	2,500.	3,500.	5,000.
1852, TEN D. Small head	1,500.	2,750.	5,200.	7,500.	—
1855, TEN D.	4,400.	7,000.	8,600.	12,000.	—

Large Head **Small Head**

	F	VF	EF	AU	UNC
1855, TWENTY DOL. Large head	—	—	—	—	—
1855, TWENTY DOL. Small head	4,000.	7,000.	13,000.	—	—

	F	VF	EF	AU	UNC
1855, 50 DOLLARS	$7,500.	$11,000.	$16,000.	$20,000.	—

KELLOGG & COMPANY
San Francisco 1854-1855

When the U.S. Assay Office ceased operations a period ensued during which no private firm was striking gold. The new San Francisco branch mint did not produce coins for some months after Curtis & Perry took the contract for the government. The lack of coin was again keenly felt by businessmen who petitioned Kellogg & Richter to "supply the vacuum" by issuing private coin. Their plea was answered on Feb. 9, 1854, when Kellogg & Co. placed their first twenty-dollar piece in circulation.

	F	VF	EF	AU	UNC
1854, TWENTY D.	$800.	$1,250.	$1,900.	$3,000.	$5,000.
1855, TWENTY D.	800.	1,250.	1,900.	3,000.	5,000.

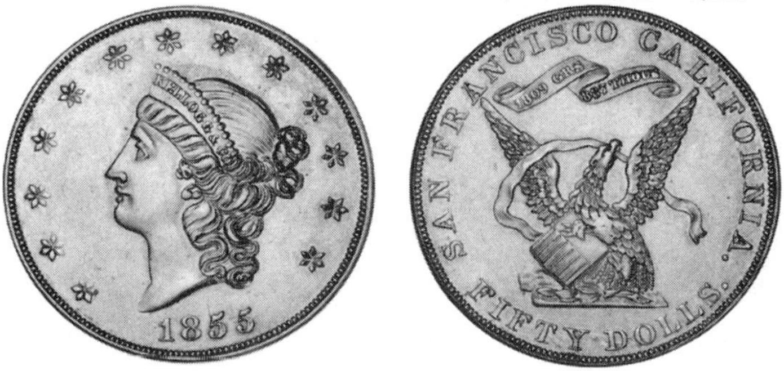

	PF
1855, FIFTY DOLLS.	—

OREGON EXCHANGE COMPANY
Oregon City, 1849
THE BEAVER COINS OF OREGON

On February 16, 1849, the legislature passed an act providing for a mint and specified five and ten dollar gold coins without alloy. Oregon City, the largest city in the territory with a population of about 1,000, was designated as the location for the mint. At the time this act was passed Oregon had been brought into the United States as a territory by act of Congress. When the new governor arrived March 2, he declared the coinage act unconstitutional.

	F	VF	EF	AU	UNC
1849, FIVE D	$6,500.	$10,000.	$17,500.	—	—
1849, TEN D	15,000.	30,000.	45,000.	$50,000.	—

MORMON GOLD PIECES
Salt Lake City, Utah 1849-1860

Brigham Young was the instigator of this coinage system and personally supervised the mint which was housed in a little adobe building in Salt Lake City. The mint was inaugurated late in 1849 as a public convenience.

	F	VF	EF	AU	UNC
1849, TWO AND HALF DOLLARS	$2,600.	$4,750.	$7,500.	$10,000.	—
1849, FIVE DOLLARS	2,500.	4,000.	5,500.	7,500.	$15,000.

	F	VF	EF
1849, TEN DOLLARS	$45,000.	$70,000.	$90,000.
1849, TWENTY DOLLARS	22,500.	37,500.	50,000.

MORMON GOLD PIECES

	F	VF	EF	AU	UNC
1850, FIVE DOLLARS	$2,750.	$4,250.	$5,750.	$8,000.	$16,000.
1860, 5D	4,750.	6,500.	12,000.	15,000.	25,000.

COLORADO GOLD PIECES

Clark, Gruber & Co. — Denver 1860-1861

Clark, Gruber and Co. was a well known private minting firm in Denver, Colo. in the early sixties.

	F	VF	EF	AU	UNC
1860, 21/2 D	$525.	$900.	$1,450.	$1,700.	$5,000.
1860, FIVE D	600.	1,100.	1,600.	1,800.	5,250.

	F	VF	EF	AU	UNC
1860, TEN D	2,800.	3,400.	5,800.	7,500.	15,000.
1860, TWENTY D	14,000.	27,000.	48,000.	55,000.	—

	F	VF	EF	AU	UNC
1861, 21/2 D	550.	900.	1,400.	1,700.	5,000.
1861, FIVE D	750.	1,150.	2,000.	2,200.	9,500.
1861, TEN D	850.	1,400.	2,200.	2,400.	7,250.

	F	VF	EF	AU
1861, TWENTY D	$2,750.	$5,000.	$12,000.	$15,000.

JOHN PARSONS & COMPANY

Tarryall Mines — Colorado 1861

Very little is known about the mint of John Parsons and Co. It probably operated in Colorado, near (the original) Tarryall, in the summer of 1861.

PIKES PEAK GOLD

	VF
(1861) Undated 21/2 D	$50,000
(1861) Undated FIVE D	60,000

J. J. CONWAY & COMPANY

Georgia Gulch, Colorado, 1861

The value of gold dust caused disagreement among the merchants and the miners in all gold mining areas. The firm of J. J. Conway & Co. solved this difficulty by bringing out its gold pieces in August, 1861.

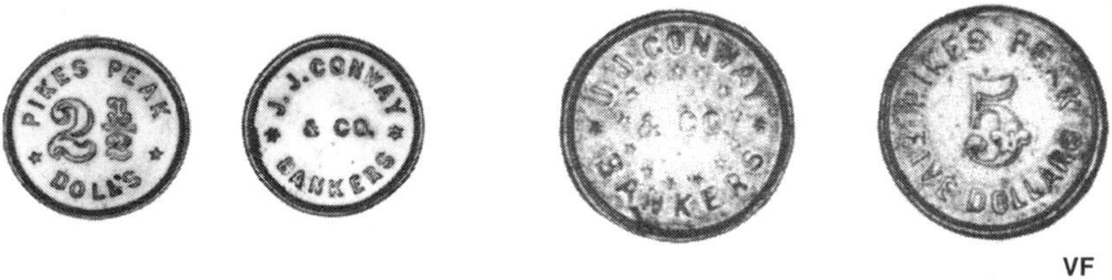

	VF
(1861) Undated 2 1/2 DOLL'S	$35,000
(1861) Undated FIVE DOLLARS	60,000

	VF
(1861) Undated TEN DOLLARS	—

CALIFORNIA SMALL DENOMINATION GOLD

There was a scarcity of small coins during the California gold rush and starting in 1852, quarter, half and dollar pieces were privately minted from native gold to alleviate the shortage. The need and acceptability of these pieces declined after 1856 and they then became popular as souvenirs. Authentic pieces all have CENTS, DOLLAR, or an abbreviation thereof on the reverse. The tokens are much less valuable. Modern restrikes and replicas have no numismatic value.

Values are only for genuine coins with the denomination on the reverse expressed as: CENTS, DOL., DOLL. or DOLLAR.

		EF-40	AU-50	MS-60
25c Octagonal:	Liberty head	$50.	$70.	$110.
	Indian head	60.	80.	120.
	Washington head	250.	350.	450.
25c Round:	Liberty head	50.	70.	110.
	Indian head	70.	100.	150.
	Washington head	300.	425.	550.
50c Octagonal:	Liberty head	70.	100.	125.
	Liberty head/eagle	400.	600.	900.
	Indian head	125.	140.	
175.50c Round:	Liberty head	70.	20.	145.
	Indian head	100.	125.	150.
$1.00 Octagonal:	Liberty head	200.	250.	300.
	Liberty head/eagle	700.	1,200.	1,700.
	Indian head	250.	350.	525.
$1.00 Round:	Liberty head	650.	850.	1,250.
	Indian head	650.	750.	1,450.

HARD TIMES TOKENS 1834–1844

During the financial crises of 1834–1844 many government coins were hoarded, and privately made tokens were used out of necessity. The so-called Hard Times Tokens of this period were slightly smaller and lighter than normal large cents. They were made of copper or brass and are of two general groups: Political tokens whose theme centered on President Jackson's fight against the United States Bank, and Tradesmen's Cards, issued by merchants. Many different designs and varieties exist. The most common pieces are valued at $4.00 Very Fine to $15.00 Ex. Fine.

CIVIL WAR TOKENS — 1861-1864

Civil War Tokens are generally divided into two groups: tradesmen's tokens, and anonymously issued pieces with political or patriotic themes. They came into existence only because of the scarcity of government coins and disappeared as soon as the bronze coins of 1864 met the public demand for small copper change.

These tokens are of great variety in composition and design. A number were more or less faithful imitations of the copper-nickel cent. A few of this type have the word "not" in very small letters above the words "ONE CENT."

	F	VF	EF	UNC
Copper or Brass Tokens	$4.	$5.	$10.	$18.
Nickel or German Silver Tokens	12.	20.	30.	45.
White Metal Tokens	14.	23.	35.	50.
Copper-Nickel Tokens	25.	35.	42.	75.
Silver Tokens	60.	85.	120.	200.

BULLION VALUE OF COINS

Common date silver coins are valued according to the price of silver bullion. In recent years the price of silver bullion has been subject to extreme fluctuation. Therefore, when you read this it is highly probable that the current bullion price may differ from the prevailing market price used in tabulating valuations of many 19th and 20th century silver coins (priced in italics) listed in this edition. The following chart will help to determine the approximate bullion value of these coins at various price levels. Or, the approximate value may be calculated by multiplying the current spot price of silver times the content for each coin as indicated below. Dealers generally purchase common silver coins at 15% below bullion value, and sell them at 15% above bullion value.

Silver Price Per Ounce	Wartime Nickel .05626 oz.	Dime .07234 oz.	Quarter .18084 oz.	Half Dollar .36169 oz.	Silver Clad Half Dollar .14792 oz.	Silver Dollar .77344 oz.
$5.00	$.28	$.36	$.90	$1.81	$.74	$3.87
5.50	.31	.40	1.00	1.99	.81	4.25
6.00	.34	.44	1.09	2.17	.89	4.64
6.50	.36	.47	1.18	2.35	.96	5.03
7.00	.40	.51	1.27	2.53	1.04	5.42
7.50	.42	.55	1.36	2.72	1.11	5.80
8.00	.45	.58	1.45	2.90	1.19	6.19

The value of common date gold coins listed in this book may be affected by the rise or fall in the price of gold bullion. Nearly all U.S. gold coins have an additional premium value beyond their bullion content, and thus are not subject to the minor variations described for silver coins. The premium amount is not necessarily tied to the bullion price of gold, but is usually determined by supply and demand levels for actual gold coins occurring in the numismatic marketplace. Because these factors can vary significantly, there is no reliable formula for calculating "percentage above bullion" prices that would remain accurate over time. For this reason the chart below lists bullion values based on gold content only. Consult your nearest coin dealer to ascertain current premium prices.

Gold Price Per Ounce	$5.00 Liberty Head 1839-1908 Indian Head 1908-1929	$10.00 Liberty Head 1838-1907 Indian Head 1907-1933	$20.00 1849-1933
$275.	$66.50	$133.03	$266.07
300.	72.56	145.13	290.25
325.	78.60	157.22	314.44
350.	84.65	169.31	338.63
375.	90.70	181.40	362.81
400.	96.75	193.50	387.00
425.	102.80	205.60	411.19
450.	108.84	217.69	435.38
475.	114.89	229.78	459.56

UNITED STATES BULLION COINS
Silver

	Mintage	UNC	PF
$1 1986	5,393,005	$11.	
$1 1986S	(1,446,778)		$20.
$1 1987	11,442,335	8.	
$1 1987S	(904,732)		20.
$1 1988	5,004,646	8.	
$1 1988S	(557,370)		45.
$1 1989	5,203,327	8.	
$1 1989S	(617,694)		25.
$1 1990	5,840,210	8.	
$1 1990S	(695,510)		25.
$1 1991	7,191,066	8.	
$1 1991S	(511,925)		32.
$1 1992	5,540,068	8.	
$1 1992S	(498,654)		30.
$1 1993	6,763,762	8.	
$1 1993P	(403,625)		200.
$1 1994	4,227,319	8.	
$1 1994P	(372,168)		90.
$1 1995	4,762,051	8.	

	Mintage	UNC	PF
$1 1995P	(395,400)		$85.
$1 1995W	(30,125)		1,500.
$1 1996	3,603,386	$20.	
$1 1996P	(473,021)		30.
$1 1997	4,295,004	8.	
$1 1997P	(429,682)		47.
$1 1998	4,847,549	8.	
$1 1998P	(452,319)		25.
$1 1999	7,408,640	8.	
$1 1999P	(549,769)		40.
$1 2000(W)	9,239,132	8.	
$1 2000P			20.
$1 2001(W)	9,001,711	8.	
$1 2001P			20.
$1 2002(W)	10,539,026	8.	
$1 2002P			20.
$1 2003(W)	8,495,008	8.	
$1 2003P			20.
$1 2004(W)		8	
$1 2004P			20.

UNITED STATES BULLION COINS
Gold

	Mintage	UNC	PF
$5 (1986)	(912,609)	$40.	
$5 (1987)	580,266	40.	
$5 (1988)	159,500	75.	
$5 (1988)P	(143,881)		$45.
$5 (1989)	264,790	42.	
$5 (1989)P	(84,924)		47.
$5 (1990)	210,210	42.	
$5 (1990)P	(99,349)		47.
$5 (1991)	165,200	50.	
$5 (1991)P	(70,334)		47.
$5 1992	209,300	40.	
$5 1992 P	(64,902)		50.
$5 1993	210,709	40.	
$5 1993P	(58,649)		50.
$5 1994	206,380	40.	
$5 1994W	(62,100)		45.
$5 1995	223,025	40.	
$5 1995W	(48,675)		45.

	Mintage	UNC	PF
$5 1996	401,964	$40.	
$5 1996W	(57,449)		$50.
$5 1997	528,266	40.	
$5 1997W	(35,164)		60.
$5 1998	1,344,520	40.	
$5 1998W	(39,706)		45.
$5 1999	2,750,338	40.	
$5 1999W	(19,919)		45.
$5 2000	569,153	40.	
$5 2000W			55.
$5 2001	269,147	40.	
$5 2001W			55.
$5 2002	230,027	40.	
$5 2002W			45.
$5 2003	245,029	40.	
$5 2003W			45.
$5 2004		40.	
$5 2004W			45.

		Mintage	UNC	PF
$10	(1986)	726,031	$100.	
$10	(1987)	269,255	100.	
$10	(1988)	49,000	100.	
$10	(1988)P	(98,028)		$125.
$10	(1989)	81,789	100.	
$10	(1989)P	(53,593)		110.
$10	(1990)	41,000	100.	
$10	(1990)P	(62,674)		110.
$10	(1991)	36,100	115.	
$10	(1991)P	(50,840)		110.
$10	1992	59,546	100.	
$10	1992 P	(42,290)		110.
$10	1993	71,864	100.	
$10	1993P	(46,271)		110.
$10	1994	72,650	100.	
$10	1994W	(47,600)		110.
$10	1995	83,752	100.	
$10	1995W	(46,825)		110.
$10	1996	60,318	100.	
$10	1996W	(37,755)		110.
$10	1997	108,805	100.	
$10	1997W	(29,984)		110.
$10	1998	309,829	100.	
$10	1998W	(29,731)		110.
$10	1999	564,232	100.	
$10	1999W	(34,410)		110.
$10	2000	128,964	100.	
$10	2000W			120.
$10	2001	71,280	100.	
$10	2001W			120.
$10	2002	62,027	100.	
$10	2002W			110.
$10	2003	74,029	100.	
$10	2003W			110.
$10	2004		100.	
$10	2004W			110.
$25	(1986)	599,566	200.	
$25	(1987)	131,255	200.	
$25	(1987)P	(143,398)		220.
$25	(1988)	45,000	200.	
$25	(1988)P	(76,528)		220.
$25	(1989)	44,829	250.	
$25	(1989)P	(44,264)		220.
$25	(1990)	31,000	250.	
$25	(1990)P	(51,636)		220.
$25	(1991)	24,100	300.	
$25	(1991)P	(53,125)		250.
$25	1992	54,404	200.	
$25	1992P	(40,982)		220.
$25	1993	73,324	200.	
$25	1993P	(43,319)		220.
$25	1994	62,400	200.	
$25	1994W	(44,100)		$220
$25	1995	53,474	$200.	
$25	1995W	(46,200)		220.
$25	1996	39,287	200.	
$25	1996W	(34,769)		220.
$25	1997	79,605	200.	
$25	1997W	(26,801)		220.
$25	1998	169,029	200.	
$25	1998W	(25,550)		220.
$25	1999	263,013	200.	
$25	1999W	(30,452)		220.
$25	2000	79,287	200.	
$25	2000W			230.
$25	2001	48,047	200.	
$25	2001W			230.
$25	2002	70,027	200.	
$25	2002W			220.
$25	2003	79,029	200.	
$25	2003W			220.
$25	2004		200.	
$25	2004W			220.
$50	(1986)	1,362,650	400.	
$50	(1986)W	(446,290)		475.
$50	(1987)	1,045,500	400.	
$50	(1987)W	(147,498)		450.
$50	(1988)	465,000	400.	
$50	(1988)W	(87,133)		450.
$50	(1989)	415,790	400.	
$50	(1989)W	(53,960)		450.
$50	(1990)	373,210	400.	
$50	(1990)W	(62,401)		450.
$50	(1991)	243,100	400.	
$50	(1991)W	(50,411)		450.
$50	1992	275,000	400.	
$50	1992W	(44,835)		450.
$50	1993	480,192	400.	
$50	1993W	(34,389)		450.
$50	1994	221,633	400.	
$50	1994W	(46,300)		450.
$50	1995	200,636	400.	
$50	1995W	(48,075)		450.
$50	1996	189,148	400.	
$50	1996W	(36,086)		450.
$50	1997	664,508	400.	
$50	1997W	(27,803)		450.
$50	1998	1,468,530	400.	
$50	1998W	(26,047)		450.
$50	1999	1,505,026	400.	
$50	1999W	(31,446)		450.
$50	2000	433,319	400.	
$50	2000W			500.
$50	2001	143,605	400.	
$50	2001W			475.
$50	2002	222,029	400.	
$50	2002W			450.
$50	2003	416,032	400.	
$50	2003W			450.
$50	2004		400.	
$50	2004W			450.

UNITED STATES BULLION PLATINUM COINS

American Eagle platinum coins are made in four denominations and sizes that are different from the similar gold coins. The one ounce coin is designated $100.00 and contains one ounce of pure platinum. Fractional denominations containing 1/2 ounce, 1/4 ounce or 1/10 ounce, are called $50, $25 and $10, respectively.

ONE OUNCE PLATINUM $100.00

	Mintage	UNC	PF
1997	56,000	$800.	
1997W	(16,000)		$810.
1998	133,002	800.	
1998W	(26,047)		810.
1999	56,707	800.	
1999W	(12,351)		810.
2000	10,003	800.	
2000W			810.
2001	14,070	800.	
2001W			810.
2002	11,502	800.	
2002W			810.
2003	8,007	800.	
2003W			810.
2004		800.	
2004W			810.

HALF-OUNCE PLATINUM $50.00

	Mintage	UNC	PF
1997	20,500	$400.	
1997W	(14,637)		$410.
1998	32,415	400.	
1998W	(13,919)		410.
1999	32,309	400.	
1999W	(11,098)		410.
2000	18,892	400.	
2000W			410.
2001	12,815	400.	
2001W			410.
2002	24,005	400.	
2002W			410.
2003	17,409	400.	
2003W			410.
2004		400.	
2004W			410.

QUARTER-OUNCE PLATINUM $25.00

	Mintage	UNC	PF
1997	27,100	$200.	
1997W	(18,726)		$210.
1998	38,887	200.	
1998W	(14,203)		210.
1999	39,734	200.	
1999W	(13,524)		210.
2000	20,054	200.	
2000W			210.
2001	21,815	200.	
2001W			210.
2002	27,405	200.	
2002W			210.
2003	25,207	200.	
2003W			210.
2004		200.	
2004W			210.

TENTH-OUNCE PLATINUM $10.00

	Mintage	UNC	PF
1997	70,250	$80.	
1997W	(37,260)		$85.
1998	39,525	80.	
1998W	(19,919)		85.
1999	55,955	80.	
1999W	(19,123)		85.
2000	34,027	80.	
2000W			85.
2001	52,017	80.	
2001W			95.
2002	23,005	80.	
2002W			90.
2003	22,007	80.	
2003W			100.
2004		80.	
2004W			100.

PROOF GOLD SETS

	PF
1987, Gold Set. $50, 25	$650.
1988, Gold Set. $50, 25, 10, 5	825.
1989, Gold Set. $50, 25, 10, 5	825.
1990, Gold Set. $50, 25, 10, 5	825.
1991, Gold Set. $50, 25, 10, 5	825.
1992, Gold Set. $50, 25, 10, 5	825.
1993, Gold Set. $50, 25, 10, 5	825.
1993, Bicentennial Gold Set. $25, 10, 5, $1 Silver Eagle and medal	450.
1994, Gold Set. $50, 25, 10, 5	825.
1995, Gold Set. $50, 25, 10, 5	825.
1995, Anniversary Gold Set. $50, 25, 10, 5 and $1 Silver Eagle	2,500.
1996, Gold Set. $50, 25, 10, 5	825.
1997, Gold Set. $50, 25, 10, 5	825.
1997, Impressions of Liberty Set. $100 platinum, $50 gold, $1 silver	1,350.
1998, Gold Set. $50, 25, 10, 5	825.
1999, Gold Set. $50, 25, 10, 5	825.
2000, Gold Set. $50, 25, 10, 5	900.
2001, Gold Set. $50, 25, 10, 5	825.
2002, Gold Set, $50, 25, 10, 5	825.
2003, Gold Set, $50, 25, 10, 5	825.
2004, Gold Set $50.00, 25.00, 10.00, 5.00	825.

Bullion values are based on spot gold at $330.00 per ounce, and silver at $4.75 per ounce.

PLATINUM

	PF
1997, Platinum Set. $100, $50, $25, $10	$1,500.
1998, Platinum Set. $100, $50, $25, $10	1,500.
1999, Platinum Set. $100, $50, $25, $10	1,500.
2000, Platinum Set. $100, $50, $25, $10	1,500.
2001, Platinum Set. $100, $50, $25, $10	1,550.
2002, Platinum Set. $100, $50, $25, $10	1,500.
2003, Platinum Set. $100, $50, $25, $10	1,500.
2004, Platinum Set, $100.00, 50.00, 25.00, 10.00	1,500.

1998

1999

2000

2001

2002

2003

INDEX